Love, Money and Obligation

Love, Money and Obligation

Transnational Marriage in a Northeastern Thai Village

Patcharin Lapanun

NUS PRESS
SINGAPORE

Published by:

NUS Press
National University of Singapore
AS3-01-02, 3 Arts Link
Singapore 117569

Fax: (65) 6774-0652
E-mail: nusbooks@nus.edu.sg
Website: http://nuspress.nus.edu.sg

ISBN 978-981-4722-91-9 (paper)

National Library Board, Singapore Cataloguing in Publication Data

Name(s): Patcharin Lapanun.
Title: Love, money and obligation: transnational marriage in a Northeastern
    Thai village / Patcharin Lapanun
Description: First edition. | Singapore: NUS Press, [2019] | Includes
    bibliographical references and index.
Identifier(s): OCN 1078380217 | ISBN 978-981-47-2291-9 (paperback)
Subject(s): LCSH: Intercountry marriage--Thailand. | Women--Marriage--
    Social aspects--Thailand. | Asians--Foreign countries.
Classification: DDC 306.84509593--dc23

All the illustrations in this book are the private collections of the author.

Cover illustration: Twilight over rice fields from airplane window (Manthakorn/
Shutterstock ID 480996391)

Typeset by: Ogma Solutions Pvt Ltd
Printed by: Ho Printing Singapore Pte Ltd

Contents

List of Illustrations

Acknowledgements

This study is the result of a long research project during which I have accumulated considerable debt to more people than I can mention here. Most of all, I owe my biggest debt to the *mia farang*, their husbands, their relatives, the residents of Na Dokmai, and the women and men whom I met and interviewed during my field research in Thailand and the Netherlands. Welcoming me into their lives and homes, they shared experiences, emotions and thoughts that I had no right to expect but without which I could never have completed this research. I hope that this book can convey my deep appreciation and respect for these individuals and their struggles to live a life that has meaning and dignity.

I am deeply grateful to Prof. Dr Oscar Salemink, Dr Lorraine Nencel, Dr Irene Stengs and Dr Chayan Vaddhanaphuti for their encouragement, inspirational advice and incisive critiques during my PhD journey. I particularly appreciate their support and concern in the period during which my mother was ill and I struggled with revising the final manuscript of my PhD project. Prof. Dr Charles F. Keyes and Dr Han ten Brummelhuis generously gave comments and criticism from the beginning of my research. I am very grateful for their insight and support. This study would not have been possible without generous funding from the Netherlands Organization for International Cooperation in Higher Education (NUFFIC) and contributions from Khon Kaen University (KKU) for which I am most grateful.

I am obliged to all friends and colleagues at the Department of Social and Cultural Anthropology, Vrije Universiteit Amsterdam who shared experiences and exchanged ideas academically or otherwise during my stay in the Netherlands. My particular thanks and appreciation go to Maaike Matelski, Joan van Wijk, Scott Dalby, Tuan Anh Nguyen, Martha Ruiz, Tom Ngo, Priscilla Koh and Thai Dang Dung. I treasure their helpfulness and precious friendship. In addition, I also enjoyed the companionship of a Thai woman/Dutch man couple, Kao and Glen, who opened their home to me and shared with me their experiences and ideas about transnational marriage. I would like to thank them.

In Thailand, I received intellectual support and valuable advice from Dr Akin Rabhibhadana and Ajarn Suriya Smuthkup, who always paid attention to my work and made time to discuss my project. I also wish to thank Dr Bonnie Brereton for helping in editing and discussing the subject of study while turning my dissertation to this book. In addition, I am grateful for all the interest, commentaries and support from my colleagues and friends from the Department of Sociology and Anthropology and the Research and Development Institute, KKU. I owe special thanks to Phi Ja who encouraged and strengthened me through the ups and downs of completing this project and who always helped in any way she could. I truly appreciate her support.

Finally, and most importantly, I would like to express my deepest gratitude to my dear family who comforted me endlessly with their affection and concern. My sister Phi Phom sustained my energy and commitment through her unfailing support. My late mother looked forward to the completion of this project and I believe that she embraces my accomplishment with enthusiasm and happiness. Therefore, I dedicate this book to her, although it cannot adequately express my gratitude and love for her.

Short Note on the Transliteration of Thai Words and Exchange Rate

For the transliteration of Thai words, I have followed the *Principles of Romanization for Thai Script by Transcription* of the Royal Institute of Thailand (1999). I have made exceptions for names of persons, villages and organisations. Here I have followed established transliterations or the preferences of the persons concerned.

The exchange rate of Thai baht to USD varied according to sources and periods of time. According to the Bank of Thailand, the average rate of exchange fluctuated between 30.39 and 34.34 baht to one USD in the years 2009–11, during which I conducted my fieldwork.

Women, Transnational Marriage and Local Dynamics

"I CAME TO PICK UP my daughter and son-in-law who are coming from Germany", the middle-aged woman standing next to me replied when I asked her reason for coming to the airport. The woman's husband, two grandchildren and several neighbours were with her.

It was late in the morning, two days before the 2008 Songkran festival,[1] and I was at Udon Thani Airport. The small arrival hall in this regional airport was crowded, as many people had come in groups from distant villages to welcome their daughters or nieces who were returning for a visit with their Western husbands. The woman I spoke with said that her daughter and son-in-law returned for a home visit annually or every other year. They usually came either at this time of the year to celebrate the Songkran festival or during the international New Year holiday.

As the couples entered the arrival hall, some of the Western men greeted those waiting for them with a handshake or a hug; others, more familiar with Thai customs, greeted them with a *wai*, the Thai way of greeting. When the German son-in-law embraced the woman with a big hug, she was visibly uncomfortable, but kept a smile on her face. After greetings were exchanged, the group of ten left for the parking lot where they all, including the mixed couple, packed themselves into a pick-up truck and drove away.

Scenes like this are familiar to anyone who travels to airports in Isan, Thailand's north-eastern region. This is true in Udon Thani (or Udon),

---

[1] The Songkran festival is 13–15 April; 13 April is the traditional New Year's Day in Thailand and Laos. It is a time for family members to get together, pay respect to elders, go to Buddhist temples, and visit friends and neighbours. The most obvious activity of Songkran is the throwing of water and so it is known as the water festival. In Thailand, April is normally the hottest month of the year. During the three days of the festival, people roam the streets with containers of water or water guns, or post themselves at the side of roads with a garden hose and soak each other and passersby.

Khon Kaen and the region's other provinces. I had often observed such scenes for some years before starting research in 2008. Travelling by plane from Bangkok to the Isan provinces, I saw countless Isan female/Western male couples, in some cases with children. The couples came from different parts of the world, and their destinations were various Isan villages, the original homes of the women. In Udon and Khon Kaen, where I have lived and visited regularly since the 1980s, the presence of local women with Western partners increased markedly in the first decade of the twenty-first century, and it is common to run into these mixed couples in shopping malls, supermarkets, hotels and restaurants, as well as entertainment and nightlife areas. Encounters like this were part of what inspired me to learn more about the particular experiences and the motivations behind these marriages.

My observation of an increase in the number of such mixed couples was substantiated by a survey conducted by the National Economic and Social Development Board (NESDB). The results showed that in Isan there were 19,594 Thai women married to non-Thai nationals, 87 per cent of whom were Western men from Europe, North America, Australia and New Zealand. These couples were concentrated primarily in three provinces, Udon, Khon Kaen and Nakhon Ratchasima, where almost half of the women originated[2] (NESDB 2004). Updated statistics from the National Statistical Office (NSO) in 2010 show that the number of Westerners residing in Isan had increased to 27,357. Ninety per cent were men who had married Isan women and 80 per cent of these men were from European countries; the rest were from North America, Australia and New Zealand.[3]

My curiosity about this social phenomenon was also kindled by the way in which these marriages were discussed and represented in the media, which usually focused exclusively on material gains for the women. Frequently the marriages were mentioned as being built on "nothing but money". This view was particularly prevalent when the women were from rural villages; they apparently made up the majority of Thai women married to foreigners. Moreover, women marrying Western men were often perceived as being associated with prostitution, a perception that originated

---

[2] Although the NESDB survey was conducted in the rural northeastern areas only, women from other regions have also married foreign men. Transnational marriage has also become increasingly popular among urban women with a good education and a professional career.

[3] http://service.nso.go.th/nso/nso_center/project/search_center/23project-th.htm, accessed 15 July 2016.

during the Vietnam War (1965–75), when many Thai women worked in the entertainment and sex industries that catered to American servicemen. I was aware of this connection; at the same time, however, I knew that not all women with a Western partner, whether from a rural or urban background, had been involved in prostitution. Likewise, while not denying an association between marriage and material gain, I asked myself: is this kind of relationship based solely on money? If not, what are the motivations and desires that encourage local women (and Western men) to opt for such a union? How are motivations and relationships shaped by local and Western cultural norms, gender fantasies, and imaginings about Western societies and lifestyles? In return, how has this kind of transnational relationship challenged or altered cultural ideas and practices pertaining to gender and marriage as well as the existing social order in rural Thai communities? These are the central questions that this book attempts to answer.

Marriages between local women and Western men have a long history in Thailand, beginning in the sixteenth century when the first Westerners came to Siam.[4] In the northeast region, interethnic marriages between women and American military men were prominent when Thailand served as a rest-and-recreation (R&R) site during the Vietnam War. What is new in the current wave of transnational marriages, however, is the over-representation of Northeastern village women.[5] Even more striking is the regularity of contact with women's families in rural Thai communities—through home visits, money transfers and communication via telephone and internet connections—which is much more prevalent now than in the past. The present situation emphasises ties and relations between those who remain in the villages and the women who engage in transnational mobility. In this context, local and global links are intensified through these marriages. Such connections evoke questions about social transformation at the local end as part and parcel of global-local dynamics (Appadurai 1996; Vertovec 2001, 2004; Abdelhady 2006). This book addresses the current dynamics and subtle shifts taking place in Isan communities generated by transnational marriages of village women. It reveals how these marriages challenge gender relations and perceptions of sexuality, marriage, and family life as well as the existing class divisions in the village. It also explores ways in which Thai women and Western men actualise their desires and negotiate social relations developed through transnational intimacy.

---

[4] Siam was the name of Thailand until 1939.

[5] The term "transnational marriage" is used with connotations that will be elaborated in the following section.

My inquiry into these contemporary marriages is informed by current scholarship on global intimacy and transnational encounters that draws on agency, gender and transnational perspectives. Such works focus on the motives, voices and experiences of women and men engaging in transnational intimate relationships in search for better life and security. Nicole Constable's work (2003) provides ground-breaking insights on international marriages. By situating mail-order brides from the Philippines and China within the political economy of globalisation, Constable argues against the portrayal of correspondence marriages within simple binary-opposition notions of victim and agent, East and West, from underdeveloped "South" to developed "North". Rather, transnational marriages are "attentive to women and men's motivations and experiences, and to subtle and complex renderings of power" (2003: 63). Denise Brennan (2004) points out that within transnational intimate networks, power is held by various actors; such power is shaped by gender, class, ethnicity, nationality and sexuality. To uncover such diverse and multifaceted power relations, we must heed the voices of women without losing sight of their vulnerabilities, and reveal women's motives, strategies and goals in transforming oppressive conditions into opportunities. Sealing Cheng (2010) brings to life the experiences of Filipina entertainers working in the bars surrounding US military bases in South Korea, revealing their desires, contradictory motives, agency and resistance to both the poverty of their homeland and the exploitation by bar owners. These works show that the women involved in transnational intimacy and the sex industry are not merely objectified subjects but also free agents who are aware of risks, marginalisation and delegitimisation within their own culture and in other societies (Brennan 2004; Cheng 2010; Constable 2003; Kempadoo 1998).

Another line of explanations describes marriage migration as commodified reproductive labour in which the brides from less-developed countries are imported to wealthier societies to uphold economic competitiveness and sustain social reproduction in middle-class families. In this context, the distinction between domestic worker and wife is blurred (Ishii 2016a; Piper and Roces 2003; Yang and Lu 2010). *Marriage Migration in Asia*, edited by Sari Ishii (2016a), suggests that marriage migrants should not be viewed as powerless and that marriage migration can also involve return or extended migrations. Other works also note a reverse pattern of gender global mobility in which men from wealthier societies move and settle in poorer countries (Oxfeld 2005; Suzuki 2005; Thai 2005). These dynamics, according to Ishii, show that "geographies of power can weaken, fade or reverse by subsequent migrations regardless of a marriage migrant's economic, national or ethnic power" (2016b: 10). In other words, the dynamics can alter geographies of power in economics, nationality or ethnicity. Similar to women's agency analysis, this perspective highlights women and men engaging in transnational intimacy and marriage.

Though the emphasis is important, I want to augment the analysis by broadening the framework to include those people who are not directly engaged in the relationships, but take part in encouraging, facilitating and contriving transnational intimacy and marriages. Nancy Abelmann and Hyunhee Kim's work (2005) is a good example, exploring the efforts of a South Korean mother to facilitate and manipulate the situation for her disabled son to marry a Filipina. While this case is specific and the mother's attempts ultimately failed, it speaks to a larger literature on migration and the "left behind", arguing that people living in migrants' home communities are not passive recipients; rather, they mediate, encourage and facilitate transnational activities and ties (Toyota, Yeoh and Nguyen 2007). Situating this work within the transnational and the "left behind" debate, apart from gender and agency perspectives, I explore the active roles and experiences of those who stay behind in accelerating and facilitating transnational marriages as well as the consequences of these marriages in women's natal communities, especially the challenges to gender and class. Specifically, I argue that women married to Western men constitute a new "class" determined by their consumption patterns and lifestyles, which set them apart from the traditional village elites.

The diverse motivations propelling women (and men) to opt for transnational marriages as well as the ways in which they materialise their desires and craft their life, discussed in Chapters Three and Four, suggest that this kind of transnational intimacy involves a much more complex set of factors than just material considerations. The normative way in which these marriages are seen as built exclusively on money is much too simplistic. Thus, this book explores the ways in which these transnational intimate relations, material considerations and the desire for a meaningful life are intertwined and how they influence the ways women and men involved in this phenomenon make sense of their lives.

Transnational Marriage and *"Mia Farang"*

Throughout this book, there are two key terms, transnational marriage and *"mia farang"*, that are used with different connotations. The term "transnational marriage" is used to signify the nature of current marriages taking place in Isan in which women and their Western partners move regularly between their residence in the husband's native land and the women's home village. These couples maintain their relationships and networks at both ends. Ties and regular contacts, either face-to-face or through such modern technologies as telephone and internet, represent one of the major differences between the current Thai-Western marriages and those of the past. The intensity and regularity of movement between specific sites, as well as communication and long-term social contact across territories of nation-states typify the nature of contemporary transnational practices (Guarnizo and Smith 1998; Portes 1997; Portes, Guarnizo, and Landdolt 1999; Vertovec 2004).

Unlike women who married American servicemen in the 1960s and 1970s, most of whom seldom returned to their village after leaving for the US, women engaged in current transnational marriages today regularly visit their home villages and stay there for periods of time while also travelling to various tourist destinations in Thailand. Currently, the couples are not only more mobile than they were in the past, but they also associate more with the local people in the women's home villages while still maintaining their lives in the husbands' countries. This dualistic frame of practice, according to Sarah Mahler (1998: 79), is the nature of the "lived reality" of globalisation and transnationalism.

The term "transnational marriage" is distinct from such terms as "mixed marriage", "intermarriage" and "cross-cultural marriage", which are normally used in a rather general sense. These terms refer to marriages between people of different ethnicities or cultures with little consideration of whether the couples are from the same or different countries. To connote that a bride and groom are from different countries, Nicole Constable (2005a) uses the term "cross-border marriage". However, all of these terms fail to consider whether the couples maintain ties in their origin and destination countries and how often they move between the settlement and home societies. Thus, use of these terms will be kept to a minimum with reference to specific contexts.

In the Thai context, "*taeng-ngan*" or marriage involves two processes: cultural rituals and registration of the marriage with the state, something that can be done either before or after the ceremony at any district office nationwide under the provisions of Thailand's 1935 marriage registration law. The rituals normally include offering bride wealth to the bride's parents, a Buddhist religious ceremony, a banquet and, in Isan culture, a *bai-si su-khwan* ceremony in which guests place a white string around the couple's wrists and bless them. A union that conforms to these standards is seen as valid and socially acceptable in rural and urban middle-class communities, whether or not it has been formally recorded by the state. However, registration is important for transnational marriages because it establishes a legal status for the non-Thai partner, and allows spouses to secure residency status and social entitlements, along with legal and civil rights. Without registration, transnational couples whose personal and family lives transcend borders could face legal complications.

A related term is *"mia farang"*. This Thai term literally means a Thai wife of a *farang* or Western man. *Farang* refers to a Westerner or a white man or woman, and in this book I use the terms *farang* and Westerner interchangeably. To villagers in Na Dokmai—the Isan village where I conducted my fieldwork—women living with and receiving financial support from their Western partners, regardless of whether they officially registered their marriage or not, are referred to as *mia farang*. *Mia farang* denotes a woman involved in a serious and long-term relationship with a Western partner. In this case, the husband is referred to as a *phua farang*. If a relationship is casual or just initiated, a Western man is referred to as a *faen farang*, meaning a Western boyfriend, while a woman is not called a *mia farang*. This practice is common in Na Dokmai. The Thai term *"phua"* denotes a more significant relationship than *faen*. However, the term *"faen"* is gender-neutral and shares the ambiguity of "husband/partner" in that *faen* can be used to refer to a husband/wife or a boyfriend/girlfriend. In this book, the terms "husband" and "partner" are alternately used to signify the seriousness of the relationships.

The category of *mia farang*, as referred to by villagers, is rather fluid and sometimes problematic. Normally, a woman is considered to be a *mia farang* as long as her relationship with a Western partner is maintained. When the relationship ends, the woman is no longer called a *mia farang*. Later, if she engages in a serious relation with another Western man, she is again referred to as a *mia farang*. However, there were some women in my study whose relationships ended and yet were continually referred to as *mia farang*. These were exceptional cases because these women had become influential figures in the village and their status as *mia farang* continued to be socially significant even though the relationship had ended.

There is another Thai term, *"phanraya farang"*, which also refers to Westerner's wives and denotes more of a sense of respect as compared to *mia farang*. The terms *phanraya* and *mia* both mean wife or wives, and *sami* and *phua* mean husband(s). From a formal point of view, there is a distinction between *phanraya* and *mia*. *Mia* generally and *mia farang* specifically can connote a lack of respect. At first, I considered using the term *phanraya farang*. When I started my fieldwork in the village, I found that villagers rarely used the term *phanraya farang*. Therefore, I changed to *mai farang* to follow that usage. For villagers in Na Dokmai, *mia farang* does not necessarily have a negative connotation and may be, to some extent, a positive appellation.

In Thai society at large, the term *mia farang* may be perceived as discriminatory as it is often associated with the term *mia chao* (hired wife) associated with American servicemen during the Vietnam War. In that specific context, a connection between women engaging in sex-related business and marrying a *farang* man was established. This social stigma has remained in the collective memory of Thai people. This perception of *mia farang* is reinforced by the fact that a route through which women of later generations met and made connections with Western men was often that of transnational tourist destinations and involved sex-related businesses, even though there are numerous other channels to enter into such marital relationships: see Chapter Four for further discussion of this issue. On another score, *mai farang* are also seen as strategic resources capable of supporting their family and community as well as social development. The ambiguous meanings of this term and the contexts in which they emerged will be discussed in Chapter Five. To avoid the derogatory connotations associated with the term, in this book *mia farang* will be used only in specific contexts with reference to particular local usages and circumstances.

Transnational Marriage in Thai and Global Contexts

The study of interethnic marriage is not a new research issue, but studying intermarriages from a transnational perspective is a recent inquiry informed by transnational migration scholarship inaugurated in the 1990s. Transnational migration scholarship grew out of a critique of the assimilation theory that dominated the literature on immigration and immigrants, especially in American society from the 1920s to the 1990s. During this period the "melting pot" metaphor was used to describe newcomers from all backgrounds putting their efforts into adapting to a new environment and eventually blending into American culture. This perspective overlooked the self-awareness of immigrants and the possibility of maintaining relationships and connections with their homeland (Glazer and Moynihan 1963; Park 1928). Drawing on assimilation explanations, scholars viewed intermarriages in Thailand as a means to integrate people from other ethnic backgrounds into Thai society and culture. G. William Skinner's classic work (1957) on the Chinese in Thai society, for instance, notes that intermarriages between Chinese male immigrants and local women were promoted, particularly during the reign of King Rama V

(1868–1910). The assimilation policy was intended to capitalise on Chinese expertise in trading, taxing and shipping, all of which were important to the country's development, especially after Siam signed the Bowring Treaty[6] in 1855. Through intermarriage, Chinese were assimilated into Thai ways of life and the third-generation descendants were generally Thai in culture and identification (Skinner 1957: 134).

In the later periods, inter- and transnational marriages in Thai society were viewed in three different ways. The first perspective involved the Thai government's hosting of American bases in the 1960s and 1970s and promoting tourism in the 1980s. These contexts created favourable circumstances for marriages between local women—particularly those working in the service, entertainment and sex industries—and foreign men. Since the 1980s, the enormous growth of tourism, a key source of Thailand's foreign exchange, has shifted to encounters between Thai women and foreign male tourists from Europe and Japan. Thai tourism, like its counterparts in the Caribbean, Latin America and Africa, tends to rely on the intimate labour of women who provide services to male tourists from the wealthier countries (Bishop and Robinson 1998; Cohen 2003; Constable 2009; Patcharin 2007; Sirijit 2014; Truong 1990).

The second perspective from which inter- and transnational marriages in Thai society were viewed was to study intermarriages within the framework of international migration, especially the transnational sex industry— viewing these marriages as a means for women to engage in the sex industry in Western countries (Pataya 1999, 2002; Supang et al. 1999). I want to expand and clarify this explanation. Experiences of the women who met their *farang* husbands by engaging in the sex industry in transnational tourist destinations such as Pattaya suggest a counter-logic to the explanation. These women were employed in sex work as a pragmatic means by which to establish transnational relationships that in many cases resulted in marriage. This insight is also reflected in Brennan's work (2004: 24), which suggests that sex work can be an "advancement" strategy for women to marry male tourists and migrate to the West as well as to provide economic stability. Similarly, Cheng views the migration of Filipina entertainers to work in South Korean bars in the hope of marrying American servicemen as a "method of setting hope in motion" (2010: 223).

---

[6] The Bowring Treaty was about trade, and its primary concern was with the permission of free trade by foreigners in Siam, which previously had been subjected to heavy royal taxes.

The third approach focuses on individual choice and agency, especially women's agency, and how such agency is facilitated and limited by local and global cultures and norms as well as by constraints and opportunities (Panitee 2009; Rattana and Thompson 2013; Sirijit and Angeles 2013). Transnational marriages are viewed as a way for women and men to empower each other and to regain their denied backgrounds and identities at home, as shown in a study of poor rural Isan women and lonely, mostly blue-collar Western men (Ratana 2010). Studies focusing on men's experiences and perspectives include Suriya Smutkupt and Pattana Kitiarsa's (2007) view of Isan female-*farang* male marriage as a "gendered orientalizing project" of men who wish to have Asian wives and develop their post-retirement life and family away from their home country. By living in Isan communities, Western men have been able to position themselves as "good providers" through manoeuvring and negotiating their sense of self and providing money (and relationships) to their wives and others in the community (Thompson, Pattana, and Suriya 2016). Their white privilege and their disadvantages as migrants are place-bound and shaped by social relations and class locations in local and global economies, which vary across social space and time (Maher and Lafferty 2014). In "Masculinity, Marriage and Migration" (2018), I also reveals both the negotiation and vulnerability of *farang* migrant men, though they are from a more advantageous position.

An assessment of studies on inter- and transnational marriages in Thai society reveals various contexts and conceptualisations of marriages between Thai women and Western men. It also highlights the fact that contemporary works consider these marriages as part of global processes facilitated by the advancement of communication and transportation technology as well as by the emergence of unbounded and fluid perceptions of different possibilities for a better life on a global scale (Appadurai 1996; Schiller, Basch and Blanc-Szanton 1992). Increasing global mobility—in the form of tourism, labour migration, business travel and study—has created favourable circumstances for women and men from different parts of the world to opt for marriage (Jones and Shen 2008). In this context, particular countries in Asia, especially Thailand, China, the Philippines and Vietnam, have become popular places of origin for marriage migrants, as well as for labour migrants looking for better opportunities (Bélanger, Lee and Wang 2011; Constable 2005a; Jones 2012; Nakamatsu 2005; Piper and Roces 2003; Yang and Lu 2010; Wang and Chang 2002). While opportunities to meet and develop transnational relationships have increased, they do not represent a "global free-for-all" phenomenon (Constable 2005a). Rather, marriage opportunities are shaped by gender, ethnicity and class, as well as by socio-economic, historical and political factors.

Literature on this topic also addresses the varied and uneven ways in which economic factors, gender expectations, racialised fantasies, familial obligations, demographic composition and personal motives come into play and shape transnational intimacy and marriage opportunities. For example, Lenore Manderson and Margaret Jolly (1997) discuss how cross-cultural liaisons between Europeans and local people in Asia and the Pacific region were influenced by confluences of cultures, erotic imaginings, border crossings and fluid terrain apart from economic incentives. Lieba Faier (2009) reveals the contradictory and ambivalent experiences of Filipina entertainers and wives in rural Japan and how these women managed to craft their lives and selves in both Japan and the Philippines through "professions of love". Such experiences reflect their financial pressure and familial obligations on the one hand and gender expectations in performing transnational labour of love on the other. Sealing Cheng (2010) also points out the variety of personal reasons prompting Filipina entertainers to choose their profession—not only economic incentives, but also personal autonomy, freedom and the hope for a better life. Hung Cam Thai's work (2008) demonstrates that marriages between Vietnamese men living in United States and women in Vietnam are facilitated by imbalanced demographic composition, gender expectations and disparities in the status of individuals in the two countries. These studies highlight the multiple, complex and sometimes intertwined factors shaping transnational intimacy and marriage. Moreover, they underline a common pattern of marriages involving brides from poorer countries and grooms from wealthier locations in the global economic hierarchy—a pattern that Constable calls "global marriage-scapes" (2005b: 3–7).

Gendered patterns in global marriage-scapes are common in labour migration as well. Transnational labour migration has involved women from Asia, Latin America and Eastern Europe who leave their homeland to find employment in North America, Western Europe and Australia, as well as wealthier countries in Asia. In many cases, the female migrants eventually marry men in the host countries (Ehrenreich and Hochschild 2002; Mahler and Pessar 2001; Piper and Roces 2003). In this sense, labour migration and marriage migration are a part of the same global processes and overlap to an extent. However, lumping domestic workers and wives into the same analytical category will distort our understanding of the experiences and realities of women of both groups. The routes and processes of migration, as well as the social relations that women encounter as migrant wives, are certainly different from those of workers, as this study aims to illustrate.

Marriage in Thai and Western Cultures: Love, Money and Sexuality

The gendered patterns of "global marriage-scapes" have often led to simplistic assumptions that portray the relationships as opportunistic: women marry to resolve economic problems, while men marry for romantic love, sex or to reassert patriarchal privileges under threat in their home countries (Davidson 1995; Garrick 2005; Ratana 2010). The normative depiction of marriages in this dichotomous fashion draws basically on Western ideas of "authentic" romantic relations based solely on romantic love. The intersection of love and money would inevitably erode the authenticity of romantic relationships. When they come into contact they contaminate each other—sentiment would be depleted by instrumental rationality, while introducing sentiment into rational transactions produces inefficiency. The cultural ideal that marriage should be about romance and not about money is widely apparent both in the academic world and beyond (Zelizer 2005: 20–6).

While love and money are considered to be mutually exclusive in Western societies, these two overlap somewhat in Thai society. The intermingling of sex, mutual affection and material resources is embedded in Thai cultural norms, manifested through various marriage customs and practices. The Thai custom of providing *sinsot* (bride wealth) by a groom to a bride's family to legitimate the marriage indicates the intersection of marital relations, material resources and sex (Lyttleton 2000; Whittaker 1999). Criteria for spouse selection always involve the considerations of the future welfare of the family (Sumalee 1995). Economic provisions in marriage are completely acceptable and, in many cases, an important reason to marry in the first place. Material support from the men is perceived as a demonstration of their love and care for women. Although this cultural idea seems to disturb Westerners, many women whom I spoke with expressed much affection and love for and from their Western partners who could economically provide for them. Marriage is thus both about money and intimate needs.

The cultural ideal emphasising romantic love as the basis for marriage in Western societies is a "modern" one that has been evolving gradually since the nineteenth century. In the sixteenth and seventeenth centuries, the family was held firmly within the matrix of a larger social order—the kin network, the wider community and ancestral traditions. With the surge of sentiment and the rise of the nuclear family, ties to the outside world were weakened, while connections binding members of the family together were reinforced. This change reversed the priorities of spouse choosing (Shorter 1975). In modern times, the cultural ideals of romantic love, personal affection and individual fulfilment have been the basis for marriage in Western societies (Lindholm 2006: 5–6; Shorter 1975: 13–15). It is this cultural ideal that the dichotomous view of marriage is based upon.

The binary explanation of marriage has been criticised by scholars, for instance Amalia Cabezas (2009), Nicole Constable (2003, 2009) and Viviana Zelizer (2005), who ask whether intimacy and money are two distinct and separate domains of social life or, in reality, intertwined and negotiated. Zelizer (2005) in particular makes this point. Through looking at how this dichotomy is approached in the literature, she points out two different ways: "hostile worlds" and "nothing but". "Hostile worlds" beliefs maintain separate boundaries between money and intimacy as they operate according to different principles. "Nothing but" views reduce intimate relations to three domains: economic rationality, culture and politics. An economic reasoning is the most common version in which love, sex and care are seen as nothing but commodities. Zelizer (2005: 20–2) argues that neither perspective can help us capture the reality of day-to-day life in which intimate relations and economic activities are blended and people are actively engaged in negotiating such combinations in constructing their social lives. She proposes alternative explanations, glossed as "connected lives" or "good matches". A good match does not necessarily mean that the match is equal and just, but that it is viable. "It gets the economic work of the relationship done and sustains the relationship" (Zelizer 2006: 307). Good matches demonstrate agreements between the partners in a relationship, and are particularly important for durable relationships such as stable marriages. Good matches also depend on meanings and practices available in the local milieu.

By raising the different cultural meanings of marriage in Thai and Western societies and Zelizer's perspective of "connected lives", I aim to reveal how love and material resources complicate the relationships developed through the current transnational intimate interactions between Thai women and Western men. This analysis allows me to move beyond the conceptualisations of inter- and transnational marriages which thus far are described in relation to colonial culture, militarisation and gendered imaginations, as well as the discourses of modernity and tradition (Cohen 2003; Constable 2005a; Enloe 2000; Stoler 1992; Tolentino 1996; Weisman 2000). My analysis focuses on the interplay between economic means, intimacy and desires to create and maintain transnational connections. I also seek to explore how such interactions and social relations are shaped by the differences between Thai and Western cultures regarding marriage and dissimilar interpretations of such cultural norms.

Motivations and the Logics of Desire

Moving away from the common assumption that views current transnational marriages in a dichotomous fashion, I explore the debates surrounding the issues of gender, race and sexuality that motivate desires and facilitate marriages between Asian women and Western men. The discussion provides a framework for an in-depth investigation in later sections.

Among scholarly works on intermarriages and border-crossing sexual encounters in an Asian context, Ann Stoler's insightful work (1992) reveals how sexuality, gender and race were linked to rules and politics, which in turn influenced individuals and families in twentieth-century Asia. Through her analysis of *métissage* (interracial unions) in French Indochina and the Netherlands Indies which gave rise to an unwanted category of *métis* (mixed bloods), Stoler points out the coexistence of inclusionary impulses and exclusionary and discriminatory practices. While colonialism generated sexual desires and fantasies among the coloniser and the colonised alike, the rejection of *métis* as a distinct legal category intensified the politics of cultural difference and confirmed the practices of imposing European superiority at the same time. Stoler's work also shows how the gendered policing of especially female sexuality was intended to keep ethnic boundaries intact, thus ensuring the endogamy of ethnic groups, which in colonial contexts overlapped with classes. Her study is one of the first academic works emphasising the intrinsic relationship between sex, gender, race, class and power in Asia. Though the investigation was of a colonial context, it sheds light on diverse circumstances and factors influencing the logics of desire and shaping conjugal relationships across borders, either by facilitating or restricting them. Stoler's work highlights the fact that motivations and aspirations associated with such relationships extend beyond love and material motives.

Similar to colonialism, militarisation has also influenced sexual desires and encouraged interracial marital relations. Constable (2003), in particular, makes this point when she describes how military experiences in the Philippines shape gender imaginations and fantasies, encouraging American men to look for Filipina spouses. Some American servicemen who served in the Philippines retained images of nurturing Filipina nurses and doctors.

These fantasies enhanced the attraction of Filipinas as prospective wives devoted to domestic tasks. Encounters between Americans and Filipinas during colonial times provided American men images of Filipinas as being more traditional, less modern and less influenced by feminism than Western women. These women were perceived as ideal wives and mothers who embraced traditional familial values. Such images of Asian women motivated Western men to look to Asia and other parts of the world for women who were thought to be committed to family values and the traditional role of a wife (Constable 2005a; Piper and Roces 2003; Thai 2008). Another view draws on Edward Said's discursive notion of "Orientalism" (1978), depicting Asia as a reflection of Western men's sexual fantasies. Such fantasies have inspired desires for transnational encounters and directed Western male tourists to travel to Asia to consume the fantasies of the eroticised Orient (Cohen 1996; Dahles 2009). Some men who marry Isan women are motivated by "certain degrees of a 'masculinity Orientalizing' style of thought and rationalization", allowing them to fulfil their exotic dream of having an Asian wife (Suriya and Pattana 2007: 3).

While men are drawn to Asian women by the expectations of "traditional values", Asian women are often attracted to Western men because of their assumptions about "modern" ways of life and more flexible gender relations in Western countries than in their own homelands. Others anticipate escaping from limited marriage opportunities at home, particularly for divorced women, women with a high education as well as those whose age renders them past "marriageability" as defined by local standards. Marrying a Western man offers women a way to grow out of these local constraints as well as to escape from gender inequalities at home (Constable 2005b; Patcharin 2012; Schein 2005; Thai 2005). Nevertheless, some women consider passion as the driving force behind their desire to marry a Western man (Constable 2003; McKay 2003). Others emphasise love in their efforts to construct and nourish new identities and gendered subjectivities in both home and host societies (Faier 2009). There has also been a growing body of literature discussing how such cognitive processes as gender imagination and fantasy as well as hope for a better life and freedom facilitate transnational marriage and migration (Cheng 2010; Ratana 2010).

The literature thus demonstrates that there are diverse factors influencing women's and men's marriage choices, posing new challenges to assumptions about love and economics. Recent scholarship emphasises the blurred boundaries between money and love and the multiple factors influencing marriage decisions and experiences. I posit that it is the combination of diverse motivations that constitute the logics of desire shaping marriage choices and experiences.

Transnational Marriage and Those Who Stay Behind

Growing out of migration scholarship, the transnational perspective offers a way out of the image of migration as a one-way process of incorporation and acculturation of migrants into host societies (Vertovec 2004). Rather, this approach looks at connections and ties that span borders. It also recognises the possibility of multi-ethnicities, multiple or hybridised identities, diversity of attachments and belongings, and multidirectional flows of imaginations, ideas and objects (Basch, Schiller and Blanc 1994; Guarnizo and Smith 1998; Kearney 1995; Vertovec 1999, 2001). The transnational approach allows us to conceive interactions and social relations in both the origin and the settlement societies rather than exclusively emphasising the receiving end (and those engaging in mobility) as key agents. In this sense, the scope of analysis is expanded to include the people living in sending communities who do not actually move, but who are involved in transnational activities in one way or another, either materially or ideationally.

Transnational connections between migrants—both labour migrants and marriage migrants—and their families in the home community take various forms, among which remittances are the most prominent. Money sent home and its use are viewed as the heart of the "migration-development nexus" (Glytsos 2002; King, Dalipaj and Mai 2006; Stahl and Arnold 1986). However, this perspective is criticised for emphasising economic benefits while downplaying the social and cultural effects of transnational practices. It also tends to treat people who stay at home solely as benefitting from remittances, while overlooking the consequences of migration on their lives beyond the alleviation of poverty. Another perspective calls for a more comprehensive social view of migration studies (Levitt 1996, 2001; Piper and Roces 2003; Piper 2009; Schuerkens 2005). Nicola Piper (2009) emphasises the effects of migration on the social fabric and transformation in the origin countries of migrants—the "social development approach to migration". Peggy Levitt (1996) also argues that migration involves not only a financial flow but also "social remittances". Social remittances refer to ideas, behaviours, lifestyles, identities and social capital that flow from receiving- to sending-country communities through practices and ties linking migrants to their home villages. The lives of local people who themselves never migrated are influenced and transformed by the transnational activities and ideologies of those who actually moved (Kyle

2000; Levitt 2001). Ratana Tosakul's work (2010) also elaborates how cross-cultural marriages between Thai women and Western men influence the dynamics of gender relations regarding sexuality and marriage in women's natal village. The reconfiguration of gender relations and norms as a result of marriage migration and transnational marriage is uncovered in other studies (Bélanger et al. 2010; Rahman 2007). The conceptualisation of migrations as a factor of social transformation in migrants' home societies is central to this approach (Schuerkens 2005).

Nevertheless, both the "social remittance" analysis and the "social development approach to migration" have been questioned for their tendency to view the people left at home as passive recipients (Toyota et al. 2007). These approaches focus on various impacts of migration on the community of origin and its residents, but shed little light on how those people left at home react to or are involved in migration processes. The relationships between the migrants and those who stay behind are in fact open-ended and multidirectional in nature. Their experiences need to be explored with an interactive perspective in the broader social, economic and political contexts (Rigg 2007). Recent migration studies address the "migration-left behind nexus" (Toyota et al. 2007: 157) and stress that we can gain new insights into migration within both internal and transnational contexts by bringing those who have remained in departure communities into view.

Relationships between migrants and those who stay in sending-country communities highlight the interplay between movement, flows, power and agency. Here, Doreen Massey's notion of "power-geometry" (1993) provides insight, especially in capturing the relationships in transnational space. Massey (1993: 59) points out that modernity, within particular conditions, has produced time-space compression—movement and communication across space which implies geographical stretching out of social relations—making transnational mobility more possible. Under these conditions, movement or flows become an important element associated with the ability to access power. However, the point of concern is not only who moves and who does not, but also who influences decisions and actions in transnational processes. Some people are involved in movement while others are not. "There are groups who really, in a sense, [are] in charge of time-space compression; who can effectively use it and turn it to [their] advantage.... But there are groups who, although doing a lot of physical moving, are not 'in charge' of the process in the same way" (Massey 1993: 61). Thus, interactions and social relations in transnational spaces are contested and complex: they involve people who initiate and participate in flows or movement as well as those who are not directly engaged in mobility. The role of people who stay behind is not that of passive recipients without agency.

Taking the "left-behind" debates into account, my approach includes local people living in rural homes as much as the women engaged in transnational marriage. Specifically, I examine how those who remain in the women's natal village mediate, encourage and participate in transnational marriage processes. Moving one step further, I also explore how transnational marriages have generated tensions affecting the social order in women's natal villages. To this end, I argue that women with Western partners constitute a distinct social category characterised by their distinctive consumption patterns and lifestyles that set them apart from the old village elites. Their improved economic well-being also allows these women to fulfil social obligations as dutiful daughters and gain social recognition. This emerging category of women challenges the existing class divisions in the village. These women make up a new "class" within the socio-economic hierarchical structure in the village reflecting their social mobility. This dynamic is a part of social transformations in contemporary Isan society and Thailand in general.

Gender and Transnational Marriage

An attempt to comprehend transnational marriages of Isan women would be difficult or impossible without understanding how cultural ascriptions of gender in Thai society consign different expectations concerning social roles and identities between women and men. The conventional explanation relates Thai ideas of gender to Buddhist beliefs. This approach is a prominent analysis of gender distinction and is in line with the feminist mainstream of the 1970s. A core argument relates the predominance of Thai women in the economic domain to their disadvantaged status in the religious world: women cannot earn the highest status, defined as the world of monkhood. Rather, they are confined to the roles of wife and/or mother (Kirsch 1982, 1985). This idea was, however, countered by Charles Keyes (1984) who argued that although women are prevented from directly accessing the spiritual power of monkhood, they enjoy a complementary status as mothers through sacrificing their sons to become monks. Moreover, a gender distinction influenced by Buddhism is inherent in the Thai cultural norm of *bun khun*—the mutual reciprocity that underlies relationships between parents and children in Thai families (Akin 1984). This cultural norm ties women to their parents and natal families physically, emotionally and materially.

Contributions to the family are a way for women to repay their moral debt to their parents, symbolising the gratitude of a dutiful daughter.

The concept of a "dutiful daughter" is a powerful one. It influences gender roles and relations and shapes women's lives in larger social contexts. Most of the studies on transnational and cross-cultural marriages of Thai women highlight their desire to fulfil expected dutiful daughter roles as a key motivation propelling them to engage in such a marital union (Panitee 2009; Ratana 2010; Sirijit 2013). Some scholars also explain prostitution in Thai society in relation to this concept as the profession enables women to fulfil this filial obligation (Muecke 1992; Sukanya 1988; Thitsa 1980; Truong 1990). Another line of explanation links commercial sex to the pattern of economic development and modernisation that creates differential opportunities between rural and urban sectors and affects the lives of rural people, especially women (Keyes 1984; Lyttleton 1994; Pasuk 1982; Yos 1992a).

Other perspectives relate gender with modernisation as well as the embodiment of Thai popular culture. Among the former view, Mary Beth Mills's ethnography (1999) of Isan female migrant workers shows how participating in wage employment in Bangkok allows these women to realise the powerful desires of being *thansamai* (modern)—consuming modern commodities (for example fashionable clothes, cosmetics and jewellery) and experiencing urban lifestyles and modern entertainment. Rural-to-urban migration also enables women to fulfil their obligation as dutiful daughters who support their parents and siblings in the rural home. The latter perspective on embodiment and subjectivity is also revealed in Mills's examination of migrants' daily life and how they perform dominant discourses of Thai modernity, especially the images of "modern women" that they would like to duplicate. These women express pride in acquiring such experiences and lifestyles (Mills 1999: 127–33). Other works illustrate the changing ideas of (female) beauty which are geared toward cultural hybridity (Van Esterik 1996). Eurasian and Amerasian physical features have become highly prized and more popular in the media and in popular discourses. The engendering of a Thai self is part and parcel of the commercialisation of beauty both in local and global contexts (Van Esterik 2000; Reynolds 1999). This transition has created a preference for children of mixed Thai-Western parents (*luk khrueng*) which has become a part of women's desires to engage in transnational marriage.

The conventional perspective framing Thai gender in relation to Buddhist beliefs helps in explaining the economic contributions and moral connections of women married to Western men to their natal family in the rural home.

The contemporary perspectives focusing on modernity and embodiment provide insight on the motivations, perceptions and actions related to marriage. All these aspects influence interactions and social relations between these women, their husbands and other social actors in the women's natal community. While acknowledging the conventional approach, I also elaborate on it by exploring how the dutiful daughter obligations reinforce the (re)production of Thai femininity and simultaneously place local men in a vulnerable situation. In other words, my analysis concentrates both on the ways in which cultural discourses of gender have shaped decisions and experiences of women and men engaging in transnational intimacy and marriage and on how such marriages challenge gender power relations at the "local end" where these marital relations are embedded.

The Research

This research was carried out in two locations: Na Dokmai, a village in Udon Thani province, and Pattaya, a transnational tourist site in Chonburi province.

Na Dokmai, the primary research site, is located 40 kilometres southwest of the city of Udon, the capital of Udon province. Pattaya, one of the most famous tourist destinations in Thailand, is located 145 kilometres southeast of Bangkok and 650 kilometres southeast of Udon (see Map 1) and, like Udon town, served as an R&R centre for the American military during the Vietnam War in the 1960s and 1970s. In addition to my studies in the two field sites in Thailand, I was also in close contact with two Thai-Dutch couples living in the Netherlands in which the wives were from Na Dokmai during the years 2007–12 when I lived there. Furthermore, I occasionally met with other Thai women and their Dutch husbands by participating in various social and cultural activities organised by Thai communities in the Netherlands, including a gathering at the Thai temple in Amsterdam for a religious ceremony. Data collected and understanding gained through these associations in the Netherlands enriched and complemented my ethnographic work.

Before deciding to locate the research site in Na Dokmai, I visited a dozen villages in Udon Thani and Khon Kaen provinces. These two provinces and Nakhon Ratchasima were home to almost half of the women with Western partners in the Northeast (NESDB 2004). Among these villages, Na Dokmai stood out in terms of the willingness of its residents to share their experiences and ideas about transnational marriage. When I introduced my research to the community leaders and local authorities, I learned that most

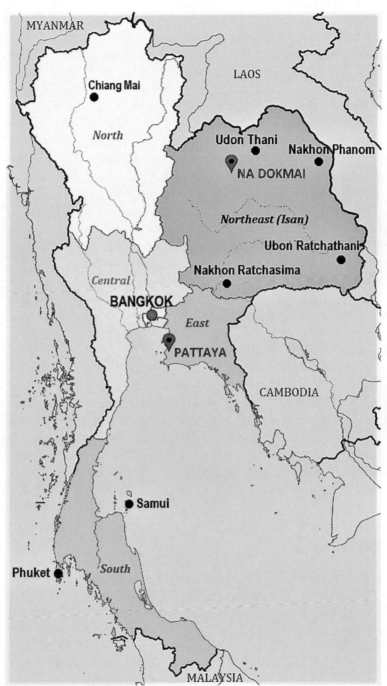

Map 1: Map of Thailand and Research Sites

of them had information and opinions about these marriages which they were willing to share with me. In January 2008, I started my first round of fieldwork and resided in the village with my research assistant until the middle of May 2008. After the first month, I decided to conduct a modest survey of background information about women married to Westerners in the village to collect demographic data and a brief history of their marriages. The survey provides relevant quantitative data to supplement ethnographic accounts. The survey results are presented in Appendix 2.

The preliminary findings led me to extend my research to Pattaya, the most popular contact zone among tourist destinations where many women from Na Dokmai had met their future *farang* husbands. There were already a considerable number of village women who had been working in Pattaya in an attempt to make connections with Western men, hoping that the relationships could eventually lead to serious commitments and marriage. For the second round of data collection, from October 2008 to May 2009, I conducted fieldwork by following village women working at a bar in Pattaya for a month. In addition, after returning to work at Khon Kaen University from 2012 to 2014, I revisited Na Dokmai on several occasions and kept contact with several villagers. Such visits and relationships allowed me to follow up on changes taking place in the village.

This research involves what George Marcus (1995) calls "multi-sited ethnography". While following the people involved in the phenomenon, it focuses on the locality where transnational marriages are embedded and where the mixed couples have resettled or have visited regularly. This strategy helps understand how the system works in translocal and transnational sites. Marcus points out various "tracking" strategies that have been employed in collecting information, including following the people, the stories, the conflicts and the metaphors that concern them. This approach shifts from the conventional ethnography of a single-sited location to multiple sites. It is particularly relevant to the study of transnational ties and activities, which cannot be fully understood within a particular single setting (Marcus 1995: 98).

While acknowledging the merits of Marcus's approach, I also take account of scholarly observations regarding the distribution of attention and (deep) involvement to maintain established standards of ethnographic research (Hannerz 1998: 248; Hendry 2003: 498). The differences in terms of fieldwork duration and number of interviews in various field sites are cases in point of an unbalanced distribution of information gained from such locations. Inevitably, these variations reflect the depth of my ethnographical data and understanding at different field sites. Thus, it is important to note here that the central concern of this research is to contribute to the local end of transnational connections—the women's natal village—while the translocal and transnational linkages provide more dynamic views and a deeper understanding of transnational processes and practices taking place at the village.

I interviewed 93 women and men, including Thais and Westerners, 86 in Na Dokmai and 7 in Pattaya (see Table 1, Appendix 1). In the village, I talked to local women and Western men involved in transnational marriages, the women's parents and siblings, as well as village leaders, residents, local government staff and school teachers. Among the 26 women involved with *farang* interviewed, 19 were having a relationship with a Westerner and 6 had already ended their relationship at the time of the interview. Five of the Western partners interviewed had resettled in the village (including one man living in a nearby village) for more than five years; the other six men were visiting their wives' home village. In Pattaya, three women interviewed were from Na Dokmai, three were from other rural villages in Northeastern provinces and one was from a village in the central region.

Identity, Relationship and the Ethnographic Experience

Before engaging in fieldwork, I presumed that it would be difficult to conduct an interview on such personal matters, given that I would be reluctant to disclose details of my own personal life. My concern in this regard was mostly about how my own background—an unmarried woman in academia who had studied overseas—would shape relationships and rapport with villagers. I soon realised that my initial concern was not entirely unjustified. In various contexts, my background created perceptions on the part of villagers regarding what kinds of information I should or should not know or ask about, as well as expectations of particular forms of assistance that I could provide them. The extent to which these expectations were realisable could have an impact on my rapport with key informants, thus affecting my access to information. Such situations required a considerable degree of management and negotiation so as to maintain good relationships.

Although my career and training are different from most of the residents in Na Dokmai, I am an Isan native and I share some commonality in terms of social and cultural characteristics as well as language—I speak the local dialect—with the villagers. This common background and my experience in conducting research in rural villages enabled me to establish research relations with the villagers fairly quickly. Good relations helped many women feel comfortable in talking with me openly. Nevertheless, these connections, created expectations which I had to deal with in some situations. For instance, I was repeatedly asked by women's parents or senior kin to help their daughters or nieces make contact with Western men. A few women who went out of their way to help me establish connections with several people in the village were serious in asking for assistance in this regard. Such requests created a situation that required negotiation, although I always obliged to help when requests involved tasks such as translating, filling in visa application forms or finding books to improve someone's English. In the eyes of the villagers, my experience of having lived abroad, my ability to communicate with Western men and my familiarity with computers and the internet qualified me as a potential agent capable of putting women in contact with Western men. Such a match-making service in the village was initiated by a local school teacher and a few teachers followed suit. I am also a teacher; in their eyes I am qualified to help them.

In order to maintain the good relationships so far developed and to avoid becoming entangled in match-making requests, I gave various (ethical) explanations. For example, I explained that there were rules I had to follow in doing research and that the request to arrange a match was against such rules. One woman said no one would check whether I followed the rules or not. So the reasons I gave did not work, and requests kept on coming. Finally, I said that they should not count on me in this matter since I could not find a Western partner for myself even though I had lived overseas for several years. Interestingly, this explanation was the most convincing one. Such requests were often brought up during the initial period of the field research. Later on they became less frequent, but every now and then they turned up again.

As the fieldwork progressed, many villagers, especially women married to *farang* men, became more at ease in talking about their lives, although there were those who showed reservations; some even refused to be interviewed. The women often shared with me their experiences of living abroad or visiting foreign countries, their connections and ties with those who stayed behind in the home village, their contributions to the village and to their parent's and sibling's households, as well as their relationships with their husbands. However, the conversation was often limited regarding issues of sexuality, which is admittedly under-represented in this book. This must have had something to do with my status as an unmarried woman. For my part, I was expected not to openly express my interest in or ask questions about sexual issues. When I tried to bring this up, the women often asked, "Are you married?" The implications were crystal clear: as an unmarried woman, I was not supposed to know about sexuality. While I was aware of this gender norm, I had presumed that they knew that it was a part of my research. However, I realised that I had made an inaccurate assumption.

In another instance, my background as an unmarried woman was used as a silencer. When I attempted to discuss with village men what a bar girl had told me about the differences between Thai and *farang* clients in terms of sexuality, I was given a look that signalled I was violating the line of "appropriate behaviour" as far as my gender and marital status were concerned. Going against this could have had a negative impact on my relationships with the informants, which inevitably would have affected my access to data. Furthermore, these encounters also reminded me of ethical considerations to the effect that villagers might be willing to share some parts of their personal lives but not others. I was respectful and appreciative of their reactions and did not push further. A few women, however, were willing to talk about sexual issues more openly. In this sense, this book represents the multilayered conversations that shaped my interactions with my research participants and the emotionally textured contexts of such relationships as much as objective information.

Overview of the Book

This book is distinct from other studies of transnational marriage and intimacy in several ways. First, it addresses the experiences and sentiments of both the people engaging in (and attempting to engage in) these transnational relationships and those living in women's natal villages, who do not directly engage in the relationship but influence and facilitate it. Their stories attest to the strength and creativity of people seeking to forge meaningful lives in the processes of social transition in the face of local and global encounters. Thus, the book adds to the body of literature about transnational intimacy and marriage by focusing on the "left-behind" population of transnationalism. Second, this book sheds light on the "local end" of transnational connections; it reveals an emergent social category in the women's natal village constituted by women with *farang* husbands. I argue that these women have created a new "class" determined by their distinctive patterns of consumption and social recognition. This dynamic challenges the village hierarchical structure and puts the village elites in a vulnerable position. Third, this study addresses the issue of transnational marriage by elaborating the binary views about materiality and intimacy within global relationship and transnational intimacies. Fourth, this book moves beyond the perspective that connects current transnational marriages in Thai society to the presence of American troops in Thailand during the Vietnam War (1965–75). It shows that the historical roots of these marriages can be traced back several centuries and that this longer history provides profound insights in terms of structural conditions in which the current popularity of transnational marriages is grounded.

The historical perspective of transnational marriages is revealed in Chapter One, which illustrates the socio-economic and political relevance of these relationships in various contexts, highlighting an extent of social recognition which the current popularity of transnational marriage is drawn on. Chapter Two focuses on transformations in Na Dokmai as a site where transnational marriages are embedded, demonstrating how the "local" and "global" articulations taking place in the village during recent decades have been intensified through transnational marriages. Chapter Three discusses the diverse and complex motivations that feed into the "logics of desire", propelling local women and Western men to engage in transnational marriage. Chapter Four examines the ways in which women realise their desires to engage in transnational marriages, focusing on Pattaya, a "space of opportunity and hope". Chapter Five turns the focus to the village setting and examines the multiplicity of images of women married to Westerners, the social relations these women are involved in, as well as the ways in which material resources and "love" have complicated the relationships within various contexts. Chapter Six focuses on the experiences of those who stay behind and the consequences of transnational marriage on the ongoing local dynamics, especially gender relations and the emergence of a new social class constituted by village women marrying *farang* husbands. Chapter Seven draws together the substantive findings presented throughout the book and highlights the contributions made by this book to the studies on transnational marriages and intimacies.

All in all, this book shows that transnational marriages have far-reaching effects that alter gender and class relations, while simultaneously contributing to lifestyle changes and transformations both in Isan society and Thailand in the face of local-global articulation.

CHAPTER ONE

Transnational Marriage in Historical Perspective

Thai society has long been familiar with intermarriages or interethnic marriages. Transnational marriages are intermarriages in the sense that they are marriages between people of different ethnicities or cultures. But transnational marriages have an extra-territorial dimension which allows husbands and wives to move between their respective countries regularly while maintaining their relationships and networks at both ends.[1] The developments over the past centuries are context-specific and the forms of marriage are different from today's transnational marriage. Embedded in its historical roots, transnational marriage as we see it today is closely connected to global trends.

Transnational marriage, like other activities and practices in the contemporary world that cross national boundaries, represents an "unbounded" and deterritorialised process (Basch et al. 1994). However, they are anchored or grounded in particular histories and places. These practices are inevitably underlined by constraints and opportunities found in the localities where they occur. As Luis Guarnizo and Michael Smith argue, "[T]ransnational practices, while connecting collectivities located in more than one national territory, are embodied in specific social relations established between specific people, situated in unequivocal localities, at historically determined times" (1998: 11). The authors also suggest that the "locality" where the activities are embedded needs to be scrutinised and further conceptualised. Suzanne Sinke (2006) shares this suggestion and posits that it is important to consider how the past and present phenomena are related or connected since these connections provide a deeper and more dynamic understanding of the contemporary phenomenon in question.

---

[1] The definitions and connotations of inter-, mixed and transnational marriage are provided in greater details in the Introduction.

In Thailand, the history of intermarriage is related to the immigration of various ethnic groups into the country. Among these groups, the Chinese represent the largest group and they were also the first to arrive in the country as early as the thirteenth century.[2] When the first Westerners arrived in Siam in the sixteenth century, the Chinese had already engaged in mining activities in the Southern region (Skinner 1957: 2–3). From the sixteenth century until the Vietnam War, Westerners in Thailand were predominantly Europeans of various nationalities. However, during the Vietnam War, American servicemen made up the majority of Westerners staying in Thailand.

Not only did the Chinese account for the highest number of immigrants, they also played a key role in various sectors of the Siamese economy, especially in trading (rice, tin and timber), shipping and taxation. As a result, the Chinese were granted high positions in the bureaucratic hierarchy such as town governors.[3] The role of Chinese immigrants was particularly evident during the reign of King Rama V (1868–1910), when they became a part of the entrepreneurial class and took up professional work as well as wage labour (Skinner 1957: 213–27). Most Chinese immigrants were male. Intermarriages between these men and Siamese women in that period were promoted under an assimilation policy, and such unions were viewed positively because of the achievements of the Chinese in economic and bureaucratic spheres. During the decades after 1910, despite the emphasis on nationalism by King Rama VI (1910–25), the Chinese continued to play key roles in the Thai economy and politics. Studies on the Chinese in Thai society and Thai-Chinese marriages have been substantially carried out elsewhere—for example Boonyong (2004), Jiemin (2003) and Skinner (1957). While acknowledging the important roles of Chinese immigrants, Thai-Chinese marriage and intermarriage between Thais and people of various ethnic groups in Thai society, this chapter focuses on Thai-Westerner marriage as most significant to the central concern of this study.

---

[2] It is noted that in Ayutthaya period (1424–1758) the immigrants included Indians, Persians, Japanese, Arab and Turks. Intermarriage between Siamese and these immigrants (and those from neighbouring countries such as Vietnam, Laos and Cambodia as well as the indigenous inhabitants in the area where Siam was situated including Mon and Khmer) was possible (Skinner 1957; Wyatt 1994).

[3] Skinner (1957: 149) notes that during the reigns of Kings Rama III and V, the governors of various towns (e.g. Songkhla, Pattani, Nakhon Ratchasima, Chanthaburi and Paknam) were Chinese immigrants or Chinese who were born locally from a Thai mother. Their accomplishment encouraged the continuation of Chinese immigration.

Most studies on intermarriage between Thai women and Westerners have centred on the period marked by the presence of American troops on Thai territory during the Vietnam War (Buapan et al. 2005; Panitee 2009; Sirijit 2009). To provide a more comprehensive overview of this type of marriage, I explore the social and political relevance of these intermarriages in the context of Thai history over three periods: the period prior to the early twentieth century, the Vietnam War era and the years since the 1980s when tourism became an important source of national revenue and prolonged associations began to be formed between local women and foreign men— mostly tourists. These periods are divided for analytical purposes; I do not mean to say that these three categories are a continuous history. Indeed, intermarriage in the period prior to the early twentieth century has less to do with Isan, as immigrants—both Westerners and those of other ethnic groups—were concentrated exclusively in the capital cities, for example Ayutthaya, Bangkok and their vicinities. In addition, the Ayutthaya kingdom did not encompass the area that is now known as Isan. However, insights on historical roots reveal social significances and meanings of inter-ethnic marriages in the contexts prior to the presence of American troops in Thailand which help shed light on why transnational marriages in the current contexts emerge, expand and are accepted relatively easily.

Thai-European Marriage Prior to the Early Twentieth Century

The Portuguese were the first Westerners in Siam, arriving in the early sixteenth century after they captured Malacca in 1511. They sent their first envoy to Ayutthaya during the reign of King Ramathibodi II (1491–1529). Portuguese merchants then began to arrive and establish residence in the kingdom. In addition to residential rights, they were also granted special trade privileges and religious liberty. In return, Siam was assured supplies of guns and bullets (Wyatt 1984: 88; Hutchison 1985: 22). Some of the Portuguese merchants took local wives. Jan Weisman (2000) notes that the first Siamese-Westerner intermarriage involved a delegation of Portuguese Catholic missionaries.[4] At the beginning of King Narai's reign (1656–88), there were as many as 2,000 Portuguese in Siam, including those whose

---

[4] These missionaries were either lay members of the church or priests. Weisman (2000: 156) notes that they were under "ecclesiastic orders not so much to proselytize the people of Ayutthaya as to marry local women and produce children to be raised from birth in the Catholic faith".

ancestors were of mixed Portuguese-Siamese parentage. However, their numbers declined after Siam signed trade agreements with various Western countries as a result of the Bowring Treaty in 1855.

As a result of the Treaty, there were also foreigners from countries such as Holland, England, China and Japan. Most of these foreigners were engaged in international trade. Arriving in a foreign land, Chinese and European traders alike wanted help to operate their businesses and to meet other needs such as housekeeping, companionship and sexual partners. Barbara Andaya (1998: 13–15) notes that forming a relationship with a local woman and recognising her as a wife was the most effective way to establish connections, as it allowed these men to obtain assistance and satisfy their sexual desires, although these marriages were temporary. The temporary marriages were critical to successful trading, not merely because of the kinship links they created but because throughout Southeast Asia it was women, not their men folk, who dominated the small trade.

Temporary marriages could not have taken place without the compliance and involvement of local women. In the case of marriages between Thai women and Chinese men, Skinner (1957: 127–8) points out that because of their involvement in trading, women preferred Chinese men, as they often knew more about the business than local men. Similarly, being involved with or marrying foreign men provided women with opportunities to access desired goods and to become an agent or a sole seller. In addition to commercial motives, temporary marriage in Southeast Asia between indigenous women and European men was boosted by the myth of Europeans as "stranger-kings" who were perceived as wealthy (Andaya 1998: 13). Gijsbert Heeck's account of the situation around 1655 indicates that Dutch VOC (Vereenigde Oost-Indische Compagnie) employees had relations with local women. These Dutch men maintained their women with "all necessities, buying or building houses for them, each according to his means" (cited in Ten Brummelhuis 1987: 59–60). The perception of Westerners as wealthy people remains relevant and is an important factor in the popularity of transnational marriage in current times.

Liaisons between foreign men and local women sometimes caused friction between local communities and European administrations. During the Ayutthaya period, there were disputes regarding authority over children (Andaya 1998; Dararat 2009). Such disputes increased with a growing number of Europeans in Siam. Accordingly, an edict forbidding Siamese women to marry foreign men was issued in the reign of King Ekathotsarot (1605–20). National security and religion were claimed as the major reasons behind the act. It was argued that a Thai woman marrying a foreign man was likely to convert to the religion of her husband. In addition, the women might reveal information affecting national security. In the law, foreign men included those from England, Holland, Java, the Malay Peninsula and India, but not Chinese. This was the first law concerning intermarriage in the legal history of Siam (Dararat 2009: 100–1).

According to the law, marriage between Siamese and Europeans was considered legal only if the following conditions were met: first, the couple had to obtain permission from the parents or the caretakers of the woman; second, the couple had to attend the customary marriage rites of both the woman and the man; and third, the couple had to sign their names in front of government officials as well as a consular representative of the husband's country (Dararat 2009: 104–8). Despite the restrictions and regulations which placed limitations and put pressure to bear on this type of relationship, there were examples of lasting and successful intermarriages whose descendants became prominent figures in government and business circles in Thai society, such as the Savetsila family,[5] descendants of Henry Alabaster, an Englishman who came to Siam as a deputy consul in 1857 and the Bunnag family whose ancestors included two Persian brothers who married Thai women (Akin 1996; Weisman 2000; Wyatt 1994).

In addition to marriage between Siamese women (of the "commoner class") and European merchants and envoys, there was also intermarriage among the elite/upper classes—the King and the royal family, royal aristocracy and noblemen.[6] Members of the upper class had ample opportunities to meet with Westerners after Siam signed trade agreements with various Western countries in 1855 as a result of the Bowring Treaty. Such opportunities were particularly evident during the reign of King Rama V (1868–10) who emphasised modern education and geared the country development toward modernisation and Westernisation. Accordingly, the government supported young men, most of them of upper-class backgrounds, to pursue a Western education. During their long study tour in the West, some of these young men formed relationships with local women. The pattern of Thai men marrying European women became common among privileged overseas students, young diplomats and other officials. At

[5] See further information in Derick Garnier's work (http://www.anglicanthai.org/alabaster.htm, accessed 27 June 2010) (site is no longer available).

[6] Akin Rabibhadana (1996) distinguishes between two classes in Thai society: the mass of the population or commoners (*phrai*) and the elite/upper class or leaders (*nai*). *Phrai* were obliged to obey orders of their *nai* and civil servants were duty-bound to obey the orders of their superiors. The upper class held political and economic power over the country while commoners served as the workforce.

this point, the roles of modernisation in encouraging interethnic marriages become clearer. Intermarriages were facilitated both through the process of supporting Thai people to obtain modern education in the Western countries and that of employing or inviting Western expertise to work in Thailand with the aim of modernising the country. Such contexts created the milieux enabling interethnic liaisons. Most Westerners arriving in Siam were merchants, envoys, diplomats, officers and experts in various fields. The backgrounds and status of these men reinforced the myth of Europeans as "stranger-kings". However, the status and image of Westerners shifted in the later periods under the contexts of militarisation, transnational tourism and globalisation.

Indeed, there was also a shift in policy regarding intermarriage that took place during the reign of King Rama VI (1910–25), who adopted a nationalistic policy in foreign affairs and placed restrictions on intermarriage. In 1914 the King gave orders to the Thai Embassies in Paris, Berlin, London, St. Petersburg and Tokyo that henceforth marriage between foreign women and members of the royal family, aristocrats, students and officials working overseas had to receive prior royal approval. Violating this rule, penalties included transfer from one country to another and withholding promotion in the case of government officials. In practice, permission was generally granted with conditions and cautions attached (Dararat 2007).

Although the common pattern of intermarriage among elites and aristocracy was Thai men marrying European women, the reversal of this gender pattern became apparent in recent years, especially when educational opportunities became more available for women. Like their male compatriots with similar backgrounds, Thai women who pursued education abroad or worked with foreigners met their future husbands in foreign settings or at local work places. Since these women were often from well-to-do families and most of them had a relatively good education, their marriages were generally not motivated by the economic status of their Western husbands. However, women with Western partners often suffered the same stigma borne by brides of American servicemen during the Vietnam War (Weisman 2000).

It is clear that intermarriage between Thais and Westerners prior to the early twentieth century was intersected by gender and class. The prevalent gender patterns of such marriages represented the opposite models between members of the elite/upper class and the commoners. While the "upper class" model became more noticeable in the later periods, the "commoner class" pattern was apparent for centuries. The phenomenon of transnational marriage of rural women in Thailand, especially in Isan in the current period, is characterised by the "commoner class" pattern. From a historical perspective, the continuation of Thai-Westerner marriage among commoners shows that Thai society has been familiar with such unions, making social acceptance of contemporary transnational marriage relatively easy.

World War II and "Siamese War Brides"

After World War II, another group of women, the "Siamese War Brides" married former prisoners of war. These women met their husbands under special circumstances and their experiences of intermarriage had little in common with those involved with or married to foreign traders and envoys, and intermarriage among the upper class. The war bride phenomenon involved a sizable number of Thai women, but literature on this subject is rather limited. The best available documentation concerns Dutch soldiers or former Dutch prisoners.[7]

Han ten Brummelhuis (1994) and Arno Ooms (2002) suggest that there were as many as 2,000 to 2,500 marriages between Thai women and former Dutch prisoners of war after World War II.[8] Some of the Thai-Dutch couples settled in Thailand; others moved to the Dutch Indies (now Indonesia), the Netherlands and other European countries. There were also Thai women who were left behind on their way to Europe, stranded in Indonesia, Singapore and Port Said in Egypt. Some of these women ended up selling sex for survival.

On 9 August 1964, the Thai-language newspaper, *Kiti Sap*, carried the headline: "Siamese Girls Who Followed Dutch Soldiers Confess Their Mistake: Instead of finding happiness with their husbands as they dreamed,

---

[7] Prisoners of World War II in Thailand included not only Dutch soldiers but also British and Australian military personnel. Captured by the Japanese army, thousands of these Allied prisoners were forced to work as labourers in constructing the railway from Kanchanaburi, Thailand to Burma to move men and supplies to the Burmese front where the Japanese were fighting the British (see further information: http://www.kanchanaburi-info.com/en/muang.html;   http://www.awm.gov.au/encyclopedia/pow/general_info.asp;   http://en.wikipedia.org/wiki/South-East Asian theatre_of_World_War_II, accessed 2 March 2012).

[8] Ooms's estimate was made by extrapolations from numbers given in newspaper articles. In 1946 alone, about 451–500 members of the Dutch Indies troops registered their marriage at the Dutch diplomatic mission in Bangkok. Citing Dutch documents, Ten Brummelhius estimates there were about 2,000 Thai-Dutch marriages from 1945 to 1947.

they became public service girls" (Ooms 2002: 106). When the news spread, popular reactions were hostile. A Dutch man accompanied by his Thai wife was assaulted by a group of youngsters in Bangkok. Some Thai columnists demanded that the government investigate such cases and bring back those who were stranded in various third countries.

It was not clear what the Thai government response was, but Ooms (2002) notes that a Dutch investigation indicated that these abandoned women did not want to be repatriated to Thailand. Rather, they tried to find some means to survive in Batavia. Some made requests to the military commanders of Batavia to track down their Dutch husbands. This situation put strains on diplomatic relations between Thailand and Holland. Dutch officials then approached the Thai press to provide them with letters from Thai women living with their Dutch partners. An official investigation involving about 100 women followed, showing that the majority of these women were living happily with their husbands although some women complained of "erotomaniac inclinations"[9] (Ten Brummelhuis 1994: 7).

Ten Brummelhuis (1994) attributes the ordeal of these Siamese brides to the prejudice of Dutch opinion associating them with the sex industry. In the eyes of ordinary Dutch people, Bangkok in those days was seen as a city of sin (an impression that still prevails today) and notorious areas like Patpong were contact zones for Western (including Dutch) men to meet up with Thai prostitutes for sexual gratification. The Siamese War Brides must have come from among these girls, so they reasoned. In reality, Thai women who married ex-Dutch prisoners of war came from diverse socio-economic backgrounds. These women, according to Ten Brummelhuis, realised that being involved in sex work is disapproved of morally in the Western view, and that a sinful past was a stigma that could not be wiped out.

On the Thai side, the reactions can be read as a nationalistic resentment about foreigners taking women out of the country. For the women, they gave reasons to justify their choice of Western partners by criticising local men for their maltreatment of their wives and their proclivity to polygamy (Ten Brummelhuis 1994). This view was shared by most women in Na Dokmai. Their perceptions and experiences of local men as "irresponsible" husbands and fathers played a key role in their search for a better life through transnational marriage.

---

[9] Erotomania is a type of delusional disorder in which a person has a delusion that a particular person is deeply in love with them (http://medical-dictionary.thefreedictionary. com/erotomaniac, accessed 25 May 2012).

The Siamese War Bride phenomenon has at least two aspects that connect to current transnational marriages. First, the war brides seem to be the first group of Thai women engaged in overseas migration through marriage, whether or not they ultimately reached their destination. Second, the ways in which Siamese War Brides were perceived and reacted to by both the Thai and Dutch sides suggest that the marriages were conceptualised beyond socio-economic, political and international-relation dimensions as previously depicted. Such reactions represented public perceptions and attitudes towards the war brides at the time. Furthermore, the brides' opinions reflected prevailing public discourses on gender, marriage and sexuality. All this indicates the multi-layered complexities of intermarriage in Thailand, and an attempt to capture this type of marriage is possible only when the multiplicity is taken into account.

The Vietnam War and Intermarriage of Rural Isan Women

The establishment of American air bases in Thailand in the mid-1960s played an important role in facilitating marriages between Thai women and American servicemen. They were different in many ways from marriages involving Europeans and Chinese migrants that took place in earlier eras, where economic and political factors played a key role. The foreign men who married Thai women at that time were persons who came to work and stayed on, and most of the mixed couples continued to live in the country after their marriage. In the Vietnam War period the American servicemen came only for war-related reasons, as with the soldiers of World War II, but in much larger numbers. If the relationship with Thai women resulted in marriage, the wife normally left her homeland to live in the US with the husband. Intermarriage in this period mainly involved women of a particular background—rural women who were mainly engaged in entertainment and commercial sex—whereas women who married foreign husbands in earlier times often came from various backgrounds and belonged to different social classes.

Unlike the Siamese War Bride phenomenon that played out exclusively in the Bangkok area—thus having little to do with Isan people—the interactions between Thai women and American servicemen during the Vietnam War took place around the US air bases in the Northeast and elsewhere. Local people had direct experiences with American servicemen; some ran small businesses, while others worked at the military bases. Many women were engaged in the service and sex industries to accommodate

American military personnel. It was during this period that residents of Na Dokmai became aware of the possibility of intermarriage, as there were village women who married American servicemen. This involvement smoothed the way for women of later generations to engage in transnational marriage in the decades that followed.

The global power of the US in the aftermath of World War II led to an expansion of its military bases in many parts of the world. In Asia, American bases were set up in Japan, Thailand, South Korea and the Philippines. By hosting the US air bases during the Vietnam War, a number of localities in Thailand were transformed into places for rest and recreation (R&R) for American soldiers fighting in Vietnam. Four out of seven US air bases were stationed in strategic areas in the Northeast while the other three were in Bangkok and other provinces in Central Thailand.[10] It is estimated that in the mid-1960s as many as 6,500 servicemen per week flocked to Thailand for R&R (Weisman 2000: 182). The total number of American troops at various locations in Thailand reached a peak of 140,000 in 1969, including those working on the bases and those coming for R&R leaves (Cohen 2003: 60). Restaurants, hotels, nightclubs, bars, massage parlours, coffee shops and brothels sprang up especially in areas surrounding the bases.[11] The establishments catering to the American military, often brightly lit and noisy, could be distinguished from brothels serving local and Chinese customers in more discreet surroundings.

The American servicemen treated their women and girls like "girlfriends" and not like prostitutes. They would openly walk hand-in-hand with them in the street (Van Esterik 2000: 175). Sometimes the relationship reached a semi-permanent stage when the woman shared a home with her American

---

[10] The four sites in Isan were located in Nakhon Ratchasima, Nakhon Phanom, Ubon Rachathani and Udon Thani provinces. The other three locations in the central region included Bangkok (Don Mueang), Nakhon Sawan (Takhli) and Chonburi (U-Tapao). It is noted that about 80 per cent of all USAF air strikes over North Vietnam originated from air bases in Thailand. At the peak in 1969, a greater number of air force men were serving in Thailand than in South Vietnam (http://en.wikipedia.org/wiki/United_States_Air_Force_in_Thailand, accessed 7 June 2008).

[11] Pasuk Phongpaichit (1982) notes that there was a tendency to separate local and foreign markets: bars, night clubs, coffee shops and massage parlours were common contact places for Thai women and foreign men, while brothels served primarily local clients. There were particular bars and massage parlours which were popular with local men as well. In addition, she also points out that although sex-for-sale existed in Thai society long before the arrival of the American troops in the 1960s, "commercial sex [in Thailand] never came close to today's scale until foreign demand for it soared in the mid-1960s" (Pasuk 1982: 17).

boyfriend for the rest of his stay in the country. This kind of relationship was dubbed "*mia chao*" (rented/hired wife): the woman would provide sexual service and do domestic work for her partner for a price. There was usually some degree of emotional involvement from both sides. Nonetheless, the relationship was understood to be a temporary one. At first glance, *mia chao* seemed to be an exotic novelty on the social scene during the Vietnam War, but arrangements made for foreign traders dating back to the early sixteenth century appear strikingly familiar: made for the length of time of a foreigner's stay in the country, they included housekeeping, trading and a sexual partner (Andaya 1998; Van Esterik 2000).

It is not known exactly how many women and girls left their villages for Udon and how many formed liaisons with or were married to American military personnel. In the case of Na Dokmai, six women from this village eventually married American GIs and left for the US with their husbands. At the time of my fieldwork these women were in their late fifties and early sixties. Their life stories recapitulate the motivations, means and meanings of their associations with American servicemen and how intermarriage was perceived and realised within a specific historical context.

The stories of Nang (56)[12] and Phin (58) illustrate the experiences of these Vietnam War-era wives. Nang's story is typical of how village women became involved with American servicemen, regardless of whether or not the relationships eventually led to marriage. Phin's story took a different course. Phin gained social recognition, especially in Na Dokmai as her improved economic situation enabled her to take care of her parents, support her siblings and make contributions to the village. Her success and consumer lifestyle inspired women of younger generations to marry a Western husband. While other GI wives, including Nang, lived in the US and rarely returned to the village for home visit, Phin came back to live in Na Dokmai after her husband passed away in 2003.

During my fieldwork, Nang did not return home so I did not meet her. Since leaving Thailand in 1973, she made only three visits, the last one in 2000. Chan (64), Nang's older sister related Nang's story to me. Conditions at the time encouraged poverty-stricken women to leave their village in search of a better life and become involved with American servicemen. These conditions and the way in which Nang searched for "better life" to support her family were also mentioned by other residents of Na Dokmai whose

---

[12] The figure after a person's name indicates his/her age in 2008 or 2009, depending on the time of the interviews.

sisters and daughters left the village and engaged in service work in Udon during the Vietnam War.

Nang's story: The quest for a "better life" through service work and sex trade

Nang, like several other girls in Na Dokmai at that time, left her home for the town of Udon in search of income to support her family. She ended up marrying James, an American soldier, and followed him to the US in 1973 after his term ended. Her sister, Chan, recalled her story:

"She left for Udon with only ten baht in her pocket. There she stayed with her friend while looking for a job. Nobody knew much about her life in the town. She left without informing anyone; my parents didn't know. They couldn't do anything, though they were worried about her. We didn't hear from her for almost two years. Then, she came home with James and told my parents that she had been living with him at Nakhon Phanom [an air base]."

Born to poor and landless parents who had six daughters and a developmentally disabled son, Nang, Chan and her sisters had to engage in wage work since they were young—soon after finishing four years of compulsory school. They worked as house maids or in the field in Na Dokmai and villages nearby. Sometimes they received rice for their labour instead of cash. Contributions from these daughters, either in cash or kind, helped the family to make ends meet. After hearing about the possibility of earning good income in the town, Nang decided to go there. First she got a job as a dishwasher in a restaurant where she met James. Later she left the restaurant and worked at a massage parlour and a bar, where she earned much more money. Meanwhile she kept seeing James, and when he was transferred to Nakhon Phanom air base she followed him there. In 1973, when James's contract ended, they departed for Florida and settled there.

Before leaving for the US, Nang took James to the village and they had a small wedding ceremony. Nang bought 50 *rai*[13] of paddy and 4 *rai* of land in the village. She gave the paddy to her sisters and brother. The piece of land in the village was offered to four of her sisters; Chan and her family have been living on this land. Nang's contribution was vital in helping her siblings and their families improve their living standards. As Chan said: "Since we have the paddy, we no longer totally depend on wage and petty trade. As we got land to grow rice, the [economic] situation of my family became much better."

In Florida, Nang ran a Thai restaurant; the business was good, but James became involved with other women working for them in the restaurant. In

---

[13] 6 *rai* equals 1 hectare.

the end the couple separated and the restaurant was closed. Later, Nang remarried and got a job at a supermarket where she kept working until recently. Chan recalled that after her divorce from James and the closure of the restaurant, Nang rarely returned to Na Dokmai. Her last visit was in 2000. "She didn't earn as much as when she ran the restaurant. This is why she couldn't afford to return home", Chan said.

Nang's story indicates that the economic hardship of her family was the main reason compelling her to leave home in search of wage work in the town and finally engage in the sex trade. Residents of Na Dokmai frequently mentioned poverty in explaining and justifying women's involvement in commercial sex during the Vietnam War. While this occupation was considered undesirable, it was often acknowledged as a necessary means for women to help their family get out of poverty. Residents of Na Dokmai, including women married to *farang* men were aware of the ambiguous attitude toward Thai women in such marriages, although many said this has changed recently.

While night-time jobs and sexual service were a common path followed by women before marrying American servicemen during the 1960s and 1970s, this was not the only path. Phin took a different route. Her story also illustrates the connections she has always maintained with her local village. Phin's contributions to her relatives and community are well recognised by residents of Na Dokmai, who often referred to her as a successful *mia farang*.

Phin's story: "Mia farang" and social recognition

Phin (58) married John, an African-American[14] computer specialist who had two grown-up children from a previous relationship. Phin is the oldest child in a family with four daughters and a son. Like Nang and other village girls of her generation, Phin has only four years of schooling. At the age of 19, she went to town to find work and got a job as a caretaker of the elderly in a family running an apartment business. There she met John, who was transferred from Ubon air base. Phin recalled: "I saw him [John] on the first day when he moved in. Later, I was told that John wanted to marry me and that he was a good guy and had a good job [a permanent position in the military]."

---

[14] Phin married a Westerner but not Caucasian or white; however villagers often referred to her husband as *farang*. For villagers of Na Dokmai, GIs are *farang* regardless of whether they are Caucasian or not. Also, Phin's husband rarely visited the village. Due to limited encounters, villagers assumed that Phin's husband is a *farang*.

Her mother did not want Phin to marry a Western man out of fear that Phin might have to leave home and live so far away, not to mention that she might be abandoned and would suffer if her husband did not take care of her. But her brother strongly supported her and asked their father to persuade their mother. Finally her parents approved and asked John to follow the Thai marriage custom by asking Phin's parents for their blessings and providing them with 50,000 baht and gold as bride wealth. They got married in May 1973. At that time, Phin was 19 and John was 47. Marrying a Westerner was quite unusual in Na Dokmai at that time. Although there were a few village women who co-habited with GIs, they would not let their parents and the people in the village know about it.

After their marriage, Phin lived with John in town. In 1975, the couple left Thailand and settled in Michigan. John retired from the military, then joined IBM until his retirement in 1990. John earned enough to allow Phin to live comfortably, to send money home to support her parents regularly and to help her siblings when they asked. She also returned for home visits every two years and built a house in Na Dokmai where Phin has been living since she returned to the village in 2003.

In 1994 John died. He left Phin with enough means to live a comfortable life. She recalled with emotion, "He talked about his pension which would be transferred to me; about the money he had in the bank. He told me to sell our house and return to Thailand if I wanted. He also said that if I meet a good man that I love, I should remarry. He was concerned about me until the last minute of his life."

Soon after her return to the village in 2003, Phin and her family organised *kathin*[15] (merit making) ceremony and afterwards she took her parents to Pattaya for a vacation. She took care of her parents until they passed away in 2005. Her improved economic situation allowed Phin to invest in various businesses. The revenue from these investments was to help her sisters and brother with supplementary income for their families. For Phin, supporting her siblings is her obligation. "We have no parents left and I am the oldest child; I have to help them", she said.

Phin also supported and played an active role in community affairs. As a main contributor to the village school's revolving fund, she always gave money when the reserve ran low. She was the driving force behind the school

---

[15] *Kathin* is a Buddhist ritual. It has to be organised within 30 days at the end of the three-month rainy season retreat. On the appointed day, robes and other necessities of temple life are offered to the monks. Today, this ritual has evolved into a multiple-day ceremony in which villagers join in the merit making. Normally, the persons or family holding a *kathin* are major contributors in making donations. This ritual is considered as great merit making especially for major sponsors. Usually, those holding a *kathin* are relatively well-to-do households (Terwiel 1994).

alumni in organising *pha pa*[16] during the New Year holiday to raise funds for educational activities and improve the school's physical environment. Phin saw her contributions as ways of making merit and believed that the offerings, in return, would give her a good life. Her generosity and good deeds were held in esteem by most of the residents in Na Dokmai whom I talked to.

Nang and Phin followed different paths to the same goal—marrying an American serviceman. However, their lives evolved quite differently after their arrival in the US. Back in their native village in Thailand, locals rarely mentioned Nang while Phin was often regarded as a "successful *mia farang*". The social recognition Phin had earned due to her economic status is based not solely on her economic improvement and her presence in the village scene, but also on her contribution to the community as well as her support of her parents and siblings.[17] Despite various differences, what these two women shared was their connection to and support of their natal families in their rural village. The contributions improved the lives of those stayed behind to different degrees.

Success stories like that of Phin were told time and again in Na Dokmai. Villagers often talked about the desirability of marrying Western men, how women with *farang* partners generously helped their families and contributed to community welfare. These accounts created high expectations among younger generations of women who staked their future on marrying a Western man. The expectations of a better future continue to propel them to take an active role in current transnational marriages. After the American forces withdrew from Thailand in the mid-1970s, the phenomenon of intermarriage was prolonged by the unprecedented expansion of global tourism.

---

[16] *Pha pa* is originally a Buddhist ritual to offer robes and necessities for the monks' personal use. Unlike *kathin, pha pa* can be organised any time of the year. This term has also been used for charitable activities such as fundraising or collecting rice, food, school materials, etc. to give to schools, social organisations and those who are in need, although they are not related to religion. These activities are considered as a way of making merit.

[17] In Phin's house and the houses of other women married to Westerners, I noticed the display of certificates of merit that showed appreciation for their contributions to the village's schools and to other community services. A sister of Sunee, another GI's wife living in Florida, mentioned with pride that Sunee donated a large sum (400,000 baht) to a village temple. This contribution was made in memory of her mother who had passed away.

Tourism and Transnational Marriage of Rural Women

Since the 1980s, Thai tourism experienced a dramatic rise in the number of foreign visitors: from 629,000 in 1970 to 2.8 million in 1986, 9.5 million in 2000 and 22.3 million in 2012, with growth strongly continuing. Among these tourists, males outnumbered females at a ratio of two to one in 2010 (Truong 1990: 277; the National Statistic Office's website).[18] Tourism became Thailand's principal source of foreign exchange. Local and foreign investors played a key role in facilitating its expansion (Bishop and Robinson 1998; Truong 1990). Tourism and the sex trade were markedly linked when tourists' demand for commercial sex was met by local supply (Cohen 1996; Dahles 2009; Ryan and Hall 2001). It was under these conditions that the tourist industry became geared to "sex tourism".

On the demand side, "sex package tours"—short trips to various destinations in Asia with the major aim of buying sex—were promoted in various European countries as well as Japan. Several European travel companies organised such tours to various Asian cities including Bangkok (Bishop and Robinson 1998; Cohen 1996). This development and the male-to-female ratio of foreign tourists noted above reflect the dominant discourse of sex tourism in which male tourists fly from developed countries to developing countries to play out their fantasies of an eroticised Orient populated by Asian women.[19] This phenomenon has been noted in various Asian destinations as well as in Africa, Latin America and the Caribbean (Dahles 2009).

The growth of (sex) tourism in Asia including Thailand was facilitated by a number of factors and conditions. Aihwa Ong (1985) views both industrialisation and prostitution in Southeast Asia as vehicles to modernisation, whereby tourism-related prostitution could be equated with industrial labour, the new form of trade in women's bodies and labour in the international division of labour. Drawing on gender perspectives and the political economy of globalisation, Sassen (2000) conceptualises the growing presence of women in the global economy, including migration and prostitution, as the feminisation of survival. Remittances from women engaging in these activities are significant resources for their households to survive and for governments to develop and modernise the countries. The recent works focus on women's agency

---

[18] http://service.nso.go.th/nso/web/statseries/statseries23.html, accessed 10 March 2016.

[19] The emerging discourse of "female sex tourism" has appeared in the literature on tourism as well, for example Cohen (1971) and De Albuquerque (1998).

and explore how women employ sex work as a vehicle to obtain a better life. These works reveal a variety of factors propelling women to engage in this profession, mainly material motivations, but also gender relations, personal autonomy, freedom and the desire for a secure life (Brennan 2004; Cabezas 2009; Cheng 2010; Faier 2009).

Apart from global economic disparities, the growth of tourism and the sex industry is also viewed in relation to the specific social and economic conditions as well as the historical developments of particular countries. In the case of Thailand, various studies reveal that the impacts of disparate development have resulted in growing inequalities and different opportunities between regions, as well as between urban and rural sectors. This disparity becomes an important factor that underlines the migration and participation of women from disadvantaged areas in the sex industry (Pasuk 1982; Yos 1992a). Various studies also indicate that since most rural-to-urban migrants have limited education and occupational skills, they have few options in urban employment and often end up in low-wage work or in the entertainment and sex industry. Many women engaged in the sex industry have previously earned their living as unskilled and semi-skilled workers as well as peddlers. The conditions of low wages/incomes and a poor working environment cause many of them to turn to commercial sex, where they can earn much more money and enjoy better working conditions, especially if they serve foreign clients (Cohen 1996; Odzer 1990; Walker and Ehrlich 1992). However, it should be noted that although a migratory path of rural women towards working in the sex industry is prevalent, this does not mean that the majority of female workers migrating to cities become prostitutes (Mills 1999; Whittaker 1999).

Entertainment and service institutions that developed to cater to American military servicemen provided the precursor for the transnational tourism expansion (Cohen 1996; Truong 1990). Such destinations as Patpong and Pattaya, the infamous sex tourist area in Bangkok and the Eastern beach resort which served as R&R sites in the 1960s and 1970s, became familiar sites where associations between the male tourists and local women took place. In the meantime, new tourist destinations such as Samui and Phuket in the southern beach resorts also blossomed and quickly became new contact zones. For local women, these tourist destinations have become "spaces of opportunity and hope" where they can meet and make connections with foreign men (cf. Brennan 2004).

Unlike the American servicemen who resided and worked in Thailand on an annual basis, tourists are likely to stay for only a short period of time, from a few days to a few weeks. However, some of these men return to the same women every year or every time they visit Thailand. Others keep communicating or sending gifts and money to the women (Cohen 1996; Walker and Ehrlich 1992). These relationships, in many cases, have resulted in long-term commitments, which was the experience of many women in Na Dokmai. In addition, the image of a "good" life and the economic improvement of women who married American servicemen also played a part in motivating women to marry a Western man. This is particularly pertinent in the case of Jit. Jit's desire to meet and make connections with Western men was largely influenced by the "good" life of Phin and her younger sister Nang. At the same time, her failed marriage with a native husband, who left her with two children to take care of, also forced Jit to find ways to earn a living and support her children. A woman of strong will, Jit headed for Bangkok and worked at a restaurant in Sukhumvit, a residential area popular with foreigners. There she met Gerhard, her future husband. Unlike the GI wives who left the village and moved abroad after their marriage, Jit and her husband decided to settle in Na Dokmai and built a house there. The couple and Jit's two children had a rather comfortable life. For village residents, Jit's story showed how marriage with a Westerner could change a woman's life, even though she encountered an uncertain future after her husband's death.

Jit's story: A successful past and an uncertain future

Jit (66), like Nang and her other sisters, began to engage in wage work at a young age. While working as a shop helper in the town of Udon, Jit got to know a woman who offered her a higher salary. She followed the woman to Yala province in the South, and worked as a maid. There she met her husband, a man working at the municipality. She lived with him for eight years, but when she learned that he had been seeing another woman, Jit took her daughter and her son, Duean and Phong, back to Na Dokmai.

After her separation, Jit had to support herself and her children. She left them with her mother and sisters and joined Nang at the Nakhon Phanom air base. There, she landed a waitress job at a restaurant. In 1973 when Nang departed with James for the US, Jit returned to Na Dokmai. It was difficult to earn an income in the village. In 1976, she headed for Bangkok looking for employment and the chance to make contact with Western men, hoping this would lead to an eventual marriage. She said, "I've learned that village women who marry *farang*, like Phin and Nang, have a 'good' life. *Farang* are wealthy. *Mia farang* can help their parents and relatives [financially] and take care of their children. So I decided to follow this path." Jit worked in a restaurant in Sukhumvit Soi 11 where she met a much younger man from Norway whom she lived with for almost a year. Because he did not take the relationship seriously, Jit left him and went back to work at the restaurant.

Just a few days after she had returned to work, Jit met Gerhard, a divorced German in his late fifties. Gerhard owned a four-storey building in Berlin that he rented out. Jit lived with Gerhard in Bangkok for two years and married him in 1980. At that time Jit was 34 and Gerhard was 60. Jit had two children living in Na Dokmai; Gerhard had a son living with his mother in Germany. The following year, they returned to live in Na Dokmai and built a spacious house with a swimming pool and a garage. Later they had a son, Jack, who lived with them in the village. Friends of their children were welcome to swim in the pool and stay overnight in the house. They also bought factory-made furniture.[20] Gerhard was the first Western man to live in the village. Their house was one of the first in the village built by a mixed couple.

While living in the village, Jit and Gerhard drove to town for their shopping almost every week. Her relatives often joined them on such trips and Gerhard would offer them a meal at a restaurant in town. Jit said, "We went to all the good restaurants in Udon." Jit also mentioned the various vacations the family enjoyed together: "We went to Samui, Phuket, Samet and Chiang Mai. The children always joined us on the trips. We ate at restaurants; the children could order whatever they wanted, never mind the cost." For Jit, living with Gerhard was the happiest and most joyful period of her life.

With Gerhard's support, Jit could meet the material desires of her children. Duean had a lot of friends and they enjoyed going out together. She often asked for money and was rarely disappointed. When asked whether Gerhard was also happy with his married life, Jit replied: "I don't know. I think he was, since we lived together for almost 20 years. He enjoyed living in the village. The last time we went to Berlin and stayed there for four months, I complained that I missed home and Thai food. He said that he too missed the village."

Gerhard returned to Germany for a few months annually. Sometimes Jit, Jack and Duean joined him. The day before his planned departure for Germany in 1998, Gerhard was hit by a truck and died a few days later. Two months after Gerhard's death, Duean, who had been ill, also died, leaving Jit a granddaughter, aged 11, who is now living in Norway with her husband. Jit admitted that after losing these two dear ones she had a nervous breakdown and began to gamble; she wasted all the money Gerhard left to her in the bank.

---

[20] In Isan villages in the early 1980s, factory-made furniture was a luxury. Now it is more common for households in Na Dokmai to have factory-made furniture, though it still indicates the economic status of the owners.

Recently Jit and Jack were living on remittances from Phong. Jack was 27 but had no job. After finishing high school in the village, he did not take college education seriously. Like his mother, Jack's life took a turn for the worse after the death of his father. Gerhard's plan for Jack to study in Germany after high school did not materialise. Jack was quite upset when he found out that the money his father left them was gone. Choked with emotion, Jit said that she felt very sorry for Jack. It was not his fault at all. Rather, she blamed herself for having failed to support him and for not being a good mother. If she could live her life again she would keep the money to support Jack's education, though he might not have been able to study in Germany as his father had wished. With a good education, Jack could have had a salaried job which would secure his future.

Jit, like Phin, was often mentioned as the first generation of women married to Westerners in the village. As she lived with her foreign husband in the village for a long time, local people could observe at first hand their comfortable way of living and how the children had benefited from Gerhard's wealth. Ironically, Jit's misfortune after Gerhard's death was largely ignored. When I brought this up, the general answer was that it had something to do with karma.[21] Jit's neighbour, a woman in her early sixties, commented that Jit's "moral merit" (bun) ended when Gerhard died; then her life took a downturn. She added that other women, like Phin are entitled to a "good life" in the present life thanks to their bun accumulated in past incarnations. Notwithstanding her difficulty in later years, in the eyes of the villagers, Jit's life with Gerhard epitomised what was good in a union between Thai women and Western men.

Among the younger generation Nid (44), a friend of Duean, said that the lifestyle of Duean and her mother Jit was very different from her own and those of other peers in the village. Duean lived in a big house with a swimming pool. She could go out whenever she wanted. She had lots of nice clothes and jewellery. "Nobody of my generation could do what Duean did. Duean couldn't have had such a good life if her mother hadn't married a farang", Nid said. Nid admitted that her decision to leave home and go to work in Bangkok was inspired, in part, by the sharp difference in living

---

[21] The Buddhist concept of karma is a result of actions in present and past lives. Good actions earn moral merit (bun); bad/wrong actions gain demerit (bap). Karma is persistently produced and reshaped throughout one's lifetime and beyond. The suffering or happiness that a person has is a result of his or her karma in past and present incarnations. One can change his or her karma by accumulating merit by moral deeds (Van Esterik 2000; Muecke 1992).

standards between Duean's family and her own. Working in a bar at Patpong enabled Nid to support her two children and her mother. There Nid met a Canadian with whom she fell in love. She lived with him for a year, but the man eventually had to return to his country. Nid was involved in "red-light" business for almost 20 years. Her mother died in a car accident in 2005, so she returned and stayed in the village to take care of her children and a handicapped sister.

Nid and a number of women in Na Dokmai became aware of the prospects of a better life through Jit's experience. There were undoubtedly others who admired Phin for her versatile social work which made her a local celebrity. Both Jit and Phin became role models by achieving their goals of marrying "good" Western men. The stories of these women circulating in the village were mainly about the successful part of their lives while their unfortunate experiences (like Jit's uncertain future) were largely overlooked.

While an increasing number of Western partners opt to settle in their wives' villages or elsewhere in Thailand, the majority of women with Western husbands in Na Dokmai left their home village to join their husband in his home country. Wherever they lived, the women always kept in contact with their families at home. Thai wives together with their foreign husbands regularly visited their home villages.

Women and Men under Transnational Marriages and Transnational Lives

Data collected in 2008 show that there were 159 women in Na Dokmai who were married to or were living with foreign men, and 22 women whose relationship had ended. These women accounted for 18 per cent of village women between the ages of 20 and 59. Their foreign partners were men from 21 nationalities. Half of the women currently in a relationship were in the 31–40 age bracket; the youngest was 18, and the oldest was 56. Most women older than 45 had four years of schooling, while the majority of younger women had between six and nine years of education.[22] There were three women with a bachelor's degree, and one of them was studying for her master's at the time of my fieldwork (see Appendix 2, Tables 1 and 2). Two-thirds of the women had been divorced or separated from a former Thai partner before marrying a Western man; about half of these women had children who had been born to a local father.

---

[22] Compulsory four-year primary education was instituted throughout the country in the 1930s. This was increased to six years in 1977 (Wyatt 1975).

About three-fourths of women who are in a relationship with Western men left their homes in the village to settle with their husbands in various countries, while one-fourth stayed with their husbands in Thailand, either in their villages or elsewhere (see Appendix 2, Table 3). The data show that these women came from diverse socio-economic backgrounds. Some were from poor families without agricultural land; others had more resources. There were also those from better-off households, with a college education and employment as school teachers, nurses, civil servants or employees of private enterprises. This diversity contrasts with the situation of the 1965–75 period, when women married to American servicemen mostly came from relatively poor households.

Most Western partners were European (81.8 per cent), particularly German, Swedish and British. Their age ranged from 27 to 73; the largest age group was the 41–50 bracket, accounting for 29 per cent. Their occupations varied: one-fifth were self-employed or career professionals while 39.6 per cent were involved in "blue-collar" work; 12.6 per cent were pensioners (see Appendix 2, Tables 4 and 5). Most of the Western men living with their Thai wives in the country were pensioners. Those still working in their own countries or elsewhere and whose wives resided in their own villages came to stay with their wives every year for periods ranging from a few weeks to six months. Some visited their wives more than once a year. While being apart, couples kept in touch via telephone or internet. Women living overseas with their husbands contacted their children, parents and relatives in the village on a regular basis; many visited their homes in the village every year or every two years. The transnational life of woman married to a Westerner was reflected in Mon's life story.

Mon's story: Transnational marriage and transnational life

In 2005 Mon (37), a divorced mother with a son (10), married Mark (47), a divorced Dutch man also with a son (16). After their marriage, the couple had a son (2). In 2007 Mon went to the Netherlands to live with Mark.

Mon was born to a poor family with three children; her parents were wage earners. Soon after finishing six years of compulsory education, she joined her parents and worked at various construction sites, including Phuket. There she found work at a supermarket and later at a bar. At Phuket, she dated an Italian and then a German man, but these relationships did not last long. She returned to Na Dokmai after breaking up with the German boyfriend. Later, she lived with a local entrepreneur, the father of her first son, whom she met while working at a café in central Thailand. He helped Mon open a shop selling cooked food. After she became pregnant, her business declined and she had to rely on her partner for support. However, he did not give Mon enough money to remit to her parents who could not work due to ill health. Eventually Mon found out that her partner had been seeing another woman. She left him and returned to Na Dokmai.

In 2004, Mon went to Phuket again and worked at a bar, where she met Mark, who was on vacation. They stayed together for most of his two-week vacation and continued their communication after he returned home. A few months later, Mon went to the Netherlands with Mark's support and worked in his parents' bakery shop during the three months of her stay in Holland. In 2005, they got married and Mon left her son with her parents and moved to the Netherlands. She called her son a few times a week. "I kept an eye on him via the telephone. We were together only a few months a year", she said. In 2008, she managed to bring him to the Netherlands.

Mark and his parents agreed to close the bakery shop and open a Thai restaurant, where Mon worked as a cook. The earnings allowed her to send money to support her parents and her siblings. Mon said, "I have to work. I can't beg Mark for money every time I want something. I don't want to live like that. It would make me feel like I have no dignity ... I'm not afraid of working hard, but I am afraid of having nothing to eat."

Before leaving for the Netherlands after her marriage, Mon bought 7 *rai* of land and built a new house. The house was designed and decorated in an urban style which set it apart from most other nearby houses. Every winter, Mon and her family returned to Na Dokmai and stayed for a couple of months. In 2009, Mark's parents also joined them and stayed for two weeks. Mon took them to various tourist sites in Thailand.

On a visit to Na Dokmai in 2008, the couple bought a 29-*rai* lot with fishing ponds and lodging facilities, located on the road from the village to the town of Udon. They wanted to turn it to a fishing resort with a restaurant and invested in its renovation. When I met Mon at the resort in January 2009, she was busy dealing with customers who came to fish and was giving instructions to her uncle and another relative who helped with the renovation. Mark remarked to me that "she is the boss". When I asked what he meant, he said, "Well, everyone here listens to her and does what she wants. In her family, her parents, sister and brother all listen to her." When the couple returned to the Netherlands, Mon's mother and sister—herself a single mother with a daughter—took care of the resort. Mon called that her sister would follow in her footsteps: marrying a "good" Dutch man she likes. If something serious develops (a long-term commitment) the sister could take her daughter to live with her in the Netherlands. Both her sister and mother agreed with this idea.

Like Phin, Mon epitomised the ideal *mia farang* in the eyes of Na Dokmai residents, especially with regard to her economic achievements. In this respect, she was an exceptional woman, having set up businesses in her own country and in the country of her husband. Mon's secure financial situation allowed her and her family to spend a few months in her native village each year. Certainly not every woman married to a Westerner and her loved ones could afford annual visits like this. However, what Mon and most women like her in Na Dokmai had in common was their effort to keep in contact with their families back home. Women's practices of maintaining and developing relationships and networks both at home and in their host countries characterise the phenomenon of transnational marriage currently taking place in Na Dokmai and elsewhere in Thai society. It is these practices that make present-day transnational marriage distinctive from intermarriage of the past.

Conclusion

Intermarriage in Thailand can be traced as far back as the thirteenth century in Thai social history and contemporary transnational marriage bears some continuity with this history, although the appearance of this marriage came much later. As Thai-Westerner intermarriage took place long before American troops set foot on Thai soil in the middle of the 1960s, it was easier for the Thai people to accept it. However, the motives and forms of today's transnational marriage are different from those in the past. The status and images of local women and Western men involved in this marriage have also shifted throughout the history. These conjugal relationships have been shaped by the intersecting of gender, class and ethnicity in specific historical contexts. Intermarriage often follows a gendered pattern and is linked closely with social class: for example, marriage between Thai women and Western (and Chinese) men was predominant among the mass of the population whereas the pattern of marriages between Thai men and Western women was observed mainly among the elite class and the royal family.

The social, political and economic meanings pertaining to intermarriage have changed over the years. Until the end of the reign of King Rama V (1910), intermarriage was seen as a means to create and strengthen economic connections for state benefits and a strategy for modernising the country. Emphasis on nationalism in the reign of King Rama VI (1910–25) made intermarriage between Thais and Westerners suspect on the grounds that it might undermine national security and subvert local religion. Laws and regulations were put in place to restrict intermarriage of Thai nationals, both commoners and members of the privileged class. In the mid-twentieth century, intermarriage between Thai women and Dutch men took place within the specific context of "Siamese War Brides". The way in which the war

brides were perceived and reacted to—by both Thai and Dutch sides—had
to do with perceptions, attitudes and ideas of people involved in and related
to this phenomenon as much as socio-economic, political and international
relation forces.

The presence of American troops in the 1960s–70s brought a new
dimension to the long history of intermarriage in Thai society that
directly relates to the current phenomenon of transnational marriage. The
experiences of village women who married American servicemen during
that period made rural women aware of the possibilities of pursuing
intermarriage as a way to escape poverty and to improve living conditions
for themselves and their families. This international association was
prolonged and even intensified in recent decades by the expansion of the
tourism industry, which transformed bustling tourist sites into contact
zones where connections between local women and the global male tourist
were initiated—connections that become permanent ties through marriage.

In the course of Thai history, intermarriage in previous eras and the
recent phenomenon of transnational marriage between Thai women and
Westerners have been taking place against the backdrop of changing national
policies and international upheavals. In the present context, the impact of
intermarriage on the local socio-economic landscape is far reaching, affecting
individual lives at the grassroots level. Marrying a *farang* has been perceived
as a means of obtaining a secure life not only for the women themselves but
also for their families. Transnational marriage that allows women to realise
this desire has been facilitated by global flows while situated in the specific
localities. To understand how local people responded to and negotiated
the transitions, the next chapter discusses the ways in which national and
international political economy shaped the lives and social landscape of Isan
villagers and the ways in which they dealt with such changes.

CHAPTER TWO

Na Dokmai: A Transnational Village

IT'S BECOME QUITE COMMON to have *farang* in this village. Currently there are about ten living here with their wives. In this *soi* (lane) alone, there are two; everybody knows them. One has lived here for many years and rarely returns to his home [country]. The other lives with his wife for some months, returns to his country [to work], then comes back to the village again. He's been doing this for years.... If you stay here until *Songkran* you will see many *farang* who come with their wives when they visit their home. Some of them return to the village every year and really enjoy *Songkran*. Some join us in dancing, drinking, *len nam* (throwing water) and going to the temple.

Mali (67) told me this while I was talking to her and her neighbour about women in Na Dokmai who married *farang* men. Another woman whose two daughters are married to Western men said that she always looked forward to their visit. The daughter living in England did not come to visit her as often as the one in Pattaya, but both called regularly and sent her money, especially on such occasions as *Songkran* and New Year. These accounts highlight the connections that link local residents of Na Dokmai to the world beyond their village and national borders.

There are three factors of particular importance that have historically linked Isan villagers to global dynamics: cash crop production, international labour migration and transnational marriage. Cash crop production connecting farmers to the world market became an integral part of rural livelihoods in Isan in the 1960s. During the next two decades, labour migration—mainly by men in pursuit of overseas employment—gradually changed the social landscape of rural Isan. In recent decades, "local" and "global" articulations have been intensified through the transnational marriage of village women. This chapter begins with a brief discussion of socio-economic and political transformation in Isan and its impacts on the lives of Isan people. The importance of kinship and Isan's matrilineal traditions in these processes of transition is also highlighted. Next, it focuses on three transitional periods in Na Dokmai.

Isan: From Rural Periphery to Transnational Region

Isan covers one-third of Thailand's land area and contains the largest proportion of the country's population. However, among the four geographical regions in Thailand, Isan has long been considered the poorest, lagging economically behind the rest of country.[1] Economic disparities were associated in part with differences in agricultural yields as those in the region were among the lowest in the country, due to generally unfertile soils and irregular rainfall patterns.

Despite its poor natural resources, this region became the country's primary producer of cassava after Isan villagers got involved in cash-crop production which became widespread after World War II. By 1985, the cassava trade had drastically expanded (Chattip 1984; Ingram 1971; Keyes 1967; Long 1966). Cash production was a major source of household income and often the only one, especially in the period before wage labour became an important component of the rural economy (Mills 1999). The expansion of cash crops and the development of Isan in the mid-twentieth century were motivated not only by economic reasons but also by national security concerns at the height of the Cold War. The political and military turmoil in Laos and Vietnam from the 1950s to the 1970s was seen as a threat to Thailand's security, which led to the establishment of US air bases during the Vietnam War.[2] The Mitraphap ("Friendship") Highway, completed in 1961 and funded by the US as part of a deal authorising the establishment of American airbases on Thai territory, connected various Isan provinces with the capital of Bangkok. Apart from this, an irrigation system and dams were built with American aid. Both the expansion of transportation and irrigation systems and the increased world market demand for agricultural products (especially cassava in the 1970s) facilitated widespread cash crop cultivation and agricultural commerce in the region.

Labour migration was another key factor contributing to the rural transformation in Isan by linking its people to centres of power in Bangkok

---

[1] That is, apart from the three predominantly ethnic Malay provinces in the Deep South: Pattani, Yala and Narathiwat.

[2] For more information about political conflicts in Laos, Vietnam and Thailand and its consequences on development policy in Thailand, see Thak Chaloemtiarana (1979) and David Wilson (1966).

and beyond. Rural-urban mobility was related to population pressures, the limited amount of arable land in rural areas and the demand for labour in the cities (Keyes 1967; Lightfoot and Fuller 1984). While there is no data available as to exactly when Isan people started to migrate in search of employment,[3] Keyes (1976) observed that significant numbers of young males (mostly aged between 20 and 29) left their home villages in Mahasarakham province to engage in wage work in Bangkok. These migrants were "temporary", going to the capital between the harvesting and planting seasons. Other studies show different migratory destinations, including various towns in the Northeast and other regions (Lightfoot and Fuller 1984; Whittaker 1999). However, Bangkok was by far the most popular destination. Interestingly, studies also indicate gender, showing that in the middle of the 1970s the number of young female migrants exceeded that of their male counterparts (Mills 1999; NSO 2003; Whittaker 1999). The NSO survey (NSO 2003) shows that in 1974, migrants in Bangkok included 33,000 females and 26,000 males and that in 1977 Isan people constituted the highest percentage of immigrants in Bangkok (45 per cent of total in-migrants). While this inter-regional migration was dominated by women, Isan men outnumbered them in international migration, especially to Middle East countries (Porpora and Lim 1987: 86–7).

International migration was fuelled by demand in the global labour market, especially in the oil-rich Middle East and high-income Asian countries, such as Taiwan, Singapore and Japan. By 1985, there were more than 200,000 Thai workers in the Middle East, most of whom were male. Female migration was restricted by the government out of fear that women might be exploited and mistreated in foreign settings (Anchalee and Nitaya 1992: 159). In recent decades, however, women's involvement in overseas employment has become more significant, although men still dominate.

In addition, out-migration of Isan villagers was spurred on by employment opportunities at R&R sites and tourist destinations. As mentioned in the previous chapter, Isan women were involved in entertainment and service work, as well as the sex industry that catered to American servicemen and foreign male tourists. Transnational connections developed from these sites and in many instances resulted in international mobility, especially through marriage.

---

[3] In fact, Isan villagers, especially men, have long been involved in long-distance mobility. However, in the past this activity involved long-distance trade rather than wage employment. Isan cattle and buffalo traders who took the animals to markets in the Central Region were well known, especially in the periods during which rice production was expanded, thus requiring more draft animals (Chatthip 1984; Pasuk and Baker 1995).

Going through the processes of transformation for more than five decades, starting from cash-crop cultivation to labour migration both internal and international, most Isan villages found themselves being marginalised and living in a cycle of poverty. Involvement in cash-crop production often brought many farmers into debt as they could not control the prices of their products. The development policies of the Thai state with emphasis on industrialisation and urban sectors also drew resources from the agricultural sector, marginalising people in rural areas and stimulating rural-to-urban migration (Mills 1999; Ratana 2010). Keyes notes that in Bangkok in the 1960s most Isan migrants were employed in lowly occupations, often at the lowest socio-economic positions of the urban ladder. These people were (and to a certain degree still are) considered inferior by urban Thais (Keyes 1967). In addition, Thongchai Winichakul (1994) also discusses the marginalised status of Isan in the context of nation-building and the construction of "Thainess" produced through the nation's "geo-body", that is, political territory practices and values. Through this process, people living in Isan, most of whom are ethnically Lao and speak Lao dialects, became "northerners" within the frame of the newly-created body of Thai nationhood. Residents of Bangkok and other regions often portray Isan and Isan villagers through negative stereotypes. The marginalised status of Isan itself provides an explanation for why a large number of Isan women have involved in transnational marriage and in international labour migration. Not surprisingly, villagers are proud of the advanced status that village women acquire by virtue of marrying Western men. I posit that these women constitute an emerging social category in the village hierarchical structure (see Chapter Six). Yet the perception of these women is still ambiguous in both the eyes of the urban middle class and the residents in women's natal village; this matter will be discussed in Chapter Five.

Na Dokmai: The Transnational Village and Its Current Context

The term "village" or "*mu baan*" used in this study to refer to Na Dokmai is different from the definition of *mu baan* used for administration purposes.[4] In referring to Na Dokmai as a "village" I wish to convey the local people's sense of belonging to the same community. Currently Na Dokmai consists

---

[4] In the Thai administration system, *mu baan* is the smallest unit of control and resource allocation. Its definition focuses on "the boundaries—physical and conceptual—of the discrete and social entity of local community" (Hirsch 1993: 2).

of slightly more than a thousand households with a population of around 4,300; the male-to-female ratio is nearly equal (49:51).

Although there is no record of its original establishment, Na Dokmai is believed to have been founded in the second decade of the twentieth century. Today, the village is well developed with good infrastructure, including a road network, electricity and a piped water system. Throughout Isan, the houses are clustered together and surrounded by rice paddies. Some of the newer houses are quite large, and are complete with lawns, gardens, garages, satellite dishes, all enclosed by fences in the front. These houses are more modern and urban in style than what one generally finds in a rural setting. Similar houses can be found on the outskirts of the village. Most of these houses belong to women married to *farang*.

Figure 2.1: The main road passing through Na Dokmai and connecting it to the town of Udon.

Na Dokmai's position at the heart of the district has transformed the village into a centre of government services and trading in the area. There are four large grocery shops, three schools, three temples, two internet cafés, and a market selling fresh and cooked food. Traders and customers involved in transactions in the market are not only residents of Na Dokmai, but also those from nearby villages. The main junction in the centre of the village

Figure 2.2: Newly-constructed houses with garages, gardens and lawns belonging to women married to *farang*.

where the market is located is particularly busy during the morning and afternoon market hours. The afternoon market starts around 4 p.m. During my stay in the village, I observed that while women went shopping for food, their Western husbands would get together to drink beer and chat outside one of the grocery shops on the corner. Whenever I was around, I always saw a few foreigners present, and there were often new faces as well. Some of these men came from nearby villages where they lived with their wives. This was where the foreign husbands got to know each other, socialise, and share experiences and information. It was also where local people learned what was happening in Na Dokmai and nearby villages, particularly about women with *farang* husbands and their husbands. People might gossip about who was visiting home, whose husband was visiting the village, who had just ended a relationship, who had a new partner, who bought or planned to buy paddy or land or to renovate her house.

Na Dokmai residents visit the town of Udon, 40 kilometres away, regularly, especially traders and shop owners who go there to buy goods which they resell in the village. A substantial number of villagers commute to Udon to work, and some parents send their children there to study in public or private schools, as they believe that the education standard there is better than at the village schools. Many women married to *farang* have their children from their former marriages study in town. It is common for residents, especially the younger generation and women living with Western partners, to go to Udon to shop, have a meal, visit entertainment sites and enjoy their leisure time.

In Na Dokmai, most households engaging in agriculture depend largely on rainfall. About 60 per cent of the households in the village own agricultural land—paddy and upland fields; half of these families hold less than 10 *rai* of land; the other half more.[5] The number of households holding less than 10 *rai* of agricultural land is slightly lower than the regional average.[6] Most households owning agricultural land cited farming as their occupation. Those having salaried jobs—selling groceries and other factory goods or running beauty salons, food stores and repair shops—indicated

---

[5] Information on land holdings is drawn from a survey of 618 households in Na Dokmai. The survey was conducted by the District Agriculture Office (DAO) in 2007.

[6] According to the 2003 agricultural census in Isan, the majority of households (60 per cent) owned 10–30 *rai* of land. Those who owned up to 10 *rai* accounted for 30 per cent. During the five-year period of 1998–2003, the number of households holding 10–30 *rai* of land declined (0.9 per cent) while those having less than 10 *rai* increased (2.4 per cent) (NSO 2003: 9, Table 1). Estimates from the survey also indicate an increase in the number of households holding up to 10 *rai*.

Figure 2.3: A "social space" where Western partners meet and socialise while waiting for their wives to buy food in the market.

these activities as their occupation. Nevertheless, farming is not a major source of income in most cases. The rice that is harvested is only enough for family consumption, while cash income comes from other sources. Wages and remittances from family members engaging in employment or living with a Western partner have become increasingly important, especially for landless farmers and families with small land holdings (less than 10 *rai*). These two groups constituted the majority of households in the village (70 per cent), including Phimon's family.

Phimon (34) and her husband (44) own 7 *rai* of paddy. Located on poorly-watered areas, the harvest was low and hardly enough for the consumption needs of a four-member household—the parents and two boys. The couple and Phimon's sister, whose husband was working abroad, farmed the land belonging to Phimon's parents. The rice harvest was shared among the households of her parents, her sister and her own. To earn cash, the couples took up various jobs. Phimon's husband often found construction work in the village and nearby areas, instead of leaving the family to work far from home. Sometimes Phimon worked alongside her husband at construction sites. She also worked as a day-labourer and occasionally sold cooked food in the village. Thanks to these diverse sources of income,

Phimon's family managed to make ends meet. Other households with small land holdings had to rely on remittances from children engaged in wage work to cover their living expenses. Families with no farm land were among the most vulnerable. Some rented paddy fields to grow rice or worked on other people's land and shared the yield. Others relied wholly on day-labour which was usually available during transplanting and harvesting times. Remittances were particularly important for those households struggling to get by.

While the majority of families have to struggle for survival, there are a number of prosperous households with large land holdings and substantial incomes from various sources. Lan's family is a case in point. Lan (63) and her husband (67) own more than 70 *rai* of land. After they stopped growing cassava, they rented out most of their land and earned both cash and extra income from a surplus of rice that they could sell. The family also started one of the first few shops in the village, selling items ranging from clothing, school materials and pots and pans to agricultural tools and religious materials. Lan's only daughter had been living in the Netherlands with her Dutch husband for 17 years. Lan did not expect regular remittances from her daughter.

Other "respectable" households in the village were those with members holding salaried jobs or those with incomes derived from a combination of agriculture and jobs such as teaching or government posts. These positions were highly regarded in the local community. An example is that of Somsri (62) and her husband, Surasak (63), who are retired teachers. Their three daughters are also teachers. Two daughters are married to local men—a teacher and an engineer; the other is married to an English man who works for a land survey company in his country. Like many households with civil service incomes, this family lives in a large house built on an extensive piece of land in the middle of the village. The family also owns 25 *rai* of farm land on which they grow fruit and rubber trees, along with 20 *rai* of paddy field which was rented out. Their rice yield is more than sufficient for their consumption and annual revenues from farming on top of their pension ensure their economic security. For this family, like Lan's, the transnational marriage of one of their daughters has little to do with economic incentives. Her story and motivations propelling her to marry an English man will be discussed in the next chapter.

Agricultural Transformation and Gender Differentiation

The commercialisation of agricultural products in Isan began with the introduction of cash crops in the late 1950s. The expansion of these crops has turned Isan into a major producer of commercial crops and linked farmers to much wider national and international political and economic arenas. Cash crop production not only affected land use patterns and household livelihoods; it also generated gender differentiation.

Thong, a Na Dokmai man in his seventies whose parents were among the first people to settle in the village, told me that by the 1960s arable land had become scarce and some farmers began to clear upland areas to grow rice and cash crops. Thong related how he and his wife engaged in household farm activities, including cash production, which they shared with Saeng and Sai.

Saeng and Sai's story: The rise and fall of cash crop production

Saeng (76) and his wife Sai (66) have six sons who are married and living with their own families; one son has health problems and moved back to live with them after his divorce. The family lives in a large house on the main road connecting the village to the town and other villages. Next to their house is a broad space where cash crops were once stored, which is now used as a parking area and playground for their grandchildren.

After Saeng married Sai in 1960, he moved to live with her in Na Dokmai. In addition to growing rice, he started cultivating jute on 16 *rai* of land. In 1970, when the price of jute went down and cassava was introduced to the region, Saeng switched to growing cassava. In the beginning the earnings were considerably higher than what he had got from jute and so the family decided to buy an additional 30 *rai* of land to grow cassava. "We spent all of our savings to buy the land", Sai said. Later, they expanded cassava cultivation to an additional 15 *rai*. Each year the family hired ten labourers, especially during the planting and harvesting periods. Earnings from this crop enabled them to build a two-story house, buy a car, and support the education of their six children. But because cassava prices declined in the late 1980s and production costs, especially wage rates, went up, they stopped growing it. That was ten years after they began. Sai explained: "When wages exceeded 100 baht per day per labourer we decided to stop. If we had kept going, the earnings might just be enough to cover wages and other costs and we would not get anything."

In 1991, they grew sugarcane, which did not require as much labour as cassava, but they could not fulfil the subcontract quota and after only one crop (lasting three years) they stopped, turning instead to eucalyptus and later to mango. The family allocated 20 *rai* of land for mango cultivation. Sai said that mangoes provided a good income and did not require many labourers, but after their son and his wife went to work in Canada two years ago leaving their two children behind, they found that taking care of the grandchildren was time consuming, and that they had to reduce their work in the mango orchard. Their income dropped to 30 per cent of what they had originally earned.

While Saeng took charge of cassava cultivation, worked in the field and made decisions about when and how much cassava to sell, Sai sometimes helped at the plantation but spent most of her time working in her vegetable and fruit garden at home and selling the products at the village market. During the mango season, she also sold mangoes at the market, which fetched higher prices than selling in bulk to traders.

Earnings from Sai's trading activity made a considerable contribution to the household's income and were used to cover day-to-day household expenses, while revenues from cash crop production went into the family's annual savings. These savings allowed Saeng and Sai to support their six sons in getting overseas employment, although they had to get extra loans to meet the high cost of these contracts. Currently, two of their sons and a daughter-in-law are working in Canada (including the couple who left two children in their care), one is in Israel and another is in Singapore. Saeng said that his sons chose wage work rather than staying in farming, and he agreed with their decision as he found that agriculture is no longer a profitable choice.

The above account illustrates how this family's livelihood has been closely linked to cash crop cultivation for a period of over 30 years, changing from crop to crop in response to market demand and price fluctuations. Not all farmers were as successful as Saeng and Sai. Income uncertainties were caused by fluctuations of commodity prices in the world market, something local producers had no way of knowing. Consequently, many farmers started to look for alternative ways of earning their living, mainly in wage employment, as in the case of the sons of Saeng and Sai. Accordingly, wage labour—predominantly linked to labour migration both within Thailand and abroad—became an important source of rural household income.

Sai's experience in petty trade was shared by other village women of her generation. Lan, for example, became involved in trading soon after finishing compulsory education and continued to do so until recently. Trading allowed her family to become one of the wealthier households in the village. Thai women's involvement in buying and selling is a sign of their control over household economics and resources (Bowie 2008: 148) and has been viewed as having contributed to their relatively independent and high status.[7] At the level of every day practices in villages like Na Dokmai, women

---

[7] However, the extent to which women and men enjoy complementary or asymmetrical status in Thai society has long been debated (Chavivun 1985; De Young 1958; Keyes 1984; Kirsch 1982, 1985; Van Esterik 1982). The arguments on gender in an agriculture-based society are often associated with Buddhism and women's and men's involvement in economic activities and other aspects of social life.

and men share many farm tasks and domestic chores and both benefit from their combined labour in the fields and in the home. The introduction of cash crops no doubt has had an impact on the livelihood and gender relations of villagers, as shown in the case of Saeng and Sai's family. Indeed, the experience of this family is shared by many villagers in Na Dokmai, although each household might engage in this production on a different scale.

As the village transforms itself, a dynamic of gender differentiation has emerged. In the past men led their families in search of farm land and engaged in cultivating rice while women focused on home grown production and selling these products, although they also helped in the fields. A shift to market agriculture allowed men to take control of cash crop production while women remained associated with home production and trading. The gender dynamic was clearly illustrated in Saeng and Sai's household. Women's roles confined to domestic and local spaces became more evident in later years as men left the village to engage in wage employment. Under this situation, support from their kinship network was vital in helping women meet filial obligations and maintain community activities.

Matrilocality and Migration

Matrilocality and the practice of matrilocal residence is widespread at the village level in Isan and other regions of Thailand (Amara 1990; De Young 1958; Mizuno 1978; Potter 1977). In his study of a rural village in Khon Kaen province, Koichi Mizuno (1978: 99) highlights key aspects of kinship as follows: celebrating weddings at the bride's house; a new couple residing temporarily in the house of the wife's parents; sons-in-law contributing their labour to the wife's parents' farms; dividing land inheritance between daughters and the youngest daughter usually remaining with the parents to care for them while receiving a portion of her parents' land and inheriting the parents' house.

Mills (1999: 17–18) also lists a range of features marking matrilocality and influencing gender roles and status. Among these are practices of land inheritance through female lineage, bride wealth payment and post-marital residence in the wife's home (at least in the initial period after marriage), all of which provide women with economic and emotional support. These customary practices are sources of female social power within village society. They allow the wife to exert considerable control over household resources and financial transactions. Mobilisation of labour and other resources is likely to be provided through the wife's kinship network. All of these factors provide the wife with emotional support, enabling her to fulfil household obligations and meet social expectations. Men, on the other hand, are dependent on their wives' families and the social network of their wives' parents for both their home and their access to agricultural land. When a man marries into a wife's family in a new village, he might experience feelings of isolation, and often the wife has to find ways to ease the pressure on her husband and mediate conflicts between him and members of her matrilineage (Bowie 2008: 139–41).

While female autonomy is supported by matrilocality and matrilineality, men gain formal authority as the role of household head is passed on to them by their father-in-law through affinial ties (Amara 1990; Potter 1977). The traditional systems mediating gender relations, however, have been changing because of development and the expansion of capitalism. Generally, government development projects recognise men as household heads while ignoring women, especially in public roles.[8] The advent of wage labour, both in agricultural and urban industrial sectors, has rewarded tasks conventionally done by men with higher wages. Also, men usually spend more time involved in wage work while women are attached to domestic responsibilities. This transition has worked to the disadvantage of women (Whittaker 1999).

In line with previous studies, the accounts provided by Na Dokmai residents illustrate the dynamics of matrilocality and matrilocal residence throughout various generations. The practices of land inheritance, for instance, have become flexible as the population increases and the size of land holdings decreases. Elderly villagers told me how in the past parents gave their land to their children, following the matrilateral inheritance rules: land was divided among daughters, whereas movable assets such as buffalo and cattle were given to sons. This pattern, however, has been shifting towards bilateral inheritance. The parents with whom I spoke said that they had given, or planned to give, their agricultural land to both their daughters and sons. Those who own too little land to divide among their children might want to give their land to the children who had contributed their labour to farming and/or who had taken care of them. Others said that the children who had financial problems should be given priority. In Na Dokmai, there

---

[8] The government supported women to work together and form "Housewives' Groups". These groups of women were encouraged to participate in processing agricultural products and making handicrafts, but opportunities to sell their products were very limited. Usually the Housewives' Groups were asked to prepare and serve food at various public functions. Whittaker (1999: 48) states that these development activities produce and reproduce an urban middle-class discourse of women as housewives and fail to recognise the important role of rural women in agricultural production.

are couples who worked on the land of the husband's parents, instead of the wife's parents. In most of these cases, land holdings of the husband's family were greater than those of the wife's parents.

Similarly, the practice of matrilocal residence has also been changing. Villagers who are in their sixties and seventies, such as Sai and Lan, said that they followed the practice of matrilocal residence. Those elderly women who did not conform to this cultural script reported that it was not possible because their parents owned only a small piece of land where their house was situated so that they could not live next door to their parents. In recent years it was more common for a new couple or a husband to leave the village to engage in wage employment in cities or overseas soon after getting married. If the husband departed, his wife usually lived with her parents.

When the husband migrated to work in the cities or overseas, the family often received support from the wife's relatives in maintaining control of their household. If the wife also had to move somewhere for work, she would leave the children under her parents' care. In this way matrilocality and matrilineality have facilitated labour migration. This support was particularly important for overseas migration, where migrants, mostly men, had to take a long leave of absence while their wives had to shoulder household burdens alone at home.

Men who are labour migrants have little time to spend with their family, and often forfeit their role of household head in taking care of their wife and children, apart from sending money. Such situations, in many cases, have had a negative impact on marriage and family life, leading eventually to marital break-up.

Labour Migration, Marriage and Family Crises

Labour migration in Isan has long been the subject of scholarly studies. However, little attention has been paid to the effects of migration on migrants' households beyond material impacts, especially in the contemporary context associated with transnationalism. Thus, this section looks at how migration has influenced migrants' marriages and resulted in family crises.

In talking about out-migration, residents of Na Dokmai often mentioned the ample employment opportunities created by the establishment of the US air base in Udon in the mid-1960s. The base provided thousands of jobs in construction, administration and service with relatively high wages. Somsri, a retired school teacher, recalled that after graduation from teachers' college, she took and passed the required exam to become a teacher. Many of her male counterparts who passed the exam did not take teaching jobs, but instead went to work at the base. A general administration job at the base would pay twice the salary of a school teacher. Income-earning opportunities were available for unskilled labourers as well. Young women, like Nang and Jit, engaged in service and entertainment work while a number of men worked at construction sites or drove pedicabs in the town. Somsri recalled that her father-in-law's pedicab rental business reached its peak during the period when GIs were stationed in the town. At that time, he had as many as 100 pedicabs and a large number of his clients were from Na Dokmai.

When the Vietnam War ended in 1975, the employment situation in the town declined. However, the growth of urban and industrial sectors provided new opportunities for rural residents looking for wage work. Nowadays in Na Dokmai most villagers—both women and men under the age of 50—have had experience working in the cities or overseas. The life histories of women married to *farang* in this study also reveal that they had migrated and taken up wage work as factory workers, maids, shop helpers, waitresses and bar girls. Those with qualifications had salaried jobs, working as accountants and sales staff. Accounts of both women and men engaged in urban or industrial employment indicated that they were motivated not only by a desire to earn a decent income, but also by the opportunity to experience city life and become *thansamai* (modern). The findings in this regard concur with Mills's work (1999) arguing that working and living in Bangkok allowed female (and male) migrants to get acquainted with new forms of entertainment and consumer commodities representing modern sophistication and self-identity.

Most of the women and men engaged in employment away from the village met their future spouses at their work places. That was the case of Phong (38), who left for the Eastern Seaboard Industrial Estate[9] a few years after finishing the ninth grade and currently works as an occupational safety staff member for a Korean company. A dozen of his male relatives now work for different companies in these areas. Some of them, like Phong, married women they met in the work place.

Employment opportunities were available to women as well. Some women left their home village to work in the cities and formed relationships with men they met at the work place. Da (38) is a case in point. A few years after finishing

---

[9] The Eastern Seaboard Industrial Estate—one of Thailand's industrial zones—is concentrated in four Eastern provinces: Chonburi (the province where Pattaya is situated), Rayong, Samut Prakan and Chachoengsao. This industrial zone is a centre for Thailand's export-oriented manufacturing and shipping industries (Industrial Estate Authority of Thailand: http://www.ieat.go.th/ieat/, accessed 18 May 2012). The availability of job opportunities has drawn people from all over the country to this economic zone.

her compulsory education (the sixth grade), Da left home for Bangkok and worked in a shop selling sweets. Then she changed to a job at a textile factory where she could earn more money with greater independence and mobility. Da met her partner, a mechanic working at the factory. They lived together for five years (1992–97) until she found out that he had been seeing another woman whom he had met before Da. She confronted him with this fact, but he kept seeing this woman, so Da left him and returned home. In 2000, she secured a three-year contract to work at a textile factory in Taiwan. After her return, she got another contract; but this time after arriving in Taiwan and working for just five days, the factory closed and she had to return home. Da later joined her friends in Pattaya and worked as a bar girl, hoping to meet a Western man with prospects of a long-term relationship.

Da's migratory and marriage experiences are shared by many women in the village. The two sisters, Kit (40) and Kan (38), also met their partners—both wage earners—while working in Bangkok. Like Da, their relationships broke up because their partners were not reliable as providers; one of them was also involved with another woman. After separating, they returned to the village to live with their parents. Kit then left her children under her parents' care and went to work in Taiwan. Both sisters eventually married Norwegian men and took their children to live with them in Norway.

The experiences of these women show how migration, marriage and kinship are closely related. When their marital relationships fail, it is common for women to turn to their parents and/or kin networks for support, without which it would be extremely difficult to shoulder the family burden. To escape such situations, women like Kit, Kan and Da came to consider transnational marriage as a choice and worked toward this goal.

Along with rural-urban migration, residents of Na Dokmai have also worked abroad. Opportunities to work overseas were plentiful in the 1980s and 1990s with an increased labour demand in the global market.[10] Despite the relatively high contract costs and the risk of being tricked by traffickers and recruiting agents, overseas contract work was perceived by villagers as a way of earning a good income. Village leaders and local government officials estimated that during the 1990s more than half of the households in Na Dokmai had at least one member engaged in overseas work at one

---

[10] Udon Thani is one of the top provinces in Isan in terms of rates of international migration. The province hosted a large company specialising in exporting labourers. In the period during which demand increased, the company provided training to teach and improve the skills of those who wanted to work abroad. A large number of villagers in Na Dokmai participated in this training and received a contract through the company. Others worked through government agencies and various private agents.

time or another. While most were men, women also participated in this employment. A number of villagers had more than one period of overseas work in various countries. Sak, for instance, had worked in three countries in a period of over ten years.

Sak's story: Engaging in overseas employment

Sak (52) and his wife Suai (46) have two children: a daughter (23) who is in her last year of college and a son (17) who is pursuing vocational education. The daughter married a Swedish man after her graduation. Sak was born and brought up in the village next to Na Dokmai. He moved to live with his wife after they got married. The house where they live and run a shop selling snacks, drinks and cooked food was given to Suai by her grandmother.

At the age of 15, Sak left home for Bangkok. "My main desire was to see Bangkok. At that time, I was not concerned much about earning money.... I knew that in Bangkok I would have to work to support myself", Sak recalled. His parents did not object to his decision, as they wanted him to get work after the harvesting season. Sak first worked at a gas station, where he received meals and accommodation. After two years, he moved on to a brewery, where he learned how to drive a car. He earned 3,000 baht per month which was a good wage at the time. Sak worked for the beer company for almost two years before returning home and joining a road construction company where he learned to extend his driving skills; he eventually was able to drive a truck, tractor, trailer and grader. These skills were assets that facilitated his overseas employment prospects.

In 1978, when he was 21, Sak secured his first one-year contract to work in Jordan as a driver at construction sites. The savings after paying for the cost of travel allowed him to apply for another job. During the years 1979–84, he got two contracts for the same job in Iraq. After that he returned to Thailand and again applied for another job. He kept applying for overseas employment as it paid much more than he could ever earn in Thailand.

While waiting for the results of his application, Sak's mother suggested he should marry, and she recommended Suai to him. At that time, he was almost 30 and Suai was 24. The two knew each other and his mother knew her mother well. In 1984, they got married, and Sak provided a bride wealth of 15,000 baht to Suai's family. Five days after the marriage ceremony, Sak went to work in Saudi Arabia and stayed there for five years without returning for home visits. Suai stayed with her parents while Sak was away. They communicated by writing letters. Suai said, "There was no telephone in the village at the time. A letter took two to three weeks to arrive. It was not like these days when *mia farang* can talk to their husbands every day. They can let their husbands know right away if something happens in the village." In discussing their marriage, Suai said that although their marriage was arranged by their mothers, Sak did not disappoint her. "I knew that he was a responsible and hard-working person", she said.

After Sak's return in 1990, the couple decided to invest in a small grocery shop which Suai had been taking care of. Later when their son began to go to school, she prepared and sold cooked food as well. Sak stuck to his occupation, driving a mini-bus serving commuters between Udon and villages in the area. He became a familiar figure among local residents and involved himself in recruiting village women to work at the bars in Pattaya and Samui. This service flourished in the beginning of the 2000s. Later he stopped driving and started the only catering business in the area, renting out amplifiers, tables, chairs, and kitchen utensils and supplying food and drinks for parties. Suai told me that *mia farang* and their families were among the main customers. On their return visits, they often organised parties to mark homecomings, farewells and birthdays. The business was successful until competitors entered the field.

Undoubtedly, Sak's overseas employment contributed substantially to his household economic security. Sak was proud of the work he had done abroad and related it to his success in the catering business and in recruiting village women to work at tourist destinations. Sak's experience is one of several success stories of international labour migration. Those who succeeded were able to buy paddy land, build or renovate their own houses and invest in business.[11] But there were many who failed and were often in debt; many lost their family fields which they had put up as collateral for an overseas contract. Nonetheless, overseas employment was perceived as an opportunity to earn a better income than working in Thailand, and returnees kept looking for an opportunity to work abroad again.

In Na Dokmai, while most of the overseas migrants were married men who left their wives and children behind, there were also some single men, like Sak, and single women who went to work abroad. Single male migrants were likely to get married soon after their return to the village. These men had obtained a certain degree of economic security and were considered potential suitors capable of taking care of a family. After getting married some men might leave their wives to continue in overseas work. Female migrants might continue their jobs after marriage and accompany their husbands but they usually returned home when they became pregnant to give birth and stayed on to bring up their child.

---

[11] Two out of four big grocery shops in the village were owned by couples whose husbands participated in overseas employment. The biggest shop was run by a couple who was involved in international labour migration.

While overseas labour connected local men to various parts of the globe and provided them with a good income, living alone away from home was not easy and many migrants experienced loneliness and frustration. Some men became involved with other women and spent their earnings on their new relationships instead of sending them home to support their wives and children. Others cut off communication with home altogether. Situations like this caused tension, worry and anger for the wives at home, often placing them in desperate situations. Without remittances from their husbands, the wives had difficulty maintaining the household and bringing up the children, as well as paying back the loans for their husbands' overseas labour contracts.

An example is the case of Mai (47), who put up her mother's paddy for collateral to get a loan of 200,000 baht for her husband to work in Brunei in 1994. A few months after his departure, he stopped communicating with her and ceased sending money home. Mai found out that he had become involved with another Thai woman whom he met in Brunei. She asked her husband to pay back the loan but he refused. "I couldn't do anything.... He always maintained that he didn't have money", Mai explained. Her mother was disappointed and afraid that she might lose her land. She was also angry at her son-in-law's behaviour. The mother-daughter relationship was under stress for years. Struggling with financial and family problems, Mai left her two sons in her sister's care and headed to Phuket in 1996 to work at a bar. She considered this choice as the only way to earn enough money to pay off the debt. There she met Tim, a Dutch man who asked her to marry him and move to the Netherlands with him. Tim also helped Mai pay off the loan so that her mother could get her land back. In 2005, Tim died; Mai remarried, again to another Dutch man who fell sick and died in 2007. After the husband's funeral Mai returned to Na Dokmai. In 2008, she went to work in Pattaya, hoping that through connections with male tourists she could return to Europe again.

Like Mai, other women in Na Dokmai faced similar problems as a result of their husbands' overseas migration. While women's accounts indicate various reasons for the popularity of transnational marriages, they also convey an image of local men as "irresponsible" since many of them fail to fulfil their family obligations, thus lending legitimacy to women's decisions to seek transnational marriages. I shall elaborate on this issue later.

Transnational Marriage and Global Connections

Thus far, one can see that there are connections between a rise in transnational marriage of village women and labour migration ventures that go awry. Despite successful migrants like Sak, there are also sad stories of women suffering from the irresponsible behaviour of local men away from home. These accounts contrast sharply with the good life and success stories of women married to *farang* circulating in the village, which generate what is perhaps an overly-optimistic view of transnational marriages and propel women to look for Western men. Some parents and senior kin whom I met were so captivated by these success stories that they urged their daughters and nieces to marry a Western partner.

The idea of transnational marriage as an alternative for women trapped in marital and family crises gave rise to the creation of recruiting agencies and match-making services by which women could make contact with Western men. These local processes were important means in initiating transnational relationships, especially in the first half of the 2000s. In many cases such connections resulted in long-term commitment and marriage.

Sak's account illustrates how he became involved in the recruiting business. While transporting passengers in his mini-bus between Udon, Na Dokmai and other villages in the area, he was often asked to take women to work in Pattaya. He did not take the requests seriously until a woman in the village next to Na Dokmai who was in a relationship with a *farang* man rented his van to move her belongings back from Pattaya because her partner wanted her to leave her job and return to the village. When Sak arrived in Pattaya, he met several women from Na Dokmai working there as bar girls who introduced him to a bar owner who told him she wanted to hire more women. From that point on, he began to take women from Na Dokmai and surrounding villages to Pattaya, and later to Samui. During the peak period in the early years of the 2000s, he made almost monthly trips transporting eight to ten women in his van. Sometimes the bar owners called him when they urgently needed girls. Sak discontinued his service a few years ago because there was another business he needed to take care of. When the service was no longer available, women interested in initiating transnational connections usually followed their friends and fellow villagers who worked or lived with their Western partners to the tourist destinations.

Sak has quite a positive view of marriages between local women and Western men. He said: "Most *farang* men accept and support children from previous relationships, but Thai men do not. It is not in our culture.... Women can also enjoy a better life and have new experiences, especially when living abroad." Sak was involved in overseas employment for ten years and he truly values the experience as it has given him new perspectives on life. Similarly, he believed that women with Western partners could also benefit from their experience living abroad.

In addition to the services provided by Sak, during 2000–03 a female school teacher took the initiative of helping village women communicate with foreign men by translating letters and messages for them. Later she offered a match-making service and gave English lessons and orientation courses in Western culture. At the peak of her work, she had approximately 80 clients, 30 of whom used her match-making services, 50 of whom used translation and training services. When she discontinued her business, another female teacher followed her footsteps, providing the same services. A few years later, she married an English man and moved to England. Other agencies did work similar to these two well-established ones.

Recently match-making services in Na Dokmai were handled by women married to *farang* and their husbands. However, demand for this service has decreased considerably because village women would rather go to tourist destinations where they can contact prospective partners face-to-face. In addition, women who used match-making services often complained that the process took longer than they expected. For their part, match-making providers explained that the process took time partly because they wanted to make sure that their clients got a "good" man who genuinely wished to establish a family and who was capable of supporting them financially. For the clients, however, a long wait meant more costs since the fee was charged on monthly basis.[12] While this kind of service in the village was declining, match-making and introduction agents were available at many internet shops in the district and provincial towns. During my fieldwork, most of the internet cafés in Udon run by mixed couples also provided such services.

The teacher who first started the match-making agency in the village considered this business as a way to protect women from being involved in prostitution as a channel to marry a *farang* man. However, the involvement of teachers in this business was viewed as "inappropriate" since it implied their support for this type of marriage which runs counter to the local expectation of teachers as role models for students. A local male leader in his fifties expressed the view that the teachers' activities in mediating

---

[12] The two main agents in the village charged an initial fee of 3,000 baht for the first three months. After that clients would be charged 1,000 baht per month. This cost did not include date arrangement or language and cultural training. Normally, the fee for date arrangement was paid directly to the agent by Western men. One of the agents in the village also charged 2 per cent of the money wired to women and when the relationship ended up in marriage; 20 per cent of bride wealth would also be charged. Similar procedures were applied by an agency in Udon run by a mixed Thai-American couple who owned an internet shop. This agency required 50 per cent of bride wealth, though they did not charge a percentage of the money wired to women.

marriage between local women and Western men might set a (bad) example for students. Some villagers and school teachers agreed with this view while others considered this involvement a personal choice that teachers, like any other village woman, were free to make. The reality was that at the time of my fieldwork, there were about five female teachers in local schools, both in Na Dokmai and the surrounding villages, who were married to Western men and some of these couples had also begun providing match-making services.

Through different paths, 159 women in Na Dokmai were married to or have had long-term relationships with foreign men from 21 countries. These ties and connections made by local women have linked a small village in Northeast Thailand to various parts of the globe. Such transnational practices have profound consequences on the perceptions and daily life of local people in the communities where ties and networks across borders are grounded. In a sense, transnational connections have also opened up spaces where local realities and global cultures meet and contest. This is a part of an ongoing process of social transformation of locality (Appadurai 1996).

Conclusion

Since the last half of the twentieth century, local residents of Na Dokmai have engaged in and negotiated a wide range of changes influencing their livelihoods and connecting them to transnational perspectives. The transformation began in the 1960s with the promotion of cash-crop production linking villagers to wider market demands driven by national and global economies. Since the 1980s, when the contribution of cash-crop production to the household economy declined, labour migration opened new opportunities for rural residents, both women and men.

While labour migration provided villagers with substantial earnings and formed an integral part of rural household economies, it also affected marriage and family life. Women in this study often attributed their domestic problems to the negative impacts of migration, pointing an accusing finger at men's irresponsibility as household providers as well as their promiscuity. Women also reported problems of financial and mental pressure, conflict with their own parents and eventual marital break-up. Transnational marriage offered an escape route for many of these women who sought to move beyond their predicaments to make a fresh start with foreigners, mainly from Western countries.

Apart from international labour migration, transnational marriages have also intensified the "local" and "global" articulation through cross-border activities and ties that women and their Western husbands continue to maintain. The ways in which these couples and local villagers have negotiated the social relations and manoeuvred tensions created by transnational marriage as well as their consequences on local cultures/norms shaping villagers' lives and the dynamic of the village socio-economic structure and social order will be revealed. In the following chapter, I shall convey some of the rich experiences of women and men involved in transnational marriage to discuss the motivations that propel them to opt for this kind of relationship.

CHAPTER THREE

Complex Motivations and the Logics of Desire

THE WEDDING OF AN ISAN woman and a Dutch man at their house in a small city near Amsterdam on 25 June 2008 brought together about ten Thai women, including me. Most came with their Dutch partners. In the late afternoon, some of us spent time cooking Thai food, eating and chatting with one another. At some point, the conversation drifted toward me when one woman asked whether I had met a Dutch man I liked and, if so, would I marry him and stay in the Netherlands after finishing my studies. While I was pondering this, she went on, "If you marry a Dutch man, you might be asked, 'Do you love him, or are you marrying him because you want to stay here?'" Suddenly, another woman who worked at a grocery store said, "Yes, my co-workers sometimes tease me about this. Once I was asked how much my husband paid to marry me. I didn't take it seriously, but this is the way they think about us."

This vignette illustrates a common assumption about marriages between women from poorer, less-developed countries with men from richer or more industrialised ones. From a migration perspective, a transnational relationship of this kind is often considered a means for women to engage in overseas work. The material incentives and the opportunity to move to and work in more desirable locations in the global hierarchy are assumed to be the woman's major motivations. Frequently, women engaged in this type of transnational relationship are assumed to be (or to have been) involved in the transnational sex industry (Pataya 2002; Piper and Roces 2003; Supang et al. 1999). The women above did not mention explicitly whether other people might think they were involved in the sex industry. Nevertheless, on other occasions, I was cautioned by Thai women married to Dutch men that if I considered marrying a Dutch man I should expect to be asked, directly or indirectly, about whether I was involved in commercial sex. This perception was pervasive regardless of the personal history, experience, educational background and qualifications of the woman in question.

Such assumptions are at odds with the modern ideal of romantic love and individual fulfilment, since economic reasons are incompatible with the Western stereotype of a love-based marriage. According to the romantic clichés, "romantic love cannot be bought and sold, love cannot be calculated, it is mysterious, true and deep, spontaneous and compelling, it can strike anyone—even the most hardened cynic can be laid low by Cupid" (Lindholm 2006: 5) This notion has helped to generate the binary opposition between romantic love and material motivation. The normative way in which transnational marriages are perceived is based on this dichotomous view.

There are, however, other factors. A more wide-reaching perspective arguing for multiple forces and flows influencing transnational practices and ties can provide insight into the motivations for women and men to engage in transnational marriages. Material gains are arguably not the sole motivation to marry. Historical and socio-cultural dimensions, desire for a better life and processes such as fantasising and strategising are powerful forces shaping transnational practices (Constable 2005a; Mahler and Pessar 2001). In addition, a gender-focused approach emphasising the impact of gender differences in the perceptions, decisions and experiences associated with transnational practices also provides insight into the complexity of transnational relationships. Constable (2003) argues against the popular perception of romantic clichés and suggests that one should look at how emotion/passion, material motivations and marriage are intertwined. Reducing these dimensions to simplistic economic motives is a serious misrepresentation.

The emergent literature on transnational intimacy poses new challenges to classic Western assumptions about romantic love and its extrication from financial motives. Cabezes's study (2009) on international tourism in Cuba and the Dominican Republic brings to light the blurred boundaries between work and romantic relationships and between love and money. Similarly, Cheng's research (2010) on Filipina entertainers points to the role of personal desire, autonomy and excitement, contrasting with the poverty and predictable abusive situations that propel them to search for work and love transnationally. She argues further that these women have accepted the risks of marginalisation and delegitimation in another culture as the costs of their desired life. Faier (2009) also reveals how intimacy is linked to and influenced by economic exchanges among Filipina bar hostesses working in rural Japan. Through exploring the performance of "emotional labour" in the bar scenes and the roles of good wife and daughter-in-law in the family,

Faier elucidates the complex meanings of "love" and the roles it plays in constructing gendered and sexualised subjectivities.

The motivations behind transnational marriage are far more complex. I seek to uncover the diverse factors and incentives that lead women in Na Dokmai and Western men to become involved in intimate relationships and to reveal how such aspirations are imaginable and realisable. Constable (2003) points out the links between political economy and the "cultural logics of desire" which form the basis upon which relationships across borders are imagined and realised. She argues that "political economy is implicated in the production and reproduction of desire and is implicated in even the most minute and intimate levels of interaction" (2003: 145). American men's attraction to Filipina was built on the idea of Asian women's commitment to traditional family values and could be traced back to historical connections between the US and these Far Eastern countries. For the women, marrying an American man was desirable for a number of reasons: "modern" ways of life in the US, constraints of norms and familial obligations in their home countries and material advantages. Yet all this did not preclude feelings of love, as revealed in the life history of a number of Filipina and Chinese women in Constable's work as well as those of women in Na Dokmai presented in this book. Thus, love and emotion are intertwined with political economy through "the cultural logics of desire" (Constable 2003: 119). I apply a similar analytical approach, but with a different emphasis. I consider historical developments of the current transnational marriages discussed in Chapter One as, in Constable's words, political economy dynamics in Thai society in the context of international relations. This chapter, therefore, focuses on how the logics of desire evolve around material resources, intimate relationships, socio-cultural dimensions, gender fantasies and feminist ideas and how these multiple motivations combine and complicate the current transnational marriage relationships.

Transcending Economic Security and Romantic Love

> My relationship with Sven started with money. I needed to support my two children and pay back a loan I had borrowed to pay the contract for my former husband to work overseas. It ended up with love.

Sa, who had been living with a Swedish pensioner named Sven since 1999, gave me this thoughtful response when I asked what motivated her to marry him, how she saw her relationship and on what foundation it was built. At a moment during our conversation, Sa reflected that she had experienced "real love", although admitting that she had told herself not to fall in love again after having gone through a terrible time with her ex-husband. The story about her relationship with Sven illustrates both the sentiments and aspirations motivating her to engage in transnational marriage.

Sa's story: It's not just about romantic love or money

Sa (43), a divorced mother with two adult sons, met Sven (70), a divorced father with three adult children, during his vacation in Pattaya, where their relationship first took root and then blossomed. They lived together in Pattaya for almost two years before moving to Na Dokmai in 2003. The couple decided to settle in the village and bought a house there, where they lived until recently. Living in the village for more than ten years, Sven rarely returned to his home country. He planned to live in the village with his wife permanently. Sa's and Sven's experiences and sentiments elucidate how their intimate relationships, the social relations they were involved in and Sa's decision to engage in transnational marriage extend beyond love and money.

Sa headed to Pattaya in 2000 after her ex-husband left her with a large debt and two sons to support. To pay off the husband's overseas employment contract, Sa had put up her house as collateral for a loan. The first contract went well, and she was satisfied with the earnings. When he decided to apply for another contract, she supported him again. This time, however, something went wrong. Sa recalled, "He didn't send any money home. When I phoned him, he said that he didn't have a job. Whenever I asked him to send money, he told me that he didn't have any money because he had no job. It wasn't just the loan I had to repay; I had to eat, feed our sons and pay for their schooling. He didn't care what happened to me or our children. He didn't care whether our house would be taken away. I couldn't make ends meet, let alone pay off the large debt to keep the house." Consequently, she decided to follow one of her friends to Pattaya and work at a bar. During her second month there, she met Sven.

After a week of living together, Sven asked Sa to stop working and marry him. She refused, however, explaining, "It was too soon. I didn't know anything about him and he didn't know enough about me either." They maintained their relationship while Sa continued working at the bar; after her three-month contract was over, she stopped working and began living with Sven. He helped Sa pay back the loan and support her children. Once when she was sick, Sven took good care of her, which impressed her immensely. "I really appreciated what he did. I have never received this kind of concern and care from anyone—my ex-husband, my parents or my siblings." Sa emphasised this point as part of the reason she continued her relationship with Sven.

Like other couples, they sometimes fought and quarrelled. In Pattaya, conflicts were often set off by distrust and misunderstanding based primarily on gossip about Sa's previous marriage among her friends who worked at the bar. The fact was that Sa had not yet officially divorced her first husband when she was living with Sven in Pattaya, which made him feel insecure about her previous relationship. After moving to Na Dokmai in 2003, they were confronted by a new set of situations, particularly the frequent requests for financial support they received from Sa's relatives, which made them feel stressed. Sa mentioned that Sven often wondered whether these people worked hard enough to help themselves. As the go-between for her husband and her relatives, Sa frequently became frustrated. "I learned that money does not always bring happiness", she said. However, the couple managed to help her relatives, although they were not able to respond to all requests and their support did not always meet the relatives' expectations. Sven realised how important it was for his wife to help her relatives and truly admired the way she handled the situation and managed the household budget. She always planned ahead, especially when large amounts of money were at stake.

Even though she did not feel much affection for Sven in the beginning, after living together for ten years and sharing both social pressure and happiness, Sa concluded that she experienced "real love" (*rak tae*). Sa appreciated the financial responsibility Sven showed her and he got along with her siblings, paid for medication and took care of her parents when they were sick. Her love for him grew on the basis of caring, understanding, mutual help and trust building, and it gradually developed into passion. Sven stated that he found Sa attractive, which is why he asked her to marry soon after he met her. Sa always took good care of him especially in recent years when he had health problems. Her care and emotional support were particularly important to him. "I can't imagine living without her", he said. "Without her I would die."

This story highlights the various motivations influencing Sa and Sven to opt for marriage. Although economic reasons did play a part, their relationship was built on diverse factors. Sven's care of her while she was sick, his support for her in fulfilling familial obligations as a mother and daughter, and his good relations with her siblings all influenced her decision to continue her relationship and eventually marry him. Similarly, Sven was deeply appreciative of the physical and emotional support Sa gave him, which had been totally lacking in his previous marriage. Sven mentioned that his ex-wife did what she wanted, and he had not expected her to take care of him. She had also been quite demanding, especially regarding financial matters, and when he could not meet her demands the relationship ended. His life with Sa was totally different, and he was very happy with his second marriage.

The gendered stereotype of Asian women, including Thai women, as being committed to the traditional role of wife and devoted to family values played a part here. This image is fostered through the experiences of Western men, like Sven, who received good care from their wives, as well as through the perceptions of local women who considered care-taking as a way of reciprocating their husbands for financial support. This gender stereotype has become a part of Western men's motivation for meeting and marrying Thai women. I asked Thomas, an English man living in Na Dokmai with his current Thai wife—his previous two marriages involved an English woman and a Thai woman—what motivates a Western man to marry a Thai woman. He replied, "Let me tell you this. If a *farang* man gets home after work and he tells his wife, 'I don't feel well. I have a headache', his *farang* wife will say: 'There's a bottle of pills on the shelf, go and get it.' But his Thai wife will give him the pills with a glass of water. Thai women know how to take care of their husbands." This is the image of Thai women in Western men's minds; it influences their marriage choices. For their part, Thai women also appreciate being cared for by their husbands (either Western or local), and this care could become a motivation contributing to the logics of desire influencing marital relations and marriage decisions, as Sa's case demonstrates. However, the image of caretaker is associated more with females than males and is particularly prevalent for Thai (and Asian) women as compared to Western women.

Physical attraction also plays an important role. The image of Asian women as typically petite, with delicate bone structure and hairless skin, is viewed as feminine. In her study of British male tourists in Pattaya, Davidson recalls the words of a respondent: "They're all like film stars or models, aren't they? It's the hair and the skin, and they're mostly always petite, you know, slim and small" (Davison 1995: 55). These men also romanticised Thai women as affectionate, respectable, innocent, loyal and natural.

As with Sa, many women married to Western men admitted that their relationships did not begin with romantic love, and that passion only came into play in later stages of their relationships. Jin (47), a woman living in a village next to Na Dokmai who married a German man and lived in Germany for ten years, said she could not imagine how husbands and wives, whether they are local or mixed couples, could live together for years without passionate ties. Jin viewed these marriages as relationships based on reciprocal support, trust, care and sexuality in which emotional attachment and passionate ties develop. She saw the care-taking and emotional support that women provided as a way to reciprocate their husbands for being financially responsible. Jin said that her husband was good to her, that he also helped her sister finish building her house and that he sometimes provided her family with financial help. Having lived together for more than ten years, Jin admitted that she eventually developed passion and emotional ties (*rak lae phukphan*) with her husband, though her relationship did not start with romantic love.

Rung (32), a divorced mother with two children aged ten and five living with her Swedish partner, also argued that local women did not marry Western men solely for economic reasons. Like Sa, Rung confessed that her relationship started with the need for money as she had to support her children after her relationship with her ex-partner had ended. Rung affirmed, however, that she would not have stayed with her Swedish partner for four years if she had not cared for him and had passion for him. If she had married only for money, her partner would not have been a good choice. In her view, even though he wasn't rich, he provided an allowance to support her children, which Rung appreciated. She explained, "The allowance isn't much, but it ensures that my children have enough to eat and that I can pay for their education. Their real father has never given his own children anything since we separated."

Interestingly, when these women talked about passion or "love", they related it to care, trust and reciprocal support—which also involved financial support from their husbands. Sa spoke of her "real love" in these terms. This meaning is different from the various definitions given to romantic love emphasising an individual's happiness and fulfilment, such as "love is blind", "love overwhelms", "a life without love is not worth living", "marriage should be for love alone, and anything less is worthless and a sham" (Lindholm 2006: 5). These diverse sayings reflect different meanings of love cross-culturally. Indeed, distinct cultural meanings of love have shaped the differences in interpreting money in relation to love. Yos (1992b) points out that in Western societies love and money are considered mutually exclusive, whereas in Thai society they overlap somewhat. He posits that "money itself cannot be distinguished from signs of affection, tender caring and love itself. Mutual or material dependence frequently engenders some sort of an emotional attachment on the part of the girl herself" (Yos 1992b: 15). Although women may enter into relationships with Western men for economic reasons, emotional attachment may develop and play an important role, thereby obscuring the line between money and love. It is on this basis that Sa, Jin, Rung and other women married to *farang* in Na

Dokmai rationalised their marital relations with their Western partners. Apart from diverse other reasons, the factors motivating women to engage in this relationship are also shaped by women's perceptions of local males and their images of Western men.

Local Male Image, Gender Imagination and the Logics of Desire

> I want a good man who is generous and warm-hearted, who is responsible for his family, accepts and supports my children and cares for my parents as well. My previous relationship [with a local man] taught me how life would be if the man doesn't take his family seriously.

This is what Nisa told me when I asked her what kind of man she was looking for and what motivated her to eventually decide to live with her Danish partner in 2004. Nisa's life story echoes the experiences of many women married to *farang* who went through difficult times with a Thai partner. These women shared similar backgrounds with Nisa in the conditions contributing to the termination of their previous relationships.

Nisa's story: "I'm looking for a man who is responsible for the family"
Nisa (33), a divorced mother with a seven-year-old daughter, met Carsten, a Danish man in his early fifties, during his vacation in Phuket in 2004. When Nisa returned to Na Dokmai, he went along and stayed with her. They had a son (2), who stayed with Nisa in the village when Carsten returned to Denmark to resume working for his parents' construction company. Carsten called via the internet to talk with them every day and managed to come and stay with Nisa and the children two or three times a year.

Previously Nisa had graduated from vocational college and gone to Bangkok to work at a textile factory where she met her ex-partner, a Thai man who was the father of her daughter. She lived with him from 1997 to 2002. The relationship went well until she found out that he was seeing another woman. Conflicts and quarrels occurred frequently. The situation became worse when she became pregnant and he did not take care of her in any way. Nisa finally left him and her job and returned to the village to live with her parents. She wanted to make sure that she could receive help and support during and after the birth of her baby. "I wasn't mistaken: he didn't show up. I struggled and supported myself all alone." Nisa brought up her daughter without any support from her husband. At one point, he asked Nisa for a reconciliation, but she did not want to go through the same experience again. As she said, "What I went through could neither be corrected nor was there anything that could make me feel better about Thai men. Believe me, many *mia farang* have the same experience."

Wanting to initiate connections with Western men, Nisa used a match-making service in the village, but none of the contacts she got this way worked out. Through long-distance communication, it was difficult to know whether the information given to her was reliable or not, so after nine months she decided to adopt a different strategy. When another village woman went to work in Phuket, Nisa went along and got a job at the same bar. During her second week there, she met Carsten and stayed with him during his time in Phuket. They got along well, and Nisa invited him to come and meet her daughter and parents in the village. Before returning to Denmark, he asked Nisa not to return to work in Phuket. He sent a regular allowance to take care of her and her daughter's living expenses. He came to stay with her in Na Dokmai whenever possible and paid for her trips to visit him in Denmark. Nisa had already been there three times when I met her.

The couple renovated the house in Na Dokmai, where Nisa lived with her parents and children. Everyone had a room, and there was a playground for the children as well. Nisa's daughter went to a private school in Udon. At first the girl commuted by minibus every day, spending nearly three hours a day commuting between home and school. In 2010, Nisa decided to move to Udon when her son reached pre-school age. She believed that the private schools in the city provided better education than the village schools. In May 2009, when I met Nisa, she was living with her two children in a rented house in town close to their children's schools. With financial support from Carsten, Nisa was able to fulfil her desire to educate her children in the best possible way. Nisa wanted to move to Denmark later so that her children could receive their education there. However, she would have to take care of the children alone if Carsten were to travel to work in other cities or other countries. She discussed this with him and they decided to wait until the children, especially their son, became older and could take care of themselves.

Thus far, Carsten has taken the family's needs seriously and sent allowances regularly. He knew that Nisa didn't work and spent her time taking care of the children. What mattered most to him was the children's well-being. He called almost every day via the internet. Both his son and stepdaughter felt that their father was not a stranger as they could talk regularly and see him through the internet. He always tried to plan his visits to the village to coincide with the children's birthdays, and if he could not be there, he never failed to give them a gift and call them on their birthdays. Nisa said that Carsten never disappointed her as her husband and the father of her children, even though they sometimes experienced conflicts and mistrust similar to those of other transnational couples.

The story highlights Nisa's experiences with her Thai ex-partner and her current Danish husband, which were so different in terms of the men's reliability and responsibility as husbands and fathers. Nisa's Thai partner failed to carry out his responsibility as a family provider and his sexual promiscuity was intolerable to her. Her experiences were similar to those of Sa, Jit, Rung and many other women married to *farang* in Na Dokmai whose marriages were fraught with crises and eventually broke up. Other women also blamed their marital troubles on their husbands' gambling and alcohol addictions. These women's accounts conveyed the image of local men as "irresponsible" with regard to their families (*mai rapphitchop khrop khrua*), which was a major factor in encouraging and legitimising women's involvement in transnational marriage. Lita, a local school teacher whose life story will be presented in the following section, talked about this image as a part of her motivation to look for a relationship with a Western man. "Most Thai men [particularly those in rural areas]", she said, "spend their earnings on drinking, gambling and enjoying other women. They don't support their families (*mai liang khrop khrua*). The family is not their priority. Women are expected to accept this male behaviour." In Lita's view, transnational marriage became an alternative choice for women whose relationships were damaged beyond repair and for those who did not want to find themselves in such situations.

While village men were aware of negative way in which they were perceived, they considered such male behaviour as a response to the pressures created by depressing conditions in their work environment, such as failure in agricultural production and other occupational setbacks, or loneliness and homesickness while working overseas and living far from home. Moreover, when village men talked about drinking, gambling and philandering, they considered it "something normal" (*pen rueang thammada*) through which they expressed their masculinity. By contrast, women regarded this behaviour as a manifestation of male irresponsibility towards their families. The different views of gender in Thai society offer insight into the marital problems faced by local women.

Gender differences are reinforced through cultural norms and institutionalised through socialisation processes. Boys are generally given much greater freedom than girls, who are assigned more household tasks and subject to stricter supervision in terms of spatial mobility and sexual activities. It is common for young men to socialise, drink alcohol and acquire sexual experience. Male peer group "outings" (*thiao*) provide opportunities for getting together, drinking alcohol and visiting entertainment locations with the possibility of seeking out prostitutes. These behaviours are seen as constituting masculinity and are accepted as a way for physical release and relaxation (Chanpen et al. 1999; Pramualratana 1992). Traditionally, polygamous relationships were commonly accepted, especially among upper-class men. Normally, the relationships involved the material support that husbands provided for their wives. In recent times, polygamy usually occurs in the form of a "minor wife" (*mia noi*). This kind of relationship has become more prevalent than it used to be among the middle and lower classes (Chanpen et al. 1999; Bencha 1992). Public opinion regarding men who have minor wives is generally negative. Thus, those who have *mia noi* make an effort to hide the relationship (Sumalee 1995). From this perspective, male behaviours, such as philandering, drinking and gambling are tightly embedded in the social fabric of Thai society. The image of local men as "irresponsible" in family matters is also rooted in cultural ideas concerning the role of husbands as breadwinners and wives as homemakers. Drawing on this cultural norm, women expect that a "good husband" first and foremost should be able to provide adequate support to his family, both financially and emotionally. Indeed, the roles of provider/breadwinner are part of a key cultural ideal that influences marital relationships and it is this ideal norm that the husbands, either local or foreign, have to negotiate (Chen, Yeoh and Zhang 2014; Maher and Lafferty 2014; Thompson et al. 2016). Men, for their part, expect their wives to be good housewives and good mothers and to understand their need to socialise with male friends. However, some men are of the view that a wife should help in contributing to household income as well (Knodel et al. 1999).

A local female school teacher in her late thirties who married a local man said that normally Thai men try to please their women during the courtship period, but after marrying or living together they are less concerned about them. Moreover, local husbands and wives are not likely to participate in shared activities: husbands would go out with their male friends, while wives would join their female peers or stay at home to take care of the children.

By contrast, women imagine Western men to be good family men and reliable providers who tend to please their wives and do things together with them and are not likely to become involved in extramarital affairs. In Na Dokmai, these images were reinforced by perceptions of how women and their *farang* partners lived their lives. Mixed-marriage couples in the village would more often do things together, such as eating out, joining communal activities and shopping. Some women in the village perceived the kind of husband-wife relations displayed by mixed couples as the ideal family lifestyle they fantasised about. The fantasising about both Western men and Western family relations fed into women's motivations to seek transnational marriage.

Interestingly, while many male villagers agreed that the image of local men as irresponsible was relevant, they did not consider it a factor that turned women away from local men and led them to transnational marriage. Rather, they claimed that the desire for wealth was the key motivation for women to engage in transnational intimacy and marriages. Apart from motivations addressed thus far, the local norms and preferences associated with marriage as well as fantasies about modernity and Western societies were also a part of the complex set of motivations that made women turn to Western men.

Local Norms and Fantasies about Modernity

> It's not easy for a woman of my age [37], living and working in a rural community, to find someone who is single and has a similar education and career background, who shares a similar lifestyle and is willing to take responsibility for his family.

These are the words of Lita, a teacher from a relatively well-to-do background who married a man from the UK. For her, material resources were less important than the search for a "suitable match" because of her background. The limited number of eligible marriage choices Lita encountered was a phenomenon shared by other Westerner's wives in the village who had similar social and economic backgrounds and who were in the same age group.

Lita's story: A local "suitable partner" is not easy to find

In May 2008, after four years of communicating through internet chatting, Lita (37) married Peter (42), an English man who worked for a land development company in his country. Lita taught at a local primary school in a village next to Na Dokmai for more than ten years. She left her secure job and her parents to live with Peter in the UK in 2009.

To provide a comprehensive picture of Lita's life story, I turn to her family background described earlier in Chapter Two. Lita was born into a "family of teachers" where both parents—currently on pension—and three daughters were teachers. Both of her sisters married Thai men and lived with their families elsewhere; only Lita stayed with her parents in the village. Her father spent his time taking care of 25 *rai* of farm land where various fruit and rubber trees were grown. The family also owned 20 *rai* of paddy land which they rented out. They lived in a spacious house on a large piece of land in the centre of the village. As a teacher in a government school, Lita earned a regular income and enjoyed other benefits such as free health care. Considering their economic background and respectable career, Lita's family was located at the top of the village hierarchy.

In 1997, a few years after she began her teaching job, her relatives urged her to see a man working at a local health centre as a marriage prospect, but Lita was not interested. Later, she was introduced to another man who worked at a local government office. After a while, she found out that he was involved with a young woman working at the same office; she then refused to see him again and ended the relationship. Lita did not date anyone after that. Her sentiment (related in the beginning of this section) is typical of the problem of finding a suitable partner in such a rural setting.

Through working with an American volunteer at her school, Lita was encouraged to improve her English ability and she often chatted via the internet. This was how her relationship with Peter started: "We chatted almost every day for years." They told each other about their families, talked about day-to-day activities and exchanged ideas about marriage between Thai women and *farang*. In 2005, Peter came to meet Lita in Na Dokmai and the following year she went to visit him in the UK for a month. She received a warm welcome from his parents.

In 2007, Peter came again and asked Lita to marry him. They married the following year. When asked why she decided to marry, Lita said, "We got along well. We had several similarities which we could always share. Before we met for the first time, he told me that he would not be surprised if I found his clothes out of style. He was not a stylish kind of person. I told him not to expect me to wear a tank top either. The way he dressed didn't bother me, but I didn't ask how he felt about mine." Peter told Lita that he was not a rich man, but he could take care of her. "We talked about his concern in this regard a few times, as he brought it up. I told him that it didn't matter to me."

Leaving home to live in the UK was a source of anxiety for both Lita and her parents. Her mother was concerned about Lita giving up a secure job and leaving her to live so far away from home. Lita had foreseen her life in the UK as being a full-time housewife, at least during the first few years. "Peter told me not to worry [about staying home with no job], he can look after me. But I don't want to be a housewife for the rest of my life. I certainly will improve my English and find a job."

Obviously, Lita's life story challenges the normative view that women from developing countries marry men from affluent countries solely because of economic incentives. Her economic and social background was rather secure. Her motivations to marry a Western man had little to do with economic gain. The limited number of marriage choices, which played a key role in motivating her to look for a Western partner, draws on the Thai cultural norm of spouse selection in which women are expected to marry a man of similar or higher socio-economic and educational background (Sumalee 1995). Following this cultural script, local marriage choices for educated women of Lita's age and relatively affluent background are rather limited.

The limitations in finding a suitable spouse locally were also experienced by Kanda (36), a nurse who was studying for a master's degree during the time I talked to her, and by other women who remained single into their thirties. In Na Dokmai, women generally marry a few years after finishing nine-year secondary school, when they are in their early twenties or younger. This observation about marriage is consistent with data from a national population survey indicating that most women in rural areas marry by their early twenties.[1] Those who continue their education may marry at an older age. After their thirties, marriage possibilities for women decline sharply. Having a relatively high education and a good social economic background, as in the cases of Lita and Kanda, might put more pressure on women to find for a local suitable match.

Another factor restricting local marriage opportunities for women, specifically those who are widowed or divorced, is the high value of chastity (and presumed virginity) attached to young womanhood. Married women were considered less desirable as spouses. In Na Dokmai, two-thirds of the 159 women married to *farang* had been divorced from a Thai partner before marrying a Western husband, and half of them had children from their previous relationships to support after the divorce. This situation left them with little chance of remarrying a "decent" Thai man. Transnational marriage provided a viable option for these women.

Furthermore, some women mentioned their preference for a Thai-Western mixed child (*luk khrueng*) as a part of their motivations to marry *farang*. Khwan (27), a dental assistant working in Pattaya who had just divorced her English husband after three years of marriage, said: "If I have children, I want a cute child with an upright nose like a Westerner's, not like mine. It is my inferiority complex really. When studying sex education at school, I learned that if I marry an Asian man, I would never get a child with a prominent nose. I kept thinking about this." Khwan talked about *luk khrueng* as attractive and representing "modernity" (*khwam thansamai*). They

---

[1] According to the survey in 1984, the average age at marriage of men and women in rural and urban areas were 24.5 and 22.4 years, respectively. In rural areas, women marry approximately 3.5 years earlier than in urban areas (Bencha 1992: 27).

could also become an actor or actress. Kanda shared Khwan's passion for *luk khrueng* which, in part, motivated her to seek connections with Western men. Kanda, like Lita, was able to use the internet to chat with Western men and through this channel she made a connection to her husband-to-be, an English man who had a PhD in information technology. After their first contact, he visited her in Thailand every two or three months for three years until they eventually got married in 2010.

Both Khwan's and Kanda's desire to have *luk khrueng* is related to Thais' craving for these children as they have acquired a privileged place in society, particularly in the media. Since the 1990s, *luk khrueng* have become a Thai public fascination. Many are popular as actors and actresses, singers, supermodels, beauty pageant contestants and social celebrities (Reynolds 1999). These new images contrast sharply with past perceptions of often marginalised Thai-American *luk khrueng* of the Vietnam War era. Weisman (2000) views the earlier *luk khrueng* as a reminder of past failures of Thai authorities in maintaining the state's control over both its socio-economic and political development and as female sexuality. Women who engaged in relationships with American servicemen were taking their sexuality into their own hands. Thai men were no longer "in charge of the preservation of Thai women's 'good' image. Rather, the thousands of Thai women who entered into unmediated (for example by fathers or other male relatives) sexual relationships with American military men were taking control of their own sexuality and images" (Weisman 2000: 8). The construction by the Thai media of *luk khrueng* as self-confident, sophisticated, beautiful and modern reflects shifting social attitudes in Thai society and in particular the notion of beauty and its commodification in Thai popular culture (Reynolds 1999; Van Esterik 1996, 2000). The current popularity of commodified *luk khrueng* images represents a reassertion of Thai control over female sexuality during another period of social and economic transformation (Weisman 2000).

Along with the current preference for *luk khrueng*, which is closely linked to ideas of modernity, women also imagine modern Western societies through various media which reinforce the popularity of the current transnational marriages. Khwan, for instance, said, "I like the modern life-styles and technologies I have seen in Hollywood movies since I was a young girl." Khwan experienced "modern life" while living in the UK with her ex-husband, which reinforced her ideas about Western society. Her fantasising about modern Western societies and her preference for *luk khrueng* played a significant part in her decision to apply for a job in Pattaya, where there were more possibilities to meet with Westerners.

The aspirations of Lita, Kanda and Khwan had less to do with material incentives than did those of other women. The associations between logics of desire and women's backgrounds become more nuanced if one takes the notion of "gendered geographies of power" (Mahler and Pessar 2001) into account. According to this idea, gender operates on multiple social scales— for example the body, the family and the state. In particular, it emphasises "social locations" of persons in shaping their perceptions, motivations and practices. The term "social locations" refers to a "person's positions within power hierarchies created through historical, political, economic, geographic, kinship-based and other socially stratifying factors" (Mahler and Pessar 2001: 445–6). In this case, the variation of women's backgrounds and characteristics constitute their "social locations", which shape their logics of desire and decisions to opt for marriage. Single, educated women with prestigious economic and social status may not be motivated by economic gain. Instead, they are driven by other factors, such as restrictive local norms and practices relating to gender, age at marriage and preferences associated with modernity. However, the primary impetus behind women's attempts to initiate this type of transnational connection, regardless of their "social locations", was the image of local men as irresponsible persons who failed to fulfil familial duties.

Gendered Stereotypes of Thai Women and Feminist Ideas

While Thai women in this study fantasised about Western men and Western society as their motivation in looking for transnational intimacy, Western men talked about images of Thais (and other Asians) that feed into their motivations in seeking relationships with Thai women. Existing studies connect Western men's desires to marry Asian women with various motivating factors. These include cultures associated with gendered images and perceptions of modernity and traditions (Constable 2005a), social and cultural norms and ideas about marriage in both women's and men's societies (Panitee 2009), men's Orientalising fantasies about Asian women (Suriya and Pattana 2007), the performances of privileged white Western masculinity (Davison 1995; Maher and Lafferty 2014) and the way in which people involved regain their denied backgrounds and identities at home (Ratana 2010). While acknowledging these explanations, I propose to examine how gendered stereotypes of Thai (and other Asian) women and gender relations in Western societies influenced by feminist ideas combine and motivate Western men to opt for transnational marriage and become empowered by it.

As mentioned, the Western men in this study often talked about gendered stereotypes of Thai women, emphasising attachment to traditional gender roles and family values as a part of their motivation to marry a Thai woman. No doubt their response was guided by common images of Thai women portrayed in the popular media. These were reinforced by stories gleaned from the experiences of their friends who married Thai women as well as those—as in the case of Sven and Thomas—who compared experiences of marriage in their home country and marriage with a Thai wife. Such experiences and perceptions must have caused these men to look for relationships developed along different lines of gender relations than those they had encountered previously. Some viewed the failure of their previous marriages as related to the greater degree of women's rights in their own home country compared to other parts of the world. Mike's account below illustrates how these perceived differences in ideas and practices of gender caused his first marriage to fail.

Mike (42), an English man who lived with his wife and a new born daughter in a village next to Na Dokmai, recounted that his first marriage came to an end because both he and his ex-wife (an English women) worked too hard and hardly had enough time for each other. They rarely went out or did things together and sometimes did not even see each other for many days. Although they lived in the same house, they were estranged from each other. They had different lives and saw things differently. They fought often and eventually divorced. Mike said that it was not necessary for his ex-wife to work so hard. With his computer science degree, he had a good job that paid well. His earnings would allow both of them to live a more than comfortable life even if she had not worked. But "she worked as hard as I did. I couldn't change her; she did what she wanted." Mike imagined that if his ex-wife had not worked so hard, they would have had more time for each other and the marriage might not have broken up.

Mike was well aware of women's rights and feminist ideas in Western societies, which are far stronger than in Thailand. Mike, like Sven and Thomas, realised that he could not expect Western women to take care of him the way Thai women would, as they were (or were thought to be) more committed to traditional gender roles. This is why statements like, "Thai women know how to take care of their husbands", often came up when we talked about Western men's motivations to meet and marry Thai women. According to Davidson (1995), British male tourists in Pattaya talked about their disappointment after being rejected by white women; this was particularly painful for men who lacked economic power, physical attraction and/or social skills. As one British tourist put it:

> English women are "hard work", in that going to discos in England is "a waste of time"... [T]he fact that "pretty" English women know they are pretty and they demand the world. (They want to marry you then soak you for every penny when they divorce you.) I'm 48, I'm balding, I'm not as trim as I was. Would a charming, beautiful, young woman want me in England? No. I'd have to accept a big, fat, ugly woman. That's all I could get (Davidson 1995: 53).

From her feminist standpoint, Davidson views this kind of misogynistic attitude as a sign of men losing their patriarchal power and threatening their notion of masculinity. Comparing their experience with women in their own societies, Western male tourists were appreciative of the ways in which they were treated by the local women they met at tourist sites. Thomas, who lived in Pattaya for some time after divorcing his previous Thai wife, recalled that many of the Western men he knew in Pattaya were quite pleased with the attention and gestures of kindness they received from the women working there. "Some told me that they felt loved. These men kept contact with the girls. Some of them eventually got married." This is the case of many women married to *farang* in Na Dokmai who met their husbands at tourist sites. There were certainly, however, countless other relationships that did not flourish or result in a long-term commitment.

Within transnational tourism settings, Cabezas (2004, 2009) suggests that one should look at how intimate relations between tourists and locals developed along the often indistinct boundaries between love, money, romance and work, and as a way for people to make sense of their own lives. Cabezas posits that by eroding these boundaries, local women shape the conditions of subordination within the global economy. In addition to this, I argue that the erosion of boundaries enables Western men to exercise a type of masculinity that some of them are unable to accomplish in their relationships with Western women in their own countries, as well as to fulfil their desire for relationships embracing traditional gender roles and family values.

Looking at how gendered stereotypes of Thai (and Asian) women, gender roles and relations in Western societies combine and affect marriage choices provides another means of revealing the complicated logics of desire fostering current transnational marriages. These nuanced explanations challenge the normative perception of these marriages in the dichotomy between romantic love and economic incentives. They emphasise, moreover, the complexity of motivations that transcend both economic motives and intimate relationships.

Conclusion

The narratives and experiences of Thai women and Western men presented in this chapter illustrate the diverse motives beyond money and "love" that prompt them to opt for marriage and complicate their desire for transnational intimacy. The motivations leading women to turn to Western men include the generally unflattering reputation of local men as irresponsible heads of family, the limitations in marriage choices influenced by local norms and practices regarding gender and marriage and women's perceptions of modernity. These factors converge in various ways which are related to women's "social locations" in the global hierarchy. Nonetheless, experiences of Thai men's irresponsibility regarding family matters have been shared among women in Na Dokmai regardless of their social and economic circumstances. As for Western men, in addition to being physically attracted to Thai women, their marriage choices are shaped by a gendered stereotyping of Thai (and other Asian) women as home-making wives who embrace traditional family values as well as gender relations in Western societies influenced by feminist ideas. These multiple factors reveal the complexity of the logics of desire propelling women and men to engage in transnational marriages.

The common assertion that women marry because of material benefits and that men marry for romantic love is thus an oversimplification that does not capture the diverse and complex motivations feeding into the logics of desire shaping marriage choices and the decisions of the women and men concerned. Another layer of the complexity of transnational marriage phenomenon is manifested through the ways in which women materialise their desires to become the wives of Western men.

CHAPTER FOUR

Becoming a Woman with a *Farang* Husband: Sexuality, Money and Intimate Relationships

ON A PATTAYA BEACH in the late morning of 15 November 2008, while I was looking at a Thai-English conversation book, a German tourist sitting next to me asked whether I could help him to communicate with a Thai woman named Tuk. He wanted to know the name and location of the bar where Tuk was working. I had a brief talk with Tuk, and we met for a longer conversation a few days later.

Tuk (39), a woman from Udon, but not from Na Dokmai, was separated from her Thai husband, the father of her daughter and son, after having lived with him for ten years. Tuk had been with him for almost three years when she first found out that he was involved with another woman. "I always hoped that he would change, but he didn't", she said with disappointment. In 2004, a year after they separated, Tuk left her children in her mother's care and went to Pattaya. There she met an English man with whom she had a relationship for a year. After a serious commitment developed, Tuk returned to her village, and her English partner sent her an allowance to cover living expenses for her and her children. He also visited her in Udon several times a year. Their relationship ended in 2006 when he returned to his ex-wife. When talking about her English ex-partner, she broke down saying, "I was heart-broken when he told me we wouldn't meet anymore." Tuk then began to sell cooked food in the village, but it was difficult to make ends meet. In 2008, she decided to return to Pattaya with the hope of establishing a relationship with a Western man again.

Tuk's account of her search for a Western man echoes that of many women in Na Dokmai and other parts of Isan. The aim of leaving home to work at tourist sites such as Pattaya was to find a long-term relationship that might eventually lead to marriage. Like Tuk, some women returned to tourist destinations several times before they could establish a serious relationship with a male tourist. Tourist sites offered these women hope that their desire to meet and establish a long-term relationship with a Western man could be realised.

Pattaya is the town in Thailand best known for the four S's—Sun, Sea, Sand and Sex—where tourists' demand for commercial sex is readily met by a local supply (Enloe 2000). The site attracts foreign tourists, primarily male, from various parts of the world. At the same time, it offers local women opportunities to fulfil their desire to create transnational connections that might result in long-term commitments. However, not all women married to *farang* initiate their transnational relationship at tourist sites. The routes to transnational marriage that women in Na Dokmai employed are similar to those described in earlier research, indicating a range of pathways by which women, especially those with rural backgrounds, meet their Western husbands (Buapan et al. 2005; NESDB 2004; Supawatanakorn, Wannapha, and Khanittha 2005; Ratana 2010). The first route consists of the informal networks that link women living with Western partners to their families, kin and friends in their home villages. Through these networks local women were put in contact with prospective partners from Western countries. The second route is that of entertainment settings and tourist destinations such as bars, nightclubs and massage parlours. Two surveys—NESDB (2004) and Supawatanakorn et al. (2005)—conducted in a number of rural villages in nine north-eastern provinces indicate that the majority of women married to Western men met their husbands while working in the service industry in various tourist destinations.[1] The third channel was through match-making and date arrangement services. This channel was commonly used by women in Na Dokmai but it was not the main path through which they met their future husbands. Fourth, some women made connections with Western men through internet chat, although this channel is limited to those with a certain degree of computer and language skills. Finally, some

---

[1] The NESDB's survey (2004), conducted in a number of villages in five provinces, reveals that 54 per cent of a total of 219 rural women who had married Western men met their husbands while working in the service industry in various tourist destinations, while 20 per cent established contact with a husband through networks of family and friends and 26 per cent met their husbands through travel and personal contacts. Another survey conducted in four provinces indicates that 58 per cent of 231 women met their Western husbands through working at tourist sites, 38 per cent through networks of friends and family and 4 per cent through match-making agents and self-introduction via the internet (Supawatanakorn et al. 2005).

women took risks and travelled abroad in order to find marriage prospects (Buapan et al. 2005).

In Na Dokmai, although many women employed multiple routes, the majority of the 159 women met their future husbands in Pattaya and other tourist destinations, including Samui and Phuket. At the time of my fieldwork, a substantial number of village women were working in Pattaya with the hope of making transnational connections that might result in a long-term relationship. Thus, I focused on Pattaya as a "space of opportunity and hope" allowing women the possibility of fulfilling their desire to marry a Western partner. The choice of Pattaya was made not only because it was the major route taken by women from Na Dokmai, but also because this tourist site allowed me to observe the daily lives of women and the strategies they employed to initiate transnational connections and negotiate long-term intimate relations.

Pattaya Paradise: A "Space of Opportunity and Hope"

Located on the coast of the Gulf of Thailand, only a two-hour drive from Bangkok (see Map 1, Introduction), Pattaya is a compact town that has everything foreign tourists could possibly want. The development of service and entertainment industries in this town began when it served as an "R&R" site for the American military in the 1960s and 1970s during the Vietnam War, and has continued since then. The promotion of the tourist industry after the American troops left has further propelled Pattaya into becoming the country's most famous beach resort, especially for foreign tourists (Bishop and Robinson 1998; Cohen 2003; Truong 1990).

Pattaya is divided into three major zones: the Northern, Central and Southern zones. North Pattaya is the area where most of the tourists are Asians; Westerners are normally concentrated in Central Pattaya, while people from the Middle East and Russia usually go to South Pattaya. Women working in these zones differ from each other in their looks. Jum (29), a freelancer at Central Pattaya beach, told me that she would not get any clients if she worked at North or South Pattaya because she is relatively slim and has dark skin. She further explained that Arab men prefer stout women and that Asian men favour women who are relatively petite with light skin. Her own physical appearance, shared with most Isan women, is attractive to Western men. My observations at the three zones confirm these differentiations, which might help shed some light on the question of gender and race in relation to sexuality on the global scale. In this study, however, I focus on Central Pattaya, where most tourists are Westerners.

Walking along the beach and the narrow lanes connecting to the beach-front road in Central Pattaya, I observed a wide range of entertainment services: bars, clubs, restaurants, discos, escort agencies and massage parlours. On the night I visited the bar where Da (38), Dao (38) and Noi (27), three friends from Na Dokmai, worked. About ten women, mostly from different Isan villages, worked there. The bar was located in a large open space together with dozens of others. This bar, like many others in the area, had a counter where patrons could talk to the women and place their orders over the counter. In the front, there were a few tables and chairs where the women sat with their customers. Some women stayed outside the bar to invite tourists passing by to come in. What differentiated the bars in the area from each other was the difference in their size. Some of the larger bars were located inside buildings and not in the open space. Business in the area was rather busy. Whenever I passed by, I always saw some women serving customers or standing outside the bars to attract tourists.

Figure 4.1: Bars in the area where Dao, Da and Noi worked.

Bars in the area where Dao, Da and Noi were working sold drinks and snacks. Customers could also take the women out. These bars did not include dancing or shows, although go-go dancing and sex performances are common in Pattaya. Normally, each bar had a "mama-san" to help the women, especially those who were new and inexperienced or who did not speak English well enough to communicate with customers. To take bar girls out, clients had to pay a bar fee of 200–500 baht (US$6–14) to the owner, in addition to a sum that was negotiated directly with the woman.[2] This fee was an important source of income for the bar. Bar girls also got a share of the fine.[3] A basic salary for a bar girl was 2,000–2,500 baht/month (US$58–73) plus a commission from drinks the customers bought for them and bar fines. However, these earnings are negligible compared to income earned by going out with customers.

In addition to jobs at familiar entertainment outlets such as bars, nightclubs, massage parlours and discos, there were other positions available: for example, shop helpers, sales staff at department stores, waitresses and house maids. These jobs also allowed women to make connections with foreign tourists that might result in sexual encounters and long-term relationships. Some of the women I met had started their career in Pattaya by engaging in such jobs and later shifted to work at the bar (or on the beach as a freelancer) so as to maximise their opportunities to make transnational connections that might lead to a serious commitment. Yet, there were also women like Dao, Da and Noi, who engaged directly in bar work.

Another group of women directly involved in the sex industry were freelancers who approached tourists in other settings, especially at the beach. While freelancing is open for any woman, many of the freelance women had prior experience working at the bars or in other entertainment and service businesses. Unlike working at the bars where women could get help from a mama-san in communicating with customers, freelancers had to be on their own so they needed to have a certain amount of experience and a good command of English to negotiate with prospective clients.

Some of these women worked freelance only in the evening (part-time), doing other jobs during the day. Others worked from noon to the next morning. Jum, a woman from Isan who had been working at Pattaya beach for almost two years, called this her "fulltime job". Normally, Jum started her work at noon and stayed at the beach until two o'clock the next morning. After going out with a client for a "short time" (a few hours), she

---

[2] Davidson (1995) notes that at go-go and live sex-show bars, a bar fee may be higher than at bars offering only drinks and snacks; it varies from 300–1,000 baht (US$9–29).

[3] Most of the bars in Pattaya, where the women I spoke with worked, charged 300 baht (US$8.50) for a bar fee; the bar owners got half of the fee and the other half went to the woman.

Figure 4.2: Women on the beach waiting to be approached.

usually returned to the beach and looked for other customers if it was not too late. But if the deal was for a "long time"[4] she stayed overnight with her client. Compared to her previous work at the discos and bars, Jum preferred freelancing because it gave her flexibility and a sense of freedom—being able to pick her clients at her own choice.

Jang (20) was another woman I met on the beach. When I saw her she was sitting and reading an English conversation book. Several Western men came and talked briefly to her then left. Jang spoke rather good English. I learned that those men had asked her to go with them, but she had declined. Jang said that "hanging out" on the beach and waiting for the right time to chat on the internet with friends from various countries that she had met in Pattaya was her routine. While waiting, she was often approached by male tourists passing by. Most often she declined their proposals. Jang stressed that she only went with the ones she liked, and continued to keep in touch with many of them through internet chatting or seeing them whenever they returned to Thailand. On occasion, these men had given her financial and emotional support. Jang emphasised that they were her friends and that she valued this kind of relationship.

Jang's account highlighted the relationships between local women and foreign male tourists that extend beyond a simple exchange of money for sex. It is likely that the men had feelings similar to hers as they continued to contact and support her. Jang's experience in this respect was shared by a number of women whose stories will be presented later in this chapter. Such accounts reveal a different picture of the prostitute-client relations than those usually portrayed in the cynical guide books written for (male sex) tourists. An example is the chauvinistic *Money Number One* (Thistlewaite 2006), which gives details about what it calls "the traps which lie waiting" for men who arrive in Pattaya to fulfil their sexual desires. The author warns particularly of various "tricks that might leave them with an empty wallet or bank account".

---

[4] The English words "short time" and "long time" were commonly used by both bar girls and freelancers. "Short time" meant a few hours while "long time" normally referred to overnight agreements. "Long time" could also mean an agreement lasting for weeks or months.

Indeed, the ways in which relationships between foreign tourists and locals can be conceptualised beyond the conventional notions of sex work[5] are described in recent literature on transnational sex tourism. Cabezas (2009) views sex tourism and romance tourism as mutually flowing into each other. Thus, she proposes to reconceptualise transnational encounters created through sexual tourism, pointing out that transnational tourism generates new patterns of sexual labour that blur the lines between work and romance, and money and love. As she puts it, "the exchange of goods and money for sexual services is not an unambiguous commercial endeavour but a discursive construction that is contested and in motion, changing across time and space" (Cabezas 2009: 4). These ideas present a re-articulation of current insights on sexualised tourism and the affective processes of globalised enterprises in tourism.

In Sosua, a transnational tourist destination in the Dominican Republic, Brennan (2004) conceptualises sex work in relation to the desire of local women to marry tourist men and to migrate off the island. The term "sexscape" is used to signify fluidity of international capital and flow on a global scale in Sosua. "Sexscapes" are defined according to three key characteristics: international travel from the developed to the developing world, consumption of paid sex and inequality. In Sosua's bar scene, European sex tourists might see Dominican sex workers as exotic and erotic and pick out one woman over another in the crowd as a commodity for their pleasure and control; but Dominican sex workers often see the men, too, as readily exploitable. In Brennan's view, the men are all potential dupes,

---

[5] The notions are victimisation and agency. The first approach is based on an assumption that all forms of sex work are oppressive and women engaging in this work are exploited by those managing the industry, mostly men. It portrays these women as victims who are forced to choose this occupation. This approach has been taken on by both feminists and activists working against the trafficking of women and supporting the abolition of prostitution (Doezema 1998; Gozdziak and Collett 2005; Murray 1998). The agency perspective emphasises that involvement in the sex industry is freely chosen by many women. This occupation can be viewed as a "potentially liberatory terrain for women" (Chapkis 1997: 1). Women working in this industry deserve the same rights as workers in other sectors. Although I agree with the women's agency approach, it does have a limitation in that it focuses exclusively on an exchange between sex and money and does not pay attention to the possibilities of the intermingling of sexuality, money and intimate relations that might lead to a long-term commitment between women in the sex industry and their clients. Each of these perspectives is relevant only when the phenomenon in question is contextually investigated, rather than assuming that all sex workers encounter the same situations and considering them as a homogenous group. Whether they are beneficial or tragic depends largely on the contexts of the women's work and their experiences, which are highly diverse.

essentially walking visas, who can help the women to leave the island and poverty (Brennan 2004: 24). Rhacle Parreñas (2011) reveals the structural conditions—poverty, cultural obligations of women to their family, limited upward opportunities in the Philippines, the anti-trafficking policy and women's liminal status as hostesses—that underlie the Filipina bar hostesses and shape the contexts of their struggles in Japan. To maximise their material gains and opportunities to make a living, these women engage in commercial flirtation with customers—looking pretty, putting them at ease, teasing and titillating them. Faier (2009) also points out how Filipina entertainers who married Japanese men skilfully employed their profession of love to construct the new gendered and sexualised subjectivities and their sense of self as modern women and wives. These works emphasise the fact that such transnational encounters can generate mutual advantages for the parties concerned and provide opportunities for participants to negotiate and extend the meaning of exchange beyond money and sex. Simultaneously, such associations also reveal gendered social relations, social inequalities and cultural meanings of intimacy (Constable 2009).

On another score, the way in which Jang talked about the relationships with her clients places emphasis more on friendship and less on sexual activity. This is a common feature shared by a number of bar girls and freelancers that I spoke with. They talked about such activities as going shopping with their customers and accompanying them to entertainment sites and tourist attractions. Instead of mentioning sex, the women used terms like "going out with clients" or "taking care of clients" in describing their work. The use of these terms and the cover stories tend to obscure the nature of the association between women sex workers and their clients. It is also an attempt to neutralise the social stigma attached to sex work. This usage only goes to show that the women (especially those from rural villages such as Na Dokmai) who engaged in this work at transnational tourist sites to realise their goal of marrying a Westerner were not naïve about their profession.

Once their dream of a long-term relationship with a Western man materialised, the women left their jobs, although they might resume this work if the relationship ended. Dao, like Tuk whose story was presented in the beginning of this chapter, left Pattaya in 1999, after developing a serious relationship with a German man. He sent her an allowance and came to stay with her in Na Dokmai a few months every year, until he died after seven years. Dao did not return to Pattaya until 2008. Still wanting to renew transnational connections Dao headed back to Pattaya, accompanied by Da and Noi. These three women, like others working in Pattaya whom I spoke with, did not talk about their work as an occupation they intended to maintain, even though earnings from the work were important for them and their family at home. Rather, the women perceived their involvement in the sex industry as a transitional moment in their transnational trajectory. In this sense, the women engaged in sex work as a pragmatic means to reach their desired end. The women remained at their job for a limited time, some as short as a few weeks or months. Having said this, I make no claim that these women represent the majority of those working in Pattaya; nevertheless, a brief and temporary engagement in this work often appeared in the life stories of the women I spoke with. Yet in Na Dokmai, there are women who remained working in Pattaya and other tourist sites for years and were not yet able to settle into a long-term transnational relationship as they wished, though they had been in relationships with foreign tourists and left their work at the site several times.

Dao, Da, Nio and the other two women from Na Dokmai who shared the same apartment were bent on exploring opportunities for a long-term relationship or marriage with Western men they met in Pattaya. Stories about Dao and Tuk, with their *farang* ex-partners, and others who had eventually married foreign tourists and migrated to the West (or Japan) must have fuelled the fantasy of many hopeful women that "anything could happen". It was convenient to overlook the disappointment and disillusion of those whose dreams had never been fulfilled, and so the image of Pattaya as a "space of opportunity and hope" remained unchanged in the eyes of many. This motivation drove women working in transnational tourist sites to strategically deploy sex work to reach their goal, reflecting the complexity of this work, which extends beyond the exchange of money for sex.

Constructing Desirable Bodies

As a "space of opportunity and hope", Pattaya has generated particular images of women (and men) working in the sex industry. Changing their appearance thus becomes a part of women's strategies to get ahead. Being attractive and appealing to tourist men is particularly important as it increases the chances for a woman to be chosen above others. The physical appearance of women, especially in a transnational tourist site like Pattaya, reflects their understanding of Western male tourists' expectations (Manderson 1992). The ways in which women dress and appear during their work contrasts sharply with representations of female gender identities outside this tourist site.

On a few occasions during my fieldwork in Pattaya, I went out with Dao, Da and Noi. They often stopped at shops selling clothes, shoes and jewellery but usually did not buy anything, claiming that the prices were unreasonably high. However, we once went to a large, newly-opened department store, where each of them bought a bagful of cosmetics. While waiting for Dao and Noi who were still in the shop, Da told me that cosmetics and clothes were the largest part of her expenses and that this spending pattern was true for all five women who shared the apartment.

That day, Dao and Noi wore shorts and T-shirts while Da wore casual slacks and a T-shirt. No one wore any makeup; all three had their hair tied in the back. This contrasted sharply with how they looked when we met the following night at the bar where they worked. Then all were dressed in the latest style complete with jewellery and stylish hairdos. Dao wore high heels and a fancy red spaghetti-top dress that just covered her knees. She was heavily made up. Noi wore very short shorts and a slinky tank top, and her face was bright with makeup. Da wore jeans and a white top. She also wore makeup and her long hair was set nicely. All three looked like different people to those I had met the day before.

A few days later when I met Dao again, I told her that I might not have recognised her if I had not known that she worked at that bar. She said that she had learned to dress and make herself look attractive when she started working in Pattaya ten years ago. As she recalled her experience then:

> My friends told me to dress up and they'd take me to see the owner of the bar where they worked. I had no idea what to wear since I didn't have any fashionable clothes. I rarely used cosmetics at home or at work [as a maid and babysitter] in Bangkok. A friend let me use hers. She made me up and set my hair. I was dressed up. I felt uncomfortable, unsure of myself. I had never dressed like this in my life. I was very shy and didn't know what to do. But I thought since my friends were dressed like this, I should do the same. That day, I got the job.

As she continued working, Dao became accustomed to the dress norms expected of women working in Pattaya, and gradually adopted them. This experience was shared by Da, who started working at a bar in Pattaya a few months before I met her in February 2008. Most of the times that we met outside her work hours Da was dressed rather casually. Even at the bar she dressed less skimpily than the other women. When I mentioned this, she said that her roommates and friends at the bar often advised her to change her look; they said she should dress "with more style" and have more "sex appeal". The roommates, two women in their early twenties, often advised her what to wear and how to dress to show her "feminine beauty". To Da, these women had a good sense of how to dress and they seemed to be confident in whatever clothes they put on, while she felt ill at ease, losing her self-esteem if she wore a spaghetti tank top, a very short skirt or hot pants, although she was aware that it was important for her job. Whether Da and Dao liked it or not, both managed to meet the expected images of bar girls in Pattaya. The construction of desirable bodies is part of the process of commodification and is reinforced by those who own or manage the businesses, such as owners of bars/nightclubs and mama-sans (Seabrook 1996).

Paradoxical as it might seem, when talking about desirable bodies of women working in Pattaya, Da commented that anyone could dress any way she wanted. If they were the subject of gossip, women in Pattaya paid no attention. This was different from what happened in Na Dokmai, where Da was quite aware of the appropriateness of her clothes and makeup. In the village, both Da and Dao rarely wore the dresses they used during their work in Pattaya. In a very real sense, their work gave them a degree of autonomy that they would not otherwise enjoy. In Thai society, a display of the female body in such a way that attracts the (male) gaze is considered inappropriate. Women who appear this way are at risk of being regarded as "bad" women. This communicative aspect of bodies is intimately connected to the pervasive view in the Thai dichotomy of "good/bad women" (Harrison 1999). However, in Pattaya, being physically attractive and sexually appealing is a part of a woman's strategy to attract male tourists, the first step in their long-term scheme of getting a Western partner. This reflects their agency, whether or not the endeavours might actually result in a serious commitment and marriage.

Negotiating Money, Sex and Marriage Possibilities

Constructing desirable bodies is part of women's complex "negotiating" processes. Another layer of the complexity of relationships between bar girls/freelancers and foreign male tourists is manifested through women's negotiations revolving around sex, material desire and possibilities for a long-term commitment and eventual marriage. Jum's case is an example. I have chosen her story not only because I knew her well, but also because her story reflects the complexity and tensions which are shared by many freelancers and bar girls in Pattaya, as well as by women married to *farang* in Na Dokmai who previously worked at tourist sites.

Jum (29) was born into a family with five children in a rural Isan village. Her brothers and sisters had married and were living with their families, leaving Jum as the main financial contributor to her parents' household. Like Dao, Da and most women married to *farang* men in Na Dokmai, Jum left her home village to engage in wage employment in the cities soon after finishing six years of compulsory schooling. She had worked as house maid, babysitter and shop assistant in various cities. Her last job before heading for Pattaya was as an assistant in a wholesale shop in Bangkok selling ready-made clothes and shoes. After the shop closed in 2006, her life in Pattaya began. At that time, she was in her mid-twenties. With the assistance of a friend's sister, Jum secured a job as a cashier in a disco. Aiming for higher earnings and maximising the opportunities to make connections with tourists, Jum left the disco and worked as a bar girl. However, the bar she worked at did not attract a lot of customers, so she resigned and started working on the beach.

On her first day as a freelancer, she met an Italian man whom she "took care of" for three weeks during his stay in Pattaya. It provided her with good earnings. Thereafter, she continued to spend time at the beach. Jum, like most women I met in Pattaya, talked about her work not just as a way to earn income, but as a means to develop transnational relationships that might lead to a serious commitment. The encounters, either on the basis of short-term or long-term deals, opened up this opportunity. Long-term relationships in particular offered a greater chance for interactions beyond just sexual service. This was precisely Jum's experience. However, long-term agreements may not be the norm for sex tourists as they usually opt for multiple partners (Bishop and Robinson 1998; Davidson 1995).

In talking about going out with clients for days or weeks, Jum explained that there was more to these associations than sexual services. She often acted as companion, tour guide and interpreter, did the shopping and sometimes tidied up the client's room. The more pleased the customers were, the better the chance that they might return again, providing more opportunities for serious commitments to develop. From a male perspective, services including both sexual and other forms of labour, as well as the ways in which the women take care of them with pleasing gestures, are often interpreted as expressions of genuine affection (Davidson 1995). These aspects make it possible for British tourists, for example, to pay for sexual services without seeing themselves as the kind of men who embrace the identity of a client. As one of the British tourist men at Pattaya put it, "They're more like girlfriends really. You do everything with them. It isn't just sex, they're not like prostitutes" (Davidson 1995: 51).

These elements and the non-contractual nature and the more open-ended of transactions in the Thai sex trade gloss over the commercial nature of the encounters (Cohen 1996; Yos 1992b). In Western countries, by contrast, sexual services are made upon an explicit agreement understood by the parties concerned—transactions normally involve an agreement to perform a specific service or task (Davidson 1995). The flexibility in the Thai sex industry provides possibilities for local women and male tourists to negotiate their relationships far beyond the usual prostitute-client encounters as imagined in popular discourses of the sex industry.

For Jum, by taking care of her clients, accompanying them and doing things with them, she learned about their character: whether they were fair, generous, picky or stingy; basically how they treated her on a personal level. Da, Dao and Tuk shared Jum's experience in this regard. According to them, some men were polite and showed concern for the women they went out with. Others only cared about what they wanted. Personal experiences like this provide important information for women to anticipate the possibility of a long-term relationship or commitment with a particular man. As Jum told me:

> I think about what kind of person a man is as much as how he looks. If I don't like his [old and unattractive] appearance, I wait to see if he is generous, polite and undemanding. If so, I overcome my dislike [of his physical appearance]. I always ask myself, "Can I trust him?" If the answer is "yes", then I could like him. It's not possible to get everything I want [a man who is good-looking, generous and not much older than me]. I look for a serious relationship and I want to be with a man that I like, not necessarily a millionaire, but one who understands and does not look down on (*du thuk*) women [working in the sex industry].

Jum's narrative reflects mixed feelings in considering choices of sexual partners. Noticeably, her criteria for a suitable long-term partner shaped her practices and the ways she dealt with customers. When going out or shopping with her clients, Jum sometimes expressed interest in such items as clothes, shoes or jewellery in order to see whether the men would offer to pay for them as gifts. If a man did not offer to pay even for a small gift, it raised the question of whether she could expect support and care from him. In this sense, the gifts (and cash) from customers are not just material items, but also gestures of generosity and expressions of affection on the part of the customers. Jum's account below of her relationships with a Belgian and a Dutch man shows how bar girls and freelancers negotiate material desire, sex and marriage.

In September 2008, Jum secured a five-day deal with a Belgian man in his forties working in Malaysia. They met a few times after the deal; then he asked her to leave her bar job and return to her home in the village. He promised to send remittances for her upkeep. Jum returned to her village home, but could not stay for long; she went back to Pattaya after a week. At home, there was nothing for her to do and she became bored. More importantly, she was worried that her parents and neighbours would ask about her work. They did not know that she worked in Pattaya. Her mother thought that she worked as a maid in the South. Soon after arriving in Pattaya, Jum ran into her Belgian boyfriend with another woman. Expecting that he was in Malaysia working, she was disappointed and decided to end the relationship. He admitted that he did not keep his promise, but said that he wanted to marry her. However, Jum declined, though he asked her several times to re-consider the proposal. She then returned to work on the beach. Her reason for turning him down was that she could not trust him as he had not done what he had told her. Ironically, she had also failed to keep her part of the deal when she came back to Pattaya without telling him.

While ending the relationship with the Belgian man, Jum began to see Rob, a retired Dutch man she met on weekends at his house. Rob had been living in Pattaya for a few years. Rob did not like going out every day like most of the Western men Jum had been associated with. Rather, he enjoyed staying at home watching television, using the computer, working in the garden and sometimes cooking. On weekends, Jum usually joined him for these activities and cleaned the house for him. Rob was generous and helped her in times of need. He always gave her pocket money when she was going home. He also paid for her parents' healthcare costs, unlike the Belgian man who neither helped with her financial needs nor gave her gifts.

After my first trip to Pattaya (8–23 November 2008), I talked to Jum on the phone several times and learned that her relationship with Rob had developed further. When I returned to Pattaya in February 2009, Jum told me that she had stopped working on the beach and had been living with Rob for almost a month. He gave her a monthly allowance which she was satisfied with. Jum admitted that after living together for a few months, she no longer viewed Rob as a client, but expected that a serious relationship would develop. However, she became doubtful after a young woman (20) whom Rob had supported earlier moved in. Rob asked Jum to take care of her. Jum admitted that she did not mind looking after her, but that she began to wonder about her relationship with Rob. In April 2009, I called Jum; she was in the village, not in Pattaya, taking care of house renovations, which Rob helped fund. I gathered from our conversation that Jum was pleased and felt more secure about her relationship with Rob. To my surprise, in June 2009, she phoned and told me that she had had a big fight with Rob. It did not involve the girl living in the house, but another woman he had been seeing lately. At that point, she left him and returned to work on the beach.

Sometimes when we talked about her clients, Jum mentioned the differences between young and old customers in relation to the sexual services these men requested. She stressed that old men, because of their physical condition, were more demanding than young men. Some older customers were fastidious and not satisfied with the services they received. This problem rarely occurred with young clients. So given the choice, she preferred a younger rather than an older client. However, her decision regarding her relationships with Rob and her Belgian boyfriend clearly indicated that age was not the sole factor; generosity and trustworthiness were important elements to be taken into account together with the possibility of a long-term commitment.

Although Jum's story did not end up like a Cinderella dream-come-true as some women married to *farang* in Na Dokmai experienced, it represents the processes that women entering into the transnational tourist scenes encounter. The women's actions and negotiations highlight their aim for future security, which extends beyond sex for money. Put differently, relationships between women in the sex industry and their clients, foreign tourists in this case, are far more complex than an exchange of money for sexual gratification. The complexity is, to some extent, shaped by Thai culture. In Thai society, the intermingling of sex, mutual affection and material resources is embedded in cultural norms, manifested through various marriage customs and practices. For example, criteria for spouse selection always involve the future welfare of the family. Similarly, the Thai cultural norm of providing *sinsot* (bride wealth) by a groom to a bride's family to legitimate the marriage indicates an intersection between marital relations, material resources and sex—an issue that will be discussed in the following chapter. Within these contexts, material support from the men is perceived in relation to their love and care for women (Lyttleton 2000; Sumalee 1995; Whittaker 1999). Women's practices of initiating connections with Western men who are perceived as potential patrons and partners are, in part, influenced by such local norms. In this light, marrying a man, either a local or a Westerner, with good economic resources is associated with culture rather than just a means to obtain material benefits.

Though many women engaged in sex work at tourist sites as a pragmatic means of seeking future security, they were not entirely free from feelings of guilt. Jum did not let her mother and neighbours know where and what kind of work she did. The guilt, in part, made her feel uncomfortable at home. Jum admitted with regret that she had not yet figured out whether she would tell her parents about her job in Pattaya, as she knew they would be disappointed. She was also concerned about reactions from the neighbours who might find her work disgraceful and would look down on her and her parents. Similarly, women in Na Dokmai who met their Western husbands in (sex) tourist sites were aware of the stigma associated with sex work. Several of them had left for Pattaya without informing their parents. Otherwise they could not have left the village. One woman recalled that she had experienced moral guilt and sorrow, especially during the first few months working in Pattaya, though she made the choice herself with the hope of changing her life. Nonetheless, there were a number of parents who supported their daughters' decision to go to Pattaya, as this route could provide security for their future (and their own welfare). Women's narratives and sentiments demonstrate that most of them knew what they were getting themselves into.

The processes in which women have engaged so as to realise their desire to have a *farang* husband are complex and involve actions and negotiations in various realms and through different means and strategies. Their negotiations in the given situations are in line with what Sherry Ortner calls "intentionality"—"a wide range of states, both cognitive and emotional, and at various levels of consciousness, that are directed forward toward some end" (2006: 134). These negotiations fit a continuum of the "hard" definitions of agency emphasising the strong role of fully conscious intentionality drawn upon desires and courses of action with intention playing a strong role.

Manipulating One's Fate: Ritual Practices

In the late afternoon of 14 November 2008, after our long conversation, I invited Jum for dinner, but she declined. She wanted to go to South Pattaya to worship the statue of Sadet Pho Krom Luang Chumporn[6] (locally called

---

[6] Sadet Pho Krom Luang Chumporn was Prince Abhakara Kiartivongse, son of King Rama V. He studied naval science in England and founded the naval base in Sattahip, which became an American air base during the Vietnam War. He was proclaimed the "Father of the Thai Navy". Krom Luang took a keen interest in herbal medicine and studied this subject by himself, then used his expertise to treat people without charging any fee. After his death in 1923, people considered him a deity. Many shrines and statues were erected throughout the country in his honour—South Pattaya is the home to one of them. His medical skills made him widely known and people have often worshipped and asked for his blessings with regard to health problems. Due to his kindness, compassion (*metta*) and divine power, people have also asked him to help in other matters as well (Saran 2003).

Krom Luang or Sadet Tia). I changed my plans and joined her. We went up to the cliff beach, where a life-size statue of Krom Luang stands on a concrete block two metres high, looking out to the ocean. On the sides and the back of the base of the statue are thousands of small figurines of horses, elephants and women that worshippers had presented to the statue. It is believed that these animal and female figurines would serve Krom Luang. Jum did not take along any figurines, but bought flowers, candles and incense at the entrance to offer to Krom Luang. I followed her.

After our worshipping, Jum said that she always asked Krom Luang for his blessings when facing critical circumstances. When her parents were sick or she was in need of money, she made her wish and prayed to Krom Luang for help. She also begged for his compassion to help her get clients, especially good-hearted ones with whom she could build a long-lasting relationship. When her requests came true, she expressed her gratitude by presenting him figurines or *phlu* (rockets usually fired as a salute). I observed people continuously coming up to worship the statue, including a few women accompanied by Western men. Jum exchanged greetings with them. I was told later that they were freelancing at the beach.

On the way, Jum mentioned that when she was unable to go up to revere Krom Luang, she would go to worship Chao Pho Ket Ngam at the spirit house on the beach just north of the central beach where she operated. She offered to take me to venerate Chao Pho and to see Pattaya before I leave in the next few days. She said that Pattaya has several interesting places where she sometimes took her clients to visit. Two days later, Jum called me telling me that she might not be able to be my guide; she was on a bus heading to her home village. I asked if anything serious was going on at home. She replied that she was just taking money to her parents and would help them in harvesting rice for a few days before returning to Pattaya. Jum further explained that she had mentioned to Rob a few times that she wanted to give money to her parents to cover the costs of rice harvesting, but he had not responded. On the day we went to worship Krom Luang, she asked him to help her out. When I dropped her off at the beach where she was based, Jum got a call from Rob asking her to meet him the following day and to bring her bank book with her as well. Then he transferred 27,000 baht to her account. She said, "Krom Luang is *saksit* (sacred); he has helped me out. I will present him *phlu* when I return to Pattaya, to thank him." When I met her in Pattaya again during my second trip in February 2009, Jum mentioned several times that I should revere Krom Luang and ask for what I wished for. Knowing that I did not want to marry a Western man, she suggested I ask

Figure 4.3: The statue of Sadet Pho Krom Luang Chumporn.

Figure 4.4: Figurines of horses, elephants and women that worshippers presented to the Sadet Pho Krom Luang Chumporn statue.

Krom Luang for help with the completion of my research. Her suggestion to me testified to the seriousness of her faith in these deities.

Jum's account stressed the importance of the spiritual dimension in her daily existence as a sex worker. In Pattaya, it is common for women working there to stop to *wai*—a Thai way of expressing respect—when passing by the spirit house of Chao Pho Ket Ngam (locally called Chao Pho) on the beach.[7] Some women dropped in to express their wishes and ask for help. The wishes they made were largely in line with those of Jum, emphasising both the desire to get (good) customers, and to reach their ultimate goal of having a long-term relationship or marrying a Western man. When their wishes came true, normally the women returned to venerate and express their gratitude to Chao Pho.

Figure 4.5: The Chao Pho Ket Ngam spirit house on Pattaya beach.

---

[7] According to a woman selling offerings in front of the spirit house, Chao Pho Ket Ngam is the spirit watching over the area and has compassion for those living and running businesses in the area. Owners of bars and other businesses in the area venerate him to ensure good fortune. However, the majority of worshippers are women working at the bars and on the beach.

Coping with uncertainties and insecurities is a permanent feature of the daily life of women working in Pattaya. There was no guarantee that they would be able to attract and finally get customers, whether they would get a good client or whether their association with a particular client would lead to a long-term commitment as they had wished. Such pervasive feelings of uncertainty and anxiety have shaped these women's day-to-day lives. Ritual practices provide them with space to manipulate uncertain circumstances, to deal with their anxieties as well as to challenge the limitations of their existence. In fact, most women married to *farang* in Na Dokmai told me that they had engaged in ritual practices before leaving the village for Pattaya and other tourist sites. It was common for these women to worship the ancestor spirits of the village (*tapu ban* or *tapu*) to ensure their success in having contacts with Western men that would eventually result in marriage.[8] The stories of villagers whose wishes came true were attributed to the spiritual deliverance of *tapu* and reinforced by such practices of worshipping.[9]

In dealing with uncertainties and risks, people often turn to spiritual interventions and ritual practices. Such practices can be interpreted as "a form of compensating for insecurity and reducing anxiety—if not seeking more security—when engaging in risky adventures" (Salemink 2010: 284). Indeed, ritual practices are common in Thai lives and are prevalent among both rural residents and the urban middle class.[10] Although these practices

---

[8] Women who employed other routes to engage transnational marriage such as match-making services and networks of kin and friends as well as those who were unsure about their future plans also expressed their wishes to the ancestor spirits and asked for their support in helping them to reach their goal.

[9] According to the intermediary of the village's guardian spirits (*chum*), a man in his sixties who had helped villagers express their wishes to the village spirits, acquiring jobs overseas and marrying a Western husband were the most common themes. The *chum* mentioned that the improvement of the house of the spirits and its landscape were made possible through donations of thankful villagers, especially Westerner's wives, whose wishes were granted by the guardian spirits. Wishes expressed to the village deity also concerned passing exams, getting promotions and having good health.

[10] Irene Stengs (2009) relates the development of the King Chulalongkorn cult among urban, middle class Thais to the "uncertainty of modernity" that many people experience. Above all, enormous economic growth in the 1980s and the 1997 economic crisis generated income inequality and marginalised large sectors of society. In this context, the expansion of worshipping the Great King highlights the experiences and feelings of uncertainties and frustrations on the level of individual daily life. In rural contexts, worshipping the ancestor spirits of the village is a common practice ensuring agricultural production, the most vital occupation of the rural residents. It is also believed that the ancestor spirits have the power to grant benevolence and reward as well as punish, to bestow individual favours and to inflict misfortune (Tambiah 1970).

have been embedded in different contexts, they share a common theme associated with the insecurity that people encounter in various dimensions of life, as well as with the auspicious and good fortune that people desire (Akin 1996; Stengs 2009; Tambiah 1970). The stories of Jum and many other women in Na Dokmai illustrate how local beliefs and practices are extended to transnational spaces where women have to cope with risk and anxieties associated with the quest for manipulating their own fate and their goal of marrying a *farang*.

Conclusion

In his study of the Thailand's Southern borderlands, Marc Askew (2006) argues for more complex cultural configurations emerging in there. The constant flow of Singaporean and Malaysian visitors to this region since the 1970s reflects its diverse images: from a dangerous area with communist insurgency and ethnic separatism to a site also associated with recreation, pleasure and religious visitation. The author argues that the borderlands are constituted by sojourners and visitors, their activities, experiences and perceptions which can be summarised as "consumption" (shopping), "blessing" (visiting temples and shrines) and "catharsis" (engaging in prostitution services and gambling). These activities are central to the reproduction of the Lower South borderland as both a sexualised and sacred space. Within the context of Pattaya, a "space of opportunity and hope", it would be a serious mistake to view women's involvement in the sex industry as only exploitative or oppressive. For these women, engaging in sex work is a pragmatic means to marrying a *farang* and thus should be understood as a transitory period of their transnational trajectory. The experiences of these women are similar to those working in the Sosua sexscape, where sex work is not simply a survival strategy, but an "advancement" strategy for them to marry male tourists and migrate off the island (Brennan 2004). Their practices are also similar to those of sex workers in other cultural contexts mentioned in the beginning of this chapter, such as the "professions of love" practised by Filipina entertainers in crafting intimate transnational relationships with their Japanese husbands (Faier 2009). Other examples are the "illicit flirtations" of Filipina hostesses discussed by Parreñas (2011) in negotiating the structural exploitative circumstances that shape their work and maximising opportunities to make a living and market their services of affection.

Women's practices reveal a high degree of "intentionality" geared toward their goal. If intentionality is reflected in actions, bar girls and freelancers working in Pattaya did put a lot of effort into constructing desirable bodies and managing liaisons with their clients to their best advantage. Their reliance on ritual practices can be seen as a way of coping with the anxieties and uncertainties inherent in their trade. Such practices and strategies are indicative of the women's determination to overcome their inferior position within the global power hierarchies dictated by gender, ethnicity and class.

These women's actions and negotiations revolve around the issues of sexuality, money and desire for a long-term commitment, which make relationships with male tourists far more ambiguous than prostitute-client associations. These practices emphasise the hazy boundaries between romance and work, between economic transactions and intimate relations. They demonstrate that sex, romance, material support and marriage are intertwined rather than separated in different spheres of life and contradict the normative cultural ideal of marriage prevalent in modern Western societies based solely on notions of romantic love (see Chapter Three).

The practice of engaging in sex work as a vehicle to enter into transnational marriage contrasts with the existing studies—for example Pataya Ruenkaew (1999) and Supang Chantavanich et al. (1999)—which claim that marriages between Thai women and Western men are a means for women to engage in sex work in Western countries. The practices described in my research call for a broader framework in studying women in the sex industry than the concepts currently used—a victimisation/oppression perspective and an approach that views sex work as an occupation based exclusively on (sexual) service and economic return. Such approaches completely ignore such aspects as meaningful relationships, affection and romance arising from interactions between sex workers and their clients. Restricting our approaches to either economic or victimisation perspectives inevitably obstructs our understanding of the complexity of the current transnational marriage phenomenon, causing us to lose sight of the ways in which women (and men) involved in this phenomenon make sense of their lives.

CHAPTER FIVE

Transnational Marriages: Images, Relationships and Practices

The lyrics of an Isan folk song, *"Khun-i-puek"* [Ms Dummy], which was quite popular in the early 2000s, reflects stereotypical images of women under transnational marriage relationships:

> Her real name is Bua-sri. Her nickname is "Dummy" for scoring last in class. Her friends call her "Ms Dummy". Her teacher is tired of her.... She never talks to anyone. Adding, subtracting, multiplying, dividing cannot get into her thick skull.... How are you going to make a living, Ms Dummy?
>
> After she finished elementary school, for several years, no one heard any news from her ... until the school's Homecoming Day when Ms Dummy appeared in the bright and colourful outfit of a high-status lady.
>
> Everyone was stunned and stared in disbelief: no one had ever dreamed of seeing her look that way. Ms Dummy is married to a *farang* husband and is wearing lots of gold jewellery that jangles loudly as she walks to the stage to present funds to the school.
>
> Although she is a dummy, she became successful and poised.... People call her the "International Dummy" who brings prestige to her natal village. You do not disappoint me, my friend. I am lucky to have a friend who is such a dummy like you.

The song ends with: "Find me a *farang* husband, will you, Ms Dummy".

The contrasting images of the young Dummy versus the mature, worldly Bua-sri are much more evident when the song is presented as a music video.[1]

---

[1] The music video provides a clearer message of what the song conveys than just hearing the CD, especially the contrasting depictions of Bua-sri as a young girl and as a fairly affluent woman who joins the school's homecoming celebrations in the company of her *farang* husband. For the video clip of *"Khun-i-puek"* ("คุณอีปึก"), see https://www.youtube.com/watch?v=BtOH91HF1p4, accessed 10 March 2016.

During my research I found that many people in Na Dokmai are familiar with this song, and although they did not remember the details, they recalled that it was about a woman whose life changed dramatically by marrying a *farang*. However, the song presents quite an extreme case, as none of the women married to *farang* whom I came to know remotely resemble Bua-sri in terms of personality or intellect. Nonetheless, the image of the woman who showed up at the school's Homecoming Day with her *farang* husband caught on with most villagers who knew this song. This chapter focuses on multiple images of such women, the local relationships they are involved in, their husbands and their fellow villagers, as well as the practices of concerned parties in managing and manoeuvring the situations they encounter at the "local end" of transnational connections.

Thus far, the ties between the people involved in transnational mobility and those who remain in migrants' home villages have been analysed through two perspectives: remittance and "social remittance"[2] (Keely and Tran 1989; Stahl and Arnold 1986; Taylor 1999; Levitt 1996, 2001). While these two forms are distinct from each other, both revolve around money either by prioritising it or discounting it. More importantly, both consider money in an economic sense, thereby limiting its meanings to economic terms. To go beyond this explanation, I have based my analysis on Zelizer's concept of "special money" (1989) emphasising the extra-economic, social basis of money marked by cultural and social structures. Zelizer proposes that the dominant utilitarian conception of market money, which reduces the qualitative distinctions of items, values and sentiments to an abstract quantity, has limitations in capturing the social meanings of money. "Special money", by contrast, is mediated through the institutionalising of controls, restrictions and distinctions in sources, uses and modes of allocation.

Applying the "special money" concept, this chapter explores the ways in which money becomes a means of representing care, love, recognition and gratitude as well as a sense of continued membership in a community.

The Multiple Images of Women Married to *Farang*

The pervasive association of Thai female sex workers with American servicemen during the Vietnam War period originated under the rubric of *mia chao*, or rented wife (see Chapter One). Such relationships re-emphasised a connection between prostitution and marriage to Western men that exists in the Thai collective memory, which even today continues to question all

---

[2] See further discussion on these two perspectives in the Introduction.

Thai-Western marriages. Regardless of what the Thai wives' backgrounds might have been, they were and still are subjected to such interpretations. The residents of Na Dokmai were well aware of the disparaging attitude towards women who married *farang*. However, among these residents were also such women and their relatives who maintained that the social stigma attached to women marrying Western husbands had been diminishing and that the change was related to the women's ability to support their natal family and kin.

Somsri, a retired school teacher whose daughter Lita married Peter, is a case in point. Somsri was worried about how Lita would be perceived by locals; she kept asking her colleagues at school if they had heard villagers gossiping about her daughter. Somsri recalled a conversation she had with Lita regarding her decision to marry Peter. "Wait until I die, then you can go marry a *farang*. I am ashamed. I see only *phuying ha kin* (prostitutes) marrying *farang*." Somsri's anxiety regarding her daughter's image reflected the lingering social stigma attached to transitional marriages at present. The concern troubling Somsri was shared among school teachers, local government staff and shop owners who often speculated about whether certain women who married *farang* were involved in the sex industry and whether they had a low level of education.

Most people I talked to about the song agreed that it reflects the lives of many women married to *farang*. However, their interpretations of it varied. Some considered it a depiction of a successful life story because the woman in the song was finally accepted by her peers. Marrying a *farang* allowed Bua-sri to improve her financial status and become a woman with a "new identity". She appeared wearing fashionable, urban-style clothes and expensive jewellery; she also made a donation to the school and gained recognition from her school friends. Her new identity contrasted sharply with her life in the past. Some women with *farang* husbands in the village said that the story was very real to them, especially with respect to how their future was being changed. The economic advancement of women with foreign husbands and their contribution to local schools and the community were perceived and acknowledged by residents of Na Dokmai, including local government staff and school teachers. But these women were still seen as having a low education—only six years of compulsory school. And some had, in fact, been involved in the sex industry.

The judgmental views toward these women were particularly prevalent in urban settings where they encountered situations in which they felt they were being looked down on. These experiences are symptomatic of social prejudices keenly felt by the women themselves, as one said, "I often got odd looks when I walked with my husband near the hotel in Udon and other places. Though they [hotel staff and guests] did not say anything, I knew they wondered if I had a background in prostitution." Another recalled, "While walking with my husband along the street, I heard a man say, 'An old cow likes young grass' (*wua kae chop kin ya on*). I knew what was on his mind. He must have thought that I was fishing for an old *farang* for money." Sirijit (2009: 137–45) has written about the bias which the wives of *farang* often encounter among urban residents, which is (re)produced through the discursive power of the urban elite; at the same time the aspirations of rural women for social and economic mobility are suppressed and invalidated. However, Sirijit looks only at the class factor in relation to rural-urban distinctions, while ignoring the class structure within rural communities, where the marriages are embedded.

The dilemma that a number of women married to Westerners and their parents have struggled over concerns the co-existence of the social stigma produced through the discourse of *mia chao* and the secure future and comfortable life that many women have obtained by being married to Western men. In addition, the local view and the central government/academic discourses also shape images of these women. In Na Dokmai the purchasing power and comfortable living they enjoyed as well as the contributions they and their husbands made to the community were apparent for all to see, although their generosity was viewed ambiguously by locals. Expressions of appreciation came particularly from community leaders; some viewed mixed couples as strategic resources for village development. The head of the sub-district municipality often associated these women and their husbands with material progress (*khwam charoen*) in the village and an improvement in the living conditions of the women's natal families. As he put it:

> Without *mia farang* and their husbands, we would not see as many cars, motor bikes and nice, big houses in the village as we do nowadays. These women take care of their parents and support their children's education. Some build a new house for their parents and send them an allowance. The women also co-operate with the community; they always contribute to its development and to village fairs.

This local leader often talked about these changes with pride. In his eyes, the growth of businesses such as grocery stores, computer shops and restaurants in the village was directly related to the consumer power of women married to *farang*, their husbands and their natal households. At the same time, the economic improvement induced mixed couples to invest in various businesses both in the village and elsewhere.

This positive local view differs sharply with the national government's standpoint and some academic discourses which look at transnational marriage in connection with problems of human trafficking and the weakening of local traditions and family values. This government discourse is persistently (re)produced through newspapers, television, websites and other forms of government-supported activities. In early 2008, a research team funded by the Ministry of Social Development and Human Security (MSO) collected information in Na Dokmai to evaluate the implementation of a government project aimed at fighting human trafficking, which suggested that there was a connection between the trafficking of women and current transnational marriages.

A female leader in Na Dokmai recalled her difficulty in making sense of the information presented at an MSO-supported training session about how marriages to *farang* men had been used to lure women into transnational prostitution. This information was at odds with what she observed in the village. She explained that most women with Western husbands and their parents had a better life, as the daughters helped build new houses, buy farm land, provide allowances and contribute to the community's prosperity. In her view, most seemed to have a good family life with their *farang* husbands. If a woman got a "bad" man—one who did not treat her well or did not care for her parents—she ended the relationship and looked for a "good" one. This perception was shared by numerous village residents.

State discourse also tends to associate transnational marriages with a decline in traditional family values. During my fieldwork in 2008, an article in the national newspaper *Kom Chad Luek* reported on this issue. The article quoted a kindergarten girl who said: "I want to be a *mia farang* when I grow up", believing that this was a means to become wealthy and to have a big house (*Kom Chad Luek*, 4 March 2008: 15). It also reported comments by various government officials and a university lecturer regarding the desire of numerous women and girls to find a *farang* husband. The lecturer's remarks were based on her research (Supawatanakorn et al. 2005), which claimed that the emphasis on economic security signals the decline of the family institution in Isan.

Women with *farang* husbands in Na Dokmai who read this article were dismayed. One commented that most of them had sought transnational marriage because of family crises, the irresponsibility of local men and a desire to take care of their parents. She asked why such women's experiences and commitments were not mentioned in the news. Another pointed out that the article dealt only with material aspects, thereby creating a negative image that they did not deserve.

Indeed, transnational marriages are shaped by other factors, among them the cultural differences between gender relations in Thai and Western societies (see Chapter Three). Thus, I suggest looking at how Thai gender relations play a role in motivating and reinforcing women to seek foreign partners and how local gender ideologies and practices have been renegotiated as a result of transnational marriages. In so doing we can better understand the impact of current transnational marriages on the dynamics of local norms and practices concerning marriage and gender rather than viewing the phenomenon solely in relation to material benefits.

While the ambivalent images of women with *farang* husbands are shaped and (re)produced through various factors and means, such as class—in the contexts of both the rural village and the rural-urban divide, as well as in government/academic discourses—these images revolve mainly around an improvement in material resources that these women gained. This improvement, however, generates expectations and influences relationships in numerous ways.

Women's Natal Family and the Notion of *Bun Khun*

When discussing their desire to find Western husbands, almost all women mentioned their wish to support their parents. In the Thai family, relationships between parents and children are determined by a cultural norm known as *bun khun*—the debt of gratitude one feels toward anyone who is good to her or him. This cultural value is applicable to all Thais regardless of social status and class position (Akin 1984; Mulder 1985).

Sons can repay the debt of gratitude to their parents, and especially to their mothers, who gave them life by being ordained as monks (and dedicating the merit made this way to their mothers). This does not mean that they no longer have to take care of and support their parents, but expectations for sons to contribute to their parental households are relatively flexible. Women, however, are not allowed to become monks as their biological role as potential mothers is believed to connect them more closely to worldly attachments. According to Kirsch (1982), this connection reflects the disadvantaged status of women in the religious world. Daughters can repay the debt of gratitude to their parents by contributing to household affairs as well as by providing material necessities and comfort to their parents. The distinction in gender roles is reinforced through socialisation processes from childhood on. Generally, girls are assigned domestic chores while boys are given more freedom. The life stories of many Na Dokmai women such as Lan, Jit and Phin, presented in Chapters One and Two reveal how these women, as young girls, helped their parents in domestic tasks and earned money by engaging in trading, working as household assistants and helping in the field. These roles reflect women's attachment to their parental household and symbolise their gratitude as dutiful daughters, a cultural ideal deeply valued in Thai society.

Parents do not expect equal assistance and support from all daughters and sons. Some parents, especially those who cannot help themselves, may rely heavily on the daily labour of one daughter while receiving financial support from other daughters and sons. Normally, daughters and sons who are relatively well-off are expected to contribute more to the parental household in terms of financial support. Conversely, children who are in difficult situations or are in need of money, may get support from their parents. In some cases, the financial burden is often borne by siblings who are in a better economic situation.

In Western societies, by contrast, there is less expectation of reciprocity between offsprings and parents. Rather, the nuclear family and the relationship between spouses are emphasised more than relations with either the wife's or husband's parents (Panitee 2009). These cultural differences sometimes make it difficult for Western partners to comply with their Thai wives' wish to contribute financially to the needs of parents, especially when demands recur regularly. Inevitably, the distinct differences in the cultural scripts can shape transnational relationships and create tensions among them and the women's parents. The experiences of Kaew and her father illustrate how *bun khun* relations generated expectations and anxieties for them.

Kaew (26), a divorced mother, lived with her six-year-old son in a traditional old wooden house on stilts with her ailing father and her mother, who were no longer able to work. This family relied on remittances sent regularly by their daughters, who had migrated to work in other provinces, and periodically from their son while Kaew took care of domestic routines. Kaew's former partner could not be relied on for support as he could not earn enough to support himself, let alone his family. Kaew had to take care of herself and their son. She also wanted to renovate her house and build a better room for her parents on the ground floor as it was difficult for her father to use the stairs because of his health problems.

Faced with these issues, Kaew decided to go to Pattaya in November 2007. There she worked in a bar where she met Bob, an Australian man in his mid-fifties. Kaew recalled her conversation with Bob and his response regarding her concern about renovating the house and her commitment to support her parents.

> He asked about my life and my family. I told him that I have a son and
> parents to look after. He didn't say much; he knew that I understood
> only a little of what he said anyway. After a week of being together, I
> returned home because my father got sick. Bob called me every day
> and asked me to stay at home, and not to return to work in Pattaya
> again. He didn't say clearly whether he would support me, but he sent
> me money. Then I stayed at home. He also sent me a gift catalogue
> and asked me to choose what I wanted [Kaew showed me a catalogue
> of jewellery, shoes, purses, etc.]. I wanted to tell him not to send me
> gifts and said that I would rather have money so that I could renovate
> my house. He came to see me in the village in March [2008] and
> stayed at a hotel in Udon, not at my house. He said that my house was
> a hut, not a house. Before leaving, he told me that he would help with
> the renovations, but it would have to be step by step.

When we met subsequently, Kaew expressed her worry about whether
Bob would keep his promise to help renovate the family house. She waited
anxiously. Her father was excited by the prospect of getting support from
Bob as he had seen many wealthy families with *farang* sons-in-law in the
village. Kaew's father said, "I don't know what will happen. It depends on
Kaew's fate."

In May 2008, when I talked to Kaew, it was still not clear whether Bob
would help her build a new house. He kept silent, but he paid for her to
visit him in Australia. During her stay in Australia, she talked to him several
times about the house. Before her return to Thailand, Bob agreed to her
request and they made a rough design of a two-story house with rooms
downstairs for her parents. The construction began in 2009 and the house
was completed in 2010; by that time Kaew and her son had already left for
Australia. For Kaew, Bob's decision to help build the house testified to his
commitment and seriousness about the relationship. This convinced her
that he would take good care of her and her son, making it easier for her to
leave the village and move to live with him in Australia.

After the family's desire for a new house was realised, there was a
financial crisis and Kaew was called upon to help the family out of this
situation. Her oldest sister, who worked in the sub-district municipal office,
decided to run in the local council election. She had a better education
than her siblings and Kaew's father thought that this background would
facilitate her political ambitions, and if this came true, she and the family
would have a better future. He supported her by putting up the family's
paddy as collateral for a loan to pay for her election campaign. However,
she was defeated and he was at risk of losing the land. He realised that
it was unlikely that she would be able to pay back the money. The only
way out was to ask Kaew for help. By the time I left the village in 2010,

it remained unclear how Kaew reacted to the crisis. The expectations for assistance from her natal family are a recurring problem for Kaew and most Westerners' wives in Na Dokmai. Generally, these women cannot ignore their elderly parents or siblings' financial troubles and they feel obligated to help. Nevertheless, the support depends on their husband's agreement, especially when it involves large sums of money, as in the case of Kaew's family. While these women conformed to their role as dutiful daughters, some complained that people in the home village, including their families, made endless demands on them, not realising how hard they had to work overseas and the effort they had to make to save enough money to remit home.

The story of Kaew and her natal family illustrates how the cultural norm of *bun khun* plays out in practice and how it shapes expectations and relationships within a woman's natal family. It also illustrates how women, in maintaining this norm, are often put under great pressure. Situations like this require adaptation and negotiation in order to maintain good relations with their partners and their kin. Sa's story, presented in Chapter Three, shows that while Sa and her partner took care of her parents, the couple was also confronted with requests for financial help from Sa's siblings which put them under considerable stress. Sa's account below is an example of how a couple managed to maintain moral ties with a woman's siblings and simultaneously keep good relations between them.

> At first, Sven didn't agree to help my siblings, although we responded to some requests. He always questioned whether they worked hard enough to help themselves. Now, he accepts it more, but requests like this often irritate him. We talked about this whenever we were asked to help. I told him that I understood him as he did a lot for my parents. But I would feel very bad if I didn't help my siblings at all. Eventually, both of us agreed that it would not be possible to respond to all demands. We help with whatever we can, though it might be much less than they expect. I feel depressed whenever I am asked for financial support, especially when it involves a large amount.

While Western partners in Na Dokmai helped their wives to fulfil filial obligations, they did not view their support from the perspective of *bun khun* reciprocity, but from a welfare-providing perspective. Thailand does not have state-provided welfare such as unemployment and old-age benefits for residents. Only those who worked as civil servants have pension and health care coverage after retirement. Most rural people, however, engage in agriculture and wage employment and do not have such social benefits. It was not until 2001 that the government implemented a health insurance scheme in which rural residents could receive affordable health care.[3] With only very limited welfare provisions, aged parents relied heavily on their children.

While Western partners assisted their wives in fulfilling their *bun khun* obligations, they were not naïve about requests for assistance. This concern was reflected in a conversation with two German men and a Swedish man getting together outside a grocery shop while waiting for their wives who were buying food in the village market. One of the German men said: "Let them [women's parents] work if they are about my age and healthy. I am working. I won't support a father-in-law in his fifties who still can work." A Swedish man added, "I told my wife I'll take good care of her old mother. But if her younger brother living with her parents doesn't work and just asks her for money, she should kick him out of the house."

Bride Wealth

Another way in which material resources can represent respect and gratitude to a women's parents as well as symbolise a man's commitment and willingness to take care of his bride is through the local practice of *sinsot* (bride wealth). This practice, its cultural meanings and its influence on transnational marital relations, illustrate how relationships mediated through transnational marriage are shaped in the context of cultural distinctions between Thai and Western society. Following Robin Fox's work (1967) on kinship and marriage, I would translate the Thai term *sinsot* as "bride wealth"—instead of "bride price" as commonly used—so as to denote the aspect of social relations within and between kin groups.[4] In Thailand,

---

[3] According to this system, when going to a public hospital, the patients pay only 30 baht per visit to cover service and medical costs. Although rural residents benefit from this system, they complain about the low quality of treatment and services compared to that of private hospitals, which are much more expensive. The complaints are particularly evident among family members of women married to *farang* who, through support of the mixed couples, sometimes visit private hospitals or clinics instead of local public hospitals or health centres.

[4] Fox suggests the different denotations of the terms "bride wealth" and "bride price". He uses the term "bride price" when discussing the exchange between women and goods under exogamy principles so as to deal with the demographic problems caused by sex-ratio imbalance (Fox 1967: 175–80), while "bride wealth" is used in the context of the discussion on lineage and descent groups as well as relationships between a groom, a bride and her children (Fox 1967: 109–20). This usage suggests that bride price is associated more with exchange, especially in terms of materials/goods and women, whereas bride wealth denotes aspects of social relations within and between kin groups. The Thai term *sinsot* denotes the latter meaning.

a man and woman can acquire social acceptance and legitimacy as a couple through a wedding ceremony and by the groom's offering bride wealth to the bride's parents. The significance of bride wealth is based not solely on economic value; it also represents the way in which the groom expresses his respect to the bride's parents, by thanking them for raising her and demonstrating to them that he has sufficient financial resources to support her after the wedding. The norm of providing bride wealth is also interpreted in connection to *bun khun* reciprocity, an opportunity for the bride to repay the debt of gratitude to her mother (Akin 1984).

In Thailand, the custom of bride wealth is maintained both in rural and urban middle-class communities, though forms of payment have become diverse (Lyttleton 2000; Sumalee 1995; Whittaker 1999). The shifts have emphasised cash, while such assets as a house, a car, gold, jewellery and other valuables are also included, especially for wealthy matches. The size of the bride wealth varies according to the social and economic standing of the bride and her family. If a bride is from a distinguished family or if she has a secure occupation, the groom has to offer an amount significant enough to impress her parents and extended family. The marriage ceremony and providing of bride wealth are more common than the formal registration of marriages, especially among rural residents. Thus, its economic significance should be taken into account in relation to its social and cultural meanings.

Thailand enacted the marriage registration law (for Thai couples) in 1935—almost four decades after the law concerning Thai-foreigner marriage was passed in 1897 (Dararat 2007: 44–7). However, the customary wedding remains important as a rite to acquire social acceptance and legitimise marriage unions. By contrast, in many Western societies such as the Netherlands, ever since the mid-twentieth century a marriage ceremony is no longer viewed as an obligation to legitimise marriage. It is common for partners to live together and to marry later, and there are cases when couples choose not to have a wedding ceremony or marriage registration (Panitee 2009). Not surprisingly, bride wealth is viewed by Westerners as a way of buying a wife. Many Western men conform to the practice, however, even if they do not agree with it.[5] The different cultural interpretations of bride wealth inevitably influence relationships among the parties concerned.

Cultural differences like this often create tensions in family and social relationships between women, their *farang* partners and the woman's

---

[5] This issue has been widely discussed online: http://www.udonmap.com/udonthaniforum/sin-sort-issue-t19318.html and http://www.talkstory.com, accessed 23 March 2011.

relatives. Such tensions appeared in the life story of Lita, presented in Chapter Three. Lita's family was among the top echelon of the village hierarchy. Both her parents were retired teachers and Lita was also a school teacher. Lita's decision to marry Peter brought much concern to her mother, who was worried whether Peter would accept and follow the local marriage ceremony and whether the value of bride wealth would be appropriate (*mo som*), in accordance with her family status. To dispel her mother's worries, Lita explained to her that Peter was well informed about Thai customs. He read and often shared with her what he learned about Thai culture. He also had several friends who had married Thai women. However, he did not tell Lita how much he would provide until a few months before the wedding, and she was not sure if he would provide an adequate amount. She did not ask him about this, explaining, "he might think that I was marrying him for his money. I just hoped that he would not upset my family as he knew about Thai customs." The amount he provided—400,000 baht plus a gold necklace and a bracelet for Lita—was not disappointing. It was the highest bride wealth in terms of cash value among the women married to *farang* in Na Dokmai I knew, as the range was between 100,000 and 400,000 baht. Usually, parents would give the gold and jewellery to their daughter and part of the money was used for the wedding ceremony and feast. In some cases, the foreign partners were expected to pay for the wedding feast apart from bride wealth.

When asked about her expectations of the value of the bride wealth, Somsri, Lita's mother, answered thoughtfully, "*Sinsot* is not a matter of money itself; however, the amount has to be *mo som* [appropriate or adequate] so that the family will not *sia na* [lose face], if it is too little." Somsri's words illustrate the concern about a family's prestige and dignity that is attached to bride wealth. Women like Lita, from a family of a relatively good socio-economic background with a college education, would become a particular target of gossip if their expectation of an adequate bride wealth were not met.

While bride wealth practice is applied to both local and transnational marriages, it is acceptable if a local man offers less than a Western man. Nevertheless, as mentioned, the value of the bride wealth has to be considered in relation to the social and economic status of the bride and her family. A school teacher from one of the well-to-do households in the village said that two years ago his daughter married a Thai man she had met while studying in college. His son-in-law provided a bride wealth of 200,000 baht and shared the cost of a wedding feast while his family took up the expenses of the marriage rite. The teacher was pleased, though he mentioned that the bride wealth was not very high compared to the cases of women who married *farang* men.

Here, the image of "better-off Westerners" has an impact on local expectations of bride wealth. While parents' anticipations are shaped by this image, they are also concerned about the ability and willingness of Western men to take care of their daughters. In the eyes of the parents, an appropriate bride wealth guarantees their daughter's good future. Wan, whose daughter had married a German man and lived in Germany since 2008, commented that most parents had only limited information about the personal and family background of the Western men who were seeing their daughters. For her, a man demonstrates that he has sufficient resources and is willing to take care of his wife by providing an adequate bride wealth, thus ensuring her future.

Wan had an experience different from that of Somsri in terms of bride wealth. For Wan, this local norm was the cause of the termination of a relationship between her daughter, Ooy, and Chris, an English man whom her daughter liked very much. Wan recalled that Ooy met Chris in Samui in 2005. They kept contact for almost a year, and Chris remitted Ooy an allowance and gave her 100,000 baht to renovate the house in the village. "They got along quite well. Chris came to be with Ooy in the village twice. He was a nice man; my daughter liked him very much, and he got along with everyone in my family." During his second visit, Chris and Ooy talked about marriage with Wan and her husband. Wan wanted them to follow Thai marriage customs and provide a bride wealth of 200,000 baht. Chris did not refuse, but before leaving the village for England he told Ooy that he did not have much money. A few weeks later, he called and informed Ooy that he could not afford to pay the bride wealth. Ooy told him to save money and they could marry when he had enough savings, but he did not agree to this. He then stopped contacting her. Wan did not know why he changed his mind; the only possibility she could imagine was that he might not want to provide the bride wealth. In any case, this brought the relationship to an end. Two years later, Ooy met Harmas, a German man at Samui, and they got married at a ceremony held in Na Dokmai. Harmas provided the bride wealth Wan requested and paid for the wedding feast as well.

Ooy's and Lita's stories show how distinctive interpretations of bride wealth based on different cultural norms in Thai and Western societies shaped relations and created tensions among these women, their parents and their partners. The various ways of negotiating and compromising in which these people engaged reflect their attempts to manage and come to terms with the differences in local and Western norms and practices regarding marriage so as to minimise tensions, maintain good relations and sustain married lives.

Trust and Sexuality

During my first interview with Nisa at her house late in the morning in February 2008, Carsten, her Danish husband, called via the internet, so I left the house to let Nisa speak to him in private. When we resumed the conversation, Nisa said that her husband regularly called, practically every day if he was at home in Denmark. She was pleased with his behaviour. Since the children could speak to him and see him through a webcam almost every day, he was not a stranger to them. When asked whether making daily calls was common among mixed couples in Na Dokmai who were living apart, Nisa replied, "Many *farang* whose wives live in the village call regularly. They want to hear from their wives. Some are afraid their wives might see other men when they are away." Tensions and questions of trust and sexuality like this often came up when I interviewed women married to Westerners about their mixed-couple unions.

At one point, Nisa mentioned that her husband was also suspicious. When calling he frequently asked her to move the webcam around. "I know that he wanted to check whether there was another man in the house. I told him, 'Don't worry. If I see another man, I will let you know and introduce him to you.'" Still Nisa's husband made this request every now and then. Nisa felt his mistrust and it disappointed her, though she knew how her husband's suspicious behaviour came about. He suffered from the effects of a previous relationship with a Thai woman who had left him to live with a local man. He did not tell her the whole story, but she became aware of it from the bits and pieces of what she heard from him. Apart from this, rumours about these women seeing local men during their husbands' absence often circulated in the village. Nisa's husband, who had spent considerable time in Na Dokmai, must have heard these stories.

Jin, who lived with her German husband in the village next to Na Dokmai, shared her experience on how this kind of rumour caused distrust for her husband and generated tensions for her. His anxiety about rumours of infidelity among women married to *farang* men made him unhappy when Jin went out with friends or relatives without his company. This made Jin feel confined, as she expressed:

> One time when I went to the temple in the morning, taking food to the monks, I returned home a bit late. He complained. He was afraid

I might be seeing other men. He always has this idea in mind and it has never changed, ever. Normally, we are together almost all the time. I rarely go out without him, but this does not change him. I don't know what to do. I often feel that I don't really have freedom. When we were in Germany, he was not like this. I sometimes went shopping alone and visited or went out with Thai friends without him. He didn't follow me on every step or keep an eye on me like he does now that we live in the village.

Other women shared Jin's feeling of being a prisoner in their own home because of distrust generated by speculations about their sexual behaviour. Some did not want to be seen in the company of friends or avoided going out altogether, especially while their husbands were staying with them in the village. The sense of confinement in this case was mainly caused by gossip about their "loose" behaviour in the past connected with the sex trade, the path that had led many women in the village to transnational marriage. This, of course, ignored the diverse routes women actually took to marry Western men and the current lives these women were living. For instance, a school teacher in his forties when talking about a woman married to a *farang* who was rumoured to be involved with a local man, said he was not surprised, and mentioned the woman's past occupation as a sex worker. A British man living with his Thai wife in the village shared a familiar saying among *farang* men: "We can take a girl from a bar, but we cannot take the bar out of her." These views reflect the social stigma linking women who have a Western partner to "sexual immorality". The stigmatisation underlines popular perceptions that once a woman has worked in the sex industry she has lost all sense of shame and can easily fall back into "sinful ways". She is compared to a drug addict. This perspective is a part of general ideas about women involved in the sex industry (Nencel 2001). Whether or not there was any truth to speculation about a woman's involvement in extramarital relations, it would cause pressure to bear on her current relationship.

Despite the tension created through distrust, some women shared the feeling of being treated differently from what they had experienced with local men. These women stated that their Western husbands respected the decisions they made about their sexuality and their bodies. Jin, for instance, said that her husband always showed his appreciation when she dressed nicely. "He'd say, 'You look beautiful', and that he wants his wife to look good. He makes me feel confident about how I dress. He doesn't complain when I spend money on clothes and cosmetics—if it doesn't occur too often. But he complains if I come home a bit later than expected." Jin also openly said that her husband has always cared about her feelings. If she didn't feel well or was tired and sometimes declined to have sex, he understood and accepted her decision. This experience was something that she had never had with her Thai husband. In this respect, I agree with Ratana (2010) that exposure to the Western culture of sexuality and marriage has made many village women find Western men more attractive than local men. These experiences also allow woman to negotiate local notions of sexuality, marriage and gender, which I will explore in the following chapter.

Transnational Marriage and Parenting

Apart from trust and sexuality, obligations of motherhood add another layer to the complex context of mixed-couple unions. In Na Dokmai, 63 per cent of women with Western husbands had had a previous relationship with a local man and 90 per cent of these women had children from a local father. For these women their wish to support their children is a part of the logics of desire propelling them to marry a Western husband. The women's aspirations in this regard are influenced by the differences in Thai and Western norms and practices concerning parental responsibility for children.

In Thai society, especially in rural areas, after a couple separates—regardless of whether or not they have formally registered their marriage—the woman is left to take care of the children, frequently without any contribution from their father. This common practice is different from norms in most Western societies where both parents, by law, are obligated to support the children until a certain age after terminating their relationship. On the basis of this Western norm, women reported that normally their *farang* husbands accepted and helped them to fulfil their maternal responsibilities, although their experiences and the level of support they received varied. These women also reported that *farang* husbands were often bothered by the fact that the ex-partners of Thai wives did not take any responsibility in providing for their own children.

In Na Dokmai, one-third of women married to *farang* men were able to take their children from previous relationships to resettle in the countries of their husbands. Those women who left children in the village under the care of their parents or siblings regularly remitted money to take care of the children's upkeep and education. Tang, a divorced mother with a daughter, who started a relationship with her German partner ten years ago, is a case in point. Tang's partner had continuously supported her daughter who was studying for a bachelor's degree at a private university in Bangkok. He provided all education expenses and living allowances. Nisa's partner also supported her daughter and their son to study in private schools in town and Nisa moved to live in town to make it easier for them to attend school. Without support from her partner, Nisa's desire to provide the best education for her children would not have been possible as she had no job.

We have seen that Thai cultural norms obligating women to support their parents are not consistent with Western norms. However, Thai ideas about women's responsibility for children are similar to Western ideas. Thus, local women's aspirations to support their children caused fewer tensions to the mixed couples' relationships compared to their desire to support their parental household. Nevertheless, not all Western partners recognised and willingly helped a woman support her children. This is the case of Khem (54), a divorced mother with two sons—now grown up, who struggled unsuccessfully for many years to get her English partner to support her sons. She finally gave up and decided to end the relationship.

Khem met Ben, an English man in his early sixties, who was a boat repairer working in Phuket in 1981. At that time Khem worked as a cook on boats taking tourists out to sea overnight. While the two lived together, both contributed their share of housekeeping. Khem sent a part of her income to support the two sons she had left in the village with her sister. Ben neither contributed to the upkeep of the children nor helped Khem's sister, who took care of her sons even when she was sick. When the sons grew up and departed for Phuket to work, Ben helped them to find jobs, but he did not allow them to stay in the house. He told Khem that he wanted them to "stand on their own feet". In 2006, when her sister died, Khem came back to the village for the funeral and did not return to Phuket. She told me her side of the story.

> Ben called me several times and asked me to return to Phuket. I was tempted, as I could earn a lot more in Phuket than in the village. But, eventually I decided to not go back to him. He needed only me, not my children, let alone my relatives. He would never help them. When his friends visited us they stayed in our house and we always took care of them and fed them good food. But my son could not stay in the house, even for a few days. I'll never forget this, ever. It's always on my mind. I felt I couldn't take it anymore when he refused to help my sister who was sick. He didn't show any concern even when he heard about her death.

Despite her partner's refusal to support her children, Khem managed to bring them up herself. However, Ben's rejection of her motherhood responsibilities not only created tensions, but also resulted in the termination of their relationship. Putting Khem's case at one end of the scale and Tang's and Nisa's cases at the other end, the experiences of most of these women were somewhere in between. Their *farang* husbands helped them in fulfilling their motherhood obligations, but might not pay for all the costs related to the children's expenses and education as Tang's and Nisa's partners did. If the women worked, they usually kept their earnings to support their children. Their partners helped pay or shared in covering the larger expenses when requests were made.

Women considered such support an expression of care and love from their *farang* husbands, who were seen as men of responsibility in contrast to unreliable local men from their previous marriages. This process illustrates how transnational marriage becomes a site where intimate relationships and material relations are intertwined. In other words, it reflects the way in which relationships revolve around money and marriage, and how money transcends its economic value to represent care, responsibility and love.

Community Contributions: Strategies and Tensions

On the early morning of 13 April 2008, I met Sa and Sven at their house to join in a *pha pa* ceremony to be held at the local Buddhist temple in the village next to Na Dokmai where Sa was born and grew up. On the way to the temple, we stopped at the house of Sa's friend, one of the main organisers, to take the donated money, which was hung on a "money tree", a small pole made from straw to which Thai bank notes were attached, to the temple (see Figure 5.1). This *pha pa* was organised by three women married to *farang* who grew up together. Two of the women lived with their husbands in Pattaya; the third was Sa who had left Pattaya and been settled in Na Dokmai for almost ten years now. The money was raised mainly from friends working and living in Pattaya. The ceremony was held during the Songkran Festival when two of the main organisers and their families from Pattaya came to the home village for an annual visit.

Pha pa is a Buddhist ritual in which monastic robes, goods for daily use and money are offered to monks. It is also a way of making merit. Being the main sponsor and organiser of *pha pa* (and *kathin*[6]) require a certain amount of resources. While drawing on the cultural idiom of Buddhist merit-making, *pha pa* carries prestige and brings honour to the organisers (Terwiel 1994)

---

[6] *Kathin* is another Buddhist ritual which has to be organised within one month after the end of the monks' rainy season retreat period. But *pha pa* can be organised at any time of the year. As noted in Chapter One (footnote 16), the term *pha pa* is also used for fundraising or collecting goods for social and charity purposes, such as giving to schools, social organisations and those who are in need, although the activities are not related to religion.

Figure 5.1: The money tree in the back of a pick-up truck, on its way to the temple.

and it also affirms a person's moral and social ties to the community and rural kin (Mills 1999). Through organising a *pha pa* trip to a village temple, female migrants can combine their desire to be "good daughters", who maintain connections and support their home village with their existence as "modern women", who challenge familiar village standards of daughterly behaviour by leaving the village to work in the city (Mills 1999: 138–46). In a different context, Marjorie Muecke (1992: 893–4) interprets participation of women working in the sex industry in *pha pa* rituals and other merit-making activities as a way to compensate for their stigmatised work and to ensure that they will not be a prostitute in their next life. Muecke views this in relation to the Buddhist law of *karma*, according to which good actions earn merit (*bun*); wrong actions result in demerit. By making merit, a person can accumulate *bun*, which can change his or her *karma* and the current life or next incarnations. Women married to Western men in Na Dokmai (and the village residents) considered merit-making activities like *pha pa* as not only a way to deal with the negative image associated with their past involvement in the sex trade, but also as an expression of their economic success and their commitment to the home village. Nonetheless, local perceptions of women's contributions are rather ambiguous.

When we arrived at the temple, the *sala* (temple hall) was crowded with villagers, many of whom had come to the temple to make merit on the occasion of Songkran. The "money tree" was put in the *sala*, between the crowd and monks (see Figure 5.2). Apart from the "money tree", there were also smaller offerings for monks wrapped in bundles containing robes, medicine, packed drinks, toothpaste, soap and detergent, etc. The religious ritual was conducted by the monks; then food was offered to them. While the monks were eating, a small group of participants, including several village leaders, and a woman, one of the organisers, took the money from the tree and counted it (see Figure 5.3). A total of about 30,000 baht had been raised, which was announced to the people gathering in the *sala* to acknowledge and publicise the good deeds of the organisers.

Sa and her friends were pleased with the contribution they had made. She mentioned that the activity was put together in such a short time, and that if there had been more time, the contribution would have been higher. The elaborate ceremony on the day the money was offered is another indication of prestige. In a different context, the ceremony is organised in such a way that allows village residents and other local people to join in. Thip, a woman married to a Briton, told me that she and another friend—a woman married to an Austrian—had organised a *pha pa* in 2006 during their home visits. Together they raised a relatively large donation (140,000 baht). The money was given to the village primary school where Thip and her friend had studied when they were young. On the evening of the ceremonial day, there was a feast at the school. Village leaders, local government staff and a number of women and their Western husbands of various nationalities were invited to participate. Residents of Na Dokmai and those from nearby villages also joined in and greatly enjoyed the performance of *mo lam* (Isan folk opera) during the banquet. The chairperson, a former Member of Parliament from Udon, was invited to thank Thip, her friend and their husbands for their contributions. The way in which Thip described the event reflected her satisfaction and pride. Thip's mother also talked proudly about her daughter's good deeds. When a *pha pa* ceremony is celebrated in such a way that allows a wide range of local people to participate—as Thip and her friend did—it provides an opportunity to enhance the women's social prestige locally.

Thip's mother, who regularly contributed to school activities, also explained that several developments and improvements in the school, such as free lunch for students, learning materials, and a fence, were possible largely because of contributions made by women and their *farang* husbands. In Na Dokmai, the appearance of a mixed couple's names as well as the

Figure 5.2: The gathering inside the *sala*.

Figure 5.3: The community leaders and one of the organisers counting the money which had been raised.

names of Thai women with a foreign last name at communal places and facilities, for example on chairs and tables in community centres, temples and local government offices was easily observed. Such contributions in many cases relieved the financial burden which would have fallen on village residents. Villagers in Na Dokmai were generally aware of and pleased about the generosity of women married to Westerners. However, the contributions were also perceived as a way the women used to gain social recognition and to obscure their background and past occupation. This view was particularly prevalent among the well-to-do and well-educated villagers, as discussed earlier.

Despite these ambiguous attitudes, the contributions generally raised expectations among local people, which brought pressure to bear on women with Western husbands especially those who had settled in the village. According to these women, they were not only expected to contribute more than other villagers, on some occasions they were also asked to provide specific items or amounts of donation. Tensions developed when they could not meet these demands. As Sa explained,

> I really feel bad, even angry at myself that I can't respond to the community requests. I've tried my best to meet these demands, but sometimes I just wasn't able to do it and contributed only what I could. You know, there is a higher expectation of *mia farang*. I don't blame anyone; I don't blame the society. My siblings and relatives also expect financial support; they all think we *mia farang* are rich. I understand them and I wish I had a lot more money so that I could help all of them and the community too.

In spite of her disappointment, Sa kept making contributions when demands were made. Sa, like many women with *farang* husbands, talked about her contribution as an affirmation of her commitment and belonging to her home village, regardless of how local people perceived it. Such a contribution is the glue that cements relations with the local folk—relations that are not always smooth, as local expectations sometimes exceed these women's financial capacities.

The social recognition that women achieved through their contributions to their community and the appreciation they gained by supporting their parents contrast sharply with the negative image of women married to *farang* (re)produced through their past connection with the sex trade. Thus, their efforts to gain recognition as generous donors and dutiful daughters can be interpreted as a strategy to offset negative images of them associated to the sex industry. Furthermore, the recognition they receive contrasts with the marginalisation experienced by those who live with their partners overseas.

Although my study does not focus on this aspect of transnational marriage, it is worth noting that many women I interviewed told me of experiences in which people suspected that they had been involved with commercial sex. It is likely that such experiences made most of the women I came to know keep silent about their lives overseas, while some talked only about the positive aspects such as "modern" lifestyle, good wages, public health care and social security. Moreover, Western partners also admitted that they tried to avoid discussing their wives' social background, nationality or the place they had met. These subjects could only bring up further inquiries and tensions, regardless of their wives' background.

Based on experiences both in the natal home village and in the host society, the community contributions that brought women with Western husbands social recognition can be read as part of their strategy to deal with negative aspects of their status. Moreover, the recognition they received underlines the connection between material resources and social recognition. Nevertheless, local people's expectations of the contributions of these women and their husbands often generated tensions for them.

Conclusion

This chapter has shown how the images of women married to Western men and the relationships and practices that they are enmeshed in revolve around their improved material situations and aspects of consumerism representing Western or middle-class lifestyles. At the same time, long-standing, unfavourable opinions of these women still exist, particularly the *mia chao* discourse that associates a woman married to a Westerner with women working in sex-related businesses. Moreover, certain state and academic discourses associate transnational marriages with human trafficking and a decline in traditional family values as well as national culture, despite the fact that these women are deemed responsible for supporting their natal household and their children. These roles and responsibilities of women are similar to those described in Nicola Piper and Mina Roces's work (2003) on Asian women and migration. These authors problematise the way in which scholarship on migration and marriage often lock women into the category of either worker or wife. They point out the multiple and unsettled categories of women—as workers, brides/wives, mothers and citizens—that female migrants negotiate and reprioritise. Such practices allow women to manoeuvre their multiple roles in the contexts of destination countries and maintain their responsibilities to those "left behind" in native home communities. Drawing on this insight, I propose that the "left-behind" perspective of transnational marriage also involves the category of women as "dutiful daughters". This category, which is highly valued in Thai society, is also a strategy in legitimating and negotiating images and relationships under transnational marriage. The fact is that women with *farang* husbands make up an inherently complex and ambiguous category. This ambiguity often causes tension between these women and the local community, driving them to seek social recognition as dutiful daughters to their parents and worthy contributors to their home community. This social recognition is important as a way of counter balancing the generally negative opinions they are subjected to.

Interactions and social relations among these women, their husbands and local people are influenced by both local and Western norms and practices concerning gender, marriage and family. Material support in mediating these relationships is essential to sustain and strengthen a marital relationship. Although the material benefits associated with current transnational marriages are apparent, the meaning of this material dimension has to be understood in relation to specific social and cultural contexts. In connection with this, the notion of "special monies" (Zelizer 1989) gives room to conceptualise material resources beyond their economic value. Thus, social meanings of money can be mediated through cultural norms, social structures, the institutionalising of controls and restrictions of resource allocation.

Guided by the notion of "special monies", this chapter has examined the cultural and social significance of material and financial support, and the ways in which they influence and shape relationships among people involved in and related to transnational marriages within various contexts. Female filial obligations based on *bun khun* reflect how women's support of parents (and siblings) symbolises their gratefulness to their parents and at the same time underline the value of dutiful daughters. Local bride wealth (*sinsot*) practices symbolise the gratitude a groom shows to his bride's parents for bringing her up and denote his willingness and ability to take care of his wife-to-be. The financial support that Western men provide to their wives to fulfil motherhood obligations towards the children of an earlier union can be seen as representing the care and love these men have for their wives. This support can positively influence relationships between mixed couples, although marital relations are also shaped by trust and sexuality. At the community level, the contributions of women with *farang* husbands to the home village reaffirm their sense of belonging and their continuation of being part of that community. These diverse social and cultural meanings of material resources testify to the complexity of the transnational marriage phenomenon involving a web of criss-crossing relationships which cannot be captured solely from an economic perspective.

The complex and multi-layered attributes of transnational marriage, the tensions that go with it, and the ongoing dynamics of local norms and practices will be the focal points of the following chapter.

CHAPTER SIX

Transnational Marriage and Local Dynamics

Current studies on transnational migration have shown that border-crossing activities, ties and networks are part of the processes of social transformation and (re)production of local communities; at the same time, these connections are influenced by global and local cultures and flows (Appadurai 1996; Levitt, DeWind, and Vertovec 2003; Vertovec 2004). The discussions in the previous chapters highlight transnational marriage as a strategy, especially for women, to interact with global dynamics and to attain a secure life. They also reveal how transnational marriage is shaped by the diversity in local and global cultures, ideas, values and practices regarding gender, marriage and family. To provide insight into the other side of the process, this chapter focuses on the effects of these marriages on local dynamics. It explores how transnational marriage both generates and challenges cultural ideas and practices pertaining to gender, marriage and class. In other words, this chapter deals with the complexity of transnational processes in the "sending" communities by examining the experiences and roles of people who stayed behind and the consequences of transnational marriage on the social order in the women's natal villages.

Recent literature on transnational processes has begun to pay more attention to the experiences of people who stay behind in relation to those who move (Bélanger et al. 2010; Ratana 2010; Toyota et al. 2007), by focusing on the connections between host and home societies through transnational social, economic, political and familial ties. This approach challenges previous contentions that regard those remaining in the home village as passive recipients while overlooking how their ideas and actions disguise the complexity of the situation and limit insight into (transnational) migration as well as transnational marriage.[1] The present chapter explores the reactions and ideas regarding transnational marriage of village women of

---

[1] See more discussion on this topic in the Introduction.

those "left behind"—local men and parents whose daughters have married a Western partner or attempted to make such a move. By drawing on their life experiences, I wish to show that those who stay behind are important actors in the transnational processes with their own agendas, which they carry out with determination.

Previous studies have explored the dynamics in "sending" communities in terms of economic improvement (King et al. 2006) and socio-economic differentiations among people living in migrants' villages (Fouron and Schiller 2001; Kyle 2000; Levitt 2001). I go a step further by focusing on the transformations and differentiations in women's natal villages in the wake of transnational marriage. Specifically, I argue that women married to Westerners constitute a distinct social category of their own within the socio-economic hierarchical structure in the village, thereby challenging the village class structure. To elaborate on this, I draw on social stratification concepts, particularly Pierre Bourdieu's notion of class distinction (1984) which views taste, manifested through consumption, as a class marker.

Local Men's Perspectives and Reactions

In the Thai context, transnational marriage might simply mean "a marriage of a Thai woman to a Western man". Indeed, how people regard such a marriage varies widely depending on their background, and gender is one of the key factors. For the women in Na Dokmai, the motivations that propel them to marry a Western partner are multiple and complex (see Chapter Three). Local men, on the other hand, view these marriages merely as a way for women to improve their economic situation and that of their families. This view, based on common sense, is predominant and is also shared by many Western people as well as by the Thai government and academic discourses (see Chapter Five). In my research some men emphasised that these marriages implied that "by nature", Thai women would feel more affection for Thai men than *farang* men. A father (32) with two children, who ran an internet shop in Na Dokmai, concurred with this viewpoint. He stated:

> If people can live a good life, nobody would want to marry a foreigner. If you come from different cultures and use different languages, it's hard to develop deep understanding and passion. I truly believe that women marry *farang* out of difficulty, not because of love. Parents and senior kin encourage their daughters and nieces to marry *farang* as the elderly are less concerned about love than a secure future.

This view was shared among many village males. A man (27) whose girlfriend, a divorced mother with two children, had left him after a one-year relationship to marry a Norwegian, sincerely believed that she did it for the future of her children, not for love. As he put it, "I understand. She wants her children to have a good education and a good future. Many women in the village marry *farang* men for the same reason." Indeed, a number of women with Western husbands acknowledged that material aspects of transnational marriage were part of what they wanted. At the same time, they also recognised other factors motivating them to turn to Western men, the major ones being local men's irresponsibility in caring for their family, and female filial obligations driven by the local norm of *bun khun*. In contrast, local men often talked about transnational marriage purely in economic terms.

However, men are not a homogenous category, and some local older men had different opinions. Their concern was with the profound impact they thought transnational marriage would have on local traditions and communities in the long term. For example, Thawe (57) speculated about changes in the physical appearance of Thai people in the future as there would be many *luk khrueng*. Thai traditions, foods, ways of life, ways of dressing and family values—including respect for the elderly, filial piety etc.—would change as a result of Western influence. Thawe claimed that villagers did not foresee these long-term effects and saw only the immediate and positive side of marrying *farang* men, that is, a means of improving one's financial circumstances.

Moreover, some men feel threatened by transnational marriage because it offers the women in their community an alternative for marital relationships beyond what is available locally. Many women in Na Dokmai, after their relationships with local men did not work out, turned to foreigners with whom they felt they could enjoy a good marriage and a secure future for themselves, their children and their natal families. In addition, transnational marriages also provide an opportunity for divorced women and widows to re-engage in a marital relationship. Such opportunities are limited in Thai cultural norm and practices, as Thai men generally do not view divorced women and widows as desirable marriage candidates.

Indeed, transnational marriage offers an alternative not only for previously married women, but also for young, single women with a higher education. The fact that an increasing number of young, well-educated women have shown interest in seeking a *farang* partner is a highly interesting development. For these women, images of local men as irresponsible and promiscuous, the limited number of marriage choices because of local norms and practices regarding gender and marriage, and their own perceptions of modernity are powerful forces that compel them to see *farang* as prospective marriage partners (see Chapter Three). In any case, transnational marriage provides women with space to negotiate gendered power relations around marital relations and sexuality. In these contexts, local men's fears of losing their partners to foreigners were manifested in such expressions as, "If I dare to argue with my wife, I'm afraid that she'll leave me to marry a *farang*", and "I don't dare to cough or sneeze. If my wife is disappointed she may leave me for a *farang*." Often these utterances were mentioned as a third person's assertion and the expressions were made in a joking manner. It is worth noting that Thais generally use humour to express emotions they feel but cannot express otherwise.

Drawing on feminist studies in the field of language, such reactions reflect men's vulnerability and insecurity. A particular area of feminist analysis of gender and humour points out how notions of masculinity and femininity are constructed and resisted through talk, especially humorous discourses (Cameron 1998; Crawford 2003; Mulkay 1988). Based on a social construction paradigm, Michael Mulkay (1988) conceptualises humour as a mode of discourse entailing the speaker's goals and intentions in particular social circumstances. Unlike serious talk emphasising objective reality and avoiding self-contradiction and ambiguity, the use of humour contains multiple interpretations of reality, paradox and ambiguity. Following this line of reasoning, it is obvious that local men's reactions reflect their realisation of the transformations that challenge existing gender relations. The responses, shrouded in an offhand and joking manner, are a reflection of insecurity and loss of control over female sexuality. This interpretation is in line with Weisman (2000) in her analysis of Thai women engaging in sexual relationships with American servicemen during the Vietnam War. Weisman argues that women's involvement in the sex trade is indicative of men's failure to control female sexuality as these women took control of their own sexuality without having recourse to mediation by their fathers or older male relatives.

The ongoing changes as reflected in men's responses to the current transnational marriages taking place in Na Dokmai underlie the gender dynamics that place local men in a vulnerable position. Whether or not local men accept or even perceive them, such changes have brought new challenges to gender relations especially with regard to marriage and sexuality.

Desired Marriage Partners

The life-stories of women married to *farang* presented in the previous chapters reveal that many of these women had gone through crises in their previous relationships with local partners. Economic insecurity, stressful relations and a partner's infidelity were the primary causes of such problems. Based on these women's experiences and local perceptions of marriage crises, there emerges a pervasive image of "irresponsible" local men who do not take family life seriously. The notion of *farang* as desirable marriage partners is rooted in this image.

Indeed, characteristics of a desirable marriage partner who is a reliable provider and a good family man are common throughout generations; Sumalee's study (1995) on love, marriage and spouse selection in twentieth-century Thai society indicates such criteria. The mothers in Na Dokmai whose daughter married a Western husband mentioned similar principles used by their own parents in considering their partners. What concerns us here is why these factors are brought up in the context of current transnational marriages and how we are to understand them in relation to gender dynamism in the current contexts of local and global encounters. These insights need to be captured in the context of (transnational) migration in relation to the local kinship system and gender on the one hand, and female filial obligations in Thai society on the other.

As explained earlier, Isan is a matrilocal society and the practice of matrilocal post-marital residence is common, although changes in this tradition have become more apparent in recent decades. This cultural norm and practice not only provides an important voice in the management of family and household economies; it also ensures physical, emotional and material support that women can obtain from their kin. This support enables a wife to manage and fulfil household responsibilities even in the absence of her husband. In this light, the cultural norm of matrilocal post-marital residence facilitates men's domestic and international migration away from home to engage in labour employment, which has become an integral part of rural household economies in Isan since the 1980s. Ironically, it is also one of the factors leading to the breakup of marriages.

With the rise of the global economy, many village men (and women) have been drawn to overseas wage employment.[2] Such work is regarded as a way to access a considerable source of income which can help improve and strengthen the household economic security. However, as described in Chapter Two, migrants and their families have diverse experiences regarding overseas employment. Many men who left their wives and children behind in the rural home could or would not fulfil their responsibility of supporting

---

[2] As addressed in Chapter Two, women are likely to return to the home village after marriage and raise their children there while men remain away in their work.

them, leaving the wives to take on the household burden alone. Some of these men, after experiencing stress and loneliness as a result of working and living away from home, spent their earnings on their own pleasure and neglected to send remittances to their families at home. Others became involved in relationships with other women. Local men, on their part, often mentioned the precariousness of their occupations, which made them stressed and put pressure on the household economy as a key factor causing marriage crisis. In any case, such experiences with past partners were common in the narratives of women who married *farang*. Situations like these tend to paint local men as "irresponsible" heads of family, an image that has been implanted in the minds of many women (and their parents). Thus, while migration provides men with opportunities to become good providers, at the same time it takes them away from their families. In this context, remittances are a key indication of their responsibility to family, while failure to send home regular remittances is indicative of irresponsibility.

Although male obligations as providers play a major role in the failure of marital relationships, the troubles women had in their relationships with local men were not only financial. These narratives reveal that male promiscuity and unfaithfulness were also to blame for earlier marital breakdowns. Many of these women ended up divorced and had to bring up their children alone. Some women complained that their husbands, apart from providing an income, did not care for their family. One woman said that she had never had a real "family life" while living with her local husband, as he rarely spent time with her and their children. Her husband lived his life outside the home. He worked at the district police station and spent his free time with his male friends while she stayed home taking care of the two children and doing domestic chores. In joining customary and communal activities, her husband went with his friends, and not with her and their children. This lifestyle was completely different from what she experienced later with her English partner with whom she always did things together, such as joining community activities, shopping and eating out. Such contrasting ways of life that women experienced, directly or indirectly, became a factor contributing to the rejection of local men and their image as "irresponsible". This image is a powerful one, as it motivated single women, some of whom were well educated and had a secure career, such as Lita and Kanda (see Chapter Three), to opt for marrying Western partners.

Suda, a school teacher in her early twenties, is another single woman who strongly felt that marrying a local man was not a feasible choice for her. Suda was fluent in English and had several American friends while studying in college. She was critical of Thai men in terms of their promiscuity, drinking and neglect of family obligations, which she found unacceptable. While rejecting such behaviour, she was attracted by the more flexible gender roles in Western society as compared to local norms, which she learned about from her friends and from movies. She expressed her sympathy for women whose husbands did not take their families seriously and who were left to shoulder their household burden alone. Suda's account shows that such male behaviour is no longer accepted, especially by women of her generation.

The emerging idea of a desired partner as someone who is reliable and a good family man has to be understood in the light of the traditional female familial obligations shaped by the Thai gender system. As discussed previously, the cultural norm of *bun khun*, which ties women to the well-being of their natal family is deeply rooted in Thai culture and is highly valued in Thai society. Ideally, the support that children provide to their parents can be in the form of labour, money or emotional ties (see Chapter Five). With economic changes and the rise of overseas and domestic migration, it is less frequent for children to contribute their labour to the parents' household. Material support and remittances have become more common, especially for female migrants (and women married to *farang*) who are more reliable than their male counterparts in sending their earnings to parents at home (Mills 1999; Whittaker 1999). Contributions from daughters with a Western husband, either regularly or on request, are increasingly important in Na Dokmai as well as in other Isan communities. Marrying a man who is a good provider enables women to fulfil *bun khun* obligations.

Moreover, transnational marriage which allows women to observe female filial duties highlights economic aspects of the constructions of femininity in the Thai context. However, in a mixed-marriage union, women are still expected to take the major responsibility for household chores and many of these women have engaged in this task. Preference for a wife who adheres to traditional gender roles and family values is a key factor motivating Western men to seek a Thai (or other Asian) partner. Most, if not all, Western partners involved in this research project expected to be cared for by their wives. This observation is consistent with Constable's comment that some Western men desire a home in which the man is "the king of his castle", where he can see himself as the dominant figure. These men look to Asia and certain other parts of the world for women who are thought to be committed to traditional family values (Constable 2003: 66). Women married to *farang* men residing in Na Dokmai as well as those living with their husbands in other parts of the world were aware of and complied with these expectations. Local men often remarked that women always took good care of their Western husbands, but they did not do the same with their local partners. Admittedly, these women viewed care-taking and household tasks as ways to reciprocate their husbands' support. Regardless of how such practices are conceived, they underline traditional female domestic roles and family values.

The idea of reliable and good family men as desirable marriage partners implies a dismissal of local men as unfit, thus legitimising women's engagement in transnational marriage. At the same time, it reinforces constructions of (Thai) femininity as it allows women to conform to female filial expectations shaped by *bun khun*, while extending their domestic roles to the wider space of a "global village" where they live with their husbands. Indeed, the idea of a desirable marriage partner is a powerful one, for it provides incentives not only to women who directly experienced marriage crises involving local men, but also to young single women. This dynamic is a part of the ongoing changes in Isan society that contribute to the popularity of transnational marriages.

The "Left Behind" and Transnational Marriage

The impact on gender relations and the dynamics in women's marriage decisions highlight some of the consequences of transnational marriages on local communities. To reveal another layer of the complex transitions in sending communities generated by international marriages, this section focuses on the involvements of the "left behind" in transnational marriage processes. By exploring the roles of women's parents, I want to show that those who stay behind are not merely passive recipients who benefit from and are influenced by financial and social remittances generated by transnational marriage and migration. Rather, the involvement of parents shows their support in materialising transnational connections as much as their determination and actions to fulfil their desired goals.

Bua, a mother in her late fifties, recounted how she had arranged for Nuan (34), her divorced daughter with a son, to marry a German man. Nuan worked as an accountant in a company in Udon after graduating from vocational college. She married a school teacher and her marriage went well until she found out that her husband had been seeing another woman. The man wanted to maintain relationships with both women, but she could not accept this idea and decided to end the relationship. Bua encouraged her daughter to re-marry and strongly suggested that she look for a Western man. Bua believed that if she married a Thai man, she would face the same problem and would suffer again. Nuan was persuaded, but she was not serious about making it happen. As Bua recounted, "Nuan said that she would not go to Pattaya, definitely not. A friend helped her to contact *farang* men through the internet. This didn't work, and for almost two years nothing happened. She didn't find any serious connections." To help her daughter, Bua turned to match-making agents by asking those who knew or had used these services. She was told about an agency in Udon run by a woman living with her German partner. Bua went there several times to get information and talk to the woman owner. Finally, she decided to use the service and paid a service charge of 120,000 baht. After paying, however, Bua kept worrying about whether such a large amount of money was well spent. Looking back, she realised that it was a substantial risk since there was no guarantee that it would work. If it didn't, she would lose her money. Fortunately, Nuan was put in contact with a German man whom she married within eight months after paying the agency. Nuan left the village for Germany in 2003 and also managed to take her son to live there with her later that year.

Bua's determination and deep involvement were instrumental in getting her daughter successfully into a transnational marriage. Cases like this encouraged other parents and elderly residents in Na Dokmai to ease the way for their daughters and nieces to pursue the transnational marital alternative. This is not to say that Bua was not aware of the social stigma attached to women marrying Western partners. However, since her daughter had suffered from a bad first marriage, she felt that if she had a happy new life with a *farang* it would outweigh the social consequences of such a union, not to mention the financial windfall that was expected to come with it. Bua anticipated that when Nuan's financial status became secure, she could contribute to her natal family. Bua was by no means a passive recipient of the benefits of a transnational marriage.

It was common for parents to be ambivalent about their daughters being the wives of *farang*. On the one hand, they believed that their daughters would have a happy and secure life by marrying a Westerner. On the other, they were worried about the social stigma attached to being married to a *farang* and about their daughters' safety while living far away in another country. This feeling was shared by many parents I spoke with, including those who were confident that their daughters were mature enough to deal with challenging situations as they arose. Nevertheless, these worries were put aside once their daughters had made up their minds to pursue their aspiration. Parents' support took various forms and with varying degrees of involvement. Usually, they helped by taking care of grandchildren when their daughters were away trying to make contact with Western men. Some helped pay for or contributed to match-making service expenses. Others were actively involved in arranging contacts or direct meetings between their daughters and prospective partners, for example Chai, who put in a great deal of effort into making it possible for his daughter to marry a *farang* man.

Chai's support for his daughter, Nam (18), a high school graduate, is a well-publicised case in Na Dokmai. During my fieldwork, I met with Chai and his wife several times, but neither of them wanted to talk about their daughter, Nam, who was preparing to visit the US, sponsored by Martin, a retired American man she had been seeing. I learned from their neighbours that Chai had tried various strategies to enable his daughter to make contact with *farang* men, though his wife had taken a rather neutral role in all this. He once took his daughter to town to meet with a man Nam had contacted on the internet and he paid for an interpreter to help his daughter communicate with the man. When women living with their husbands overseas returned to the village on their home visits, he would ask them to introduce *farang* men to his daughter. In mid-2009, after Chai rented out his van to Martin, he put him in touch with his daughter through a woman in the village who was married to an American man. Nam met with Martin while he stayed in the village, and after returning to the US, Martin continued to communicate with her, sending money for her expenses and her English language courses. He also offered to pay for her to visit him in the US, but Nam's visa application was not approved. Nam then reapplied. To prepare for her visit to the US, Nam went to Bangkok to take English courses. A female relative of Chai's wife told me that Chai was satisfied with the "progress" his daughter had made so far. He also predicted that Nam would have a good future as Martin seemed to be a reliable person, as shown by his support for her and especially the efforts he made to get her to go to the US.

The villagers, for their part, often raised questions about the wide age gap between Nam and Martin. The issue was about happiness versus a secure life. A woman in her forties, whose daughter was a good friend of Nam's, commented on the rashness of Chai's attitude. "Nam just finished school and has not had a chance to learn how life is. I don't agree with what her father has done. I feel sorry for Nam, really. I can't imagine how an 18-year-old girl will be happy with a man in his sixties. He is older than her father; he belongs to her grandfather's generation." The woman pointed out that parents sometimes focus more on a good financial future rather than the personal feelings and happiness of their daughters. Chai's hopes for his daughter to have a secure life were apparent. But in steering his daughter towards a transnational marital relationship, no doubt he also wished to reap benefits for himself, as he had seen similar cases in the village—the same motives shared by Bua. Obviously, Chai and Bua, the ones who stayed behind, were active actors in facilitating and encouraging this transnational process that had been transforming Isan communities.

Parents' roles in transnational marriage were sometimes criticised in terms of morality when they encouraged and provided the means for their daughters to go and work at notorious tourist destinations like Pattaya that served as contact zones (see Chapter Four). The principal of the local primary school said that support from parents and elderly kin for women to work in Pattaya in search of marital possibilities with Western men is immoral since it sets a bad example for young girls, making them think the quick way to get rich is to marry a *farang* by whatever means, including selling their bodies. While this view was shared by most villagers, some said that although working in a place like Pattaya might be an "immoral" practice, it was "morally justified" since it allowed women to earn money to support their parents. Those parents who encouraged their daughters to go to Pattaya saw this as the most practical way to make initial contact even though they were aware of the social stigma attached to women working there.

The ways in which parents were involved in their daughters' transnational marriages indicate that they were active players with their own motives and agendas, which they carried out with determination. Although they were "left behind", their actions demonstrate that they were by no means passive bystanders, but that they not only influenced but also benefitted from transnational activities. An important question is whether such active involvement also implies parents' authority over children, especially with regarding their choices of partners and female sexual behaviour.

Parents' Authority, Daughters' Choices of Marriage Partner and Female Sexuality

In talking about parents' authority in the context of transnational marriage, parents often compared the ways in which women married to *farang* chose their partners with their own experiences while they were young. Kham (79), a widow whose daughter had married a Belgian man and lived with him in his home country for 12 years, recalled that her parents selected a husband for her out of four men who proposed to her—a teacher, a folk healer, a farmer and the son of a local trader. The farmer, her late husband, was chosen since her parents wanted a good labourer who could help with the household farming. Kham accepted her parents' choice without any fuss, as she explained, "This [arranged marriage] is the way it was at that time.... [P]arents and the elderly always said that by living together, we [the couple] would eventually love each other." This experience was shared by Noi (62), a widow whose two daughters were married to *farang*, a Greek and a Briton. Noi was married to a man who had been in the monkhood for many years; her parents chose him for this reason. They believed that through ordination, he had become a "mature man", able to take care of a family of his own. Noi went along with her parents' decision. The arranged marriages worked well for both women and lasted until their husbands passed away. Parents' influence on their children's choice of marriage and the criteria for selecting a son-in-law used by Kham's and Noi's parents are different from those of their daughters' generation. Today, agricultural skills are no longer an important factor in selecting a son-in-law; instead, parents generally appreciate a man with a good job and/or a secure economic situation as well as ability and willingness to take care of his family.

With regard to spouse selection, Noi recounted that she had nothing to do with her daughters' choice of partners. Both of them met their husbands through an agency in Bangkok while they worked as babysitters. Noi did not know how well her daughters got to know these men. She only heard about them through her daughters and met them for the first time when they came to the village with the women. She could not communicate with the sons-in-law because of the language barrier. Likewise, Kham was not involved in her daughter's relationship with her Belgian husband. "They met in Bangkok while I was in the village. He asked to marry my daughter the first time I met him. I didn't know much about him. My daughter chose him, and then they got married." The decline of parental authority over their children's choice of spouses is shared by most parents of women married to *farang* in Na Dokmai, including those who encouraged their daughters to go and work in Pattaya in order to contact Western men. A mother in her late fifties, whom I first met in Pattaya when she was visiting her daughter who worked there as a bar girl, admitted that she had encouraged her to go there to look for a "good" *farang* man who would take care of her and her son from a previous marriage. Her daughter had had several relationships with different *farang* partners during her four years of working in Pattaya. The woman said she had no influence on her daughter's decision concerning the men she associated with. She rarely met these men in order to get to know them, and moreover, she could not communicate with them as she could speak only Thai.

Generally, the decline in authority over children's choice of partner was common among parents including those with daughters (and sons) working away from home. Studies on migration reveal that when away from their natal home, women are able to exercise a high degree of autonomy over their decisions and actions, free from supervision by parents and elderly kin (Mills 1999; Sobieszczyk 2002). In the case of transnational marriage, parents' authority is negligible since their daughters not only reside in a distant place, but they also associate with men of other cultures and languages that parents know nothing about. Decisions about personal relationships and eventual marriage are almost entirely in the daughters' hands. Despite their efforts to pave the way for their daughters to meet prospective foreign partners, parents have little say in the final outcome. This situation allows women to enjoy a certain degree of freedom over their decisions and actions in the search for suitable foreign partners, although they remain tied to their parental home through the ethics of *bun khun* relations.

One issue that often came up when talking about parents' authority in relation to women's marriage choices and sexual behaviour concerned gossip about "sexual immorality" of women married to *farang*. Chan, a woman in her mid-sixties, alleged that the woman living in a house opposite hers had been seeing a local Thai man while her *farang* husband was away. This kind of gossip caused concern to the parents of the woman but they could not do anything about the situation. In Chan's words: "The parents can't do anything. They have to follow their daughter's wishes since this *mia farang* supports the whole family. She built a new house where she lives with her parents and her two daughters [from a *farang* father]. She provides allowances to her parents and helped her siblings financially." Indeed, the responses to rumours like this are varied. Some villagers spoke of this situation as a woman's choice and explained that these women had done so much for their natal family, thus they could have their wishes met as well. Others related the speculation to the wide gap between the ages of the mixed couple. A local school teacher, commenting on parents' support of their daughters working in Pattaya, said that apart from the loss of parental authority over their children, such rumours reflected the moral deprivation within the community. For him, the blame should be not just on the women who were said to be involved in extramarital relationships but also on their lovers since these men, too, played a part in the decline of morality.

The roles of parents in transnational marriage reveal that the ones "left behind" are actually active players in these transnational engagements. However, this does not imply that parents have authority over women's choices of marriage partners. On the contrary, most parents have experienced a decline in their ability to influence their daughters' decisions in this respect as well as in supervising female sexual behaviour. This paradox is part of ongoing social transformations at the local end of transnational processes, particularly in villages like Na Dokmai where transnational marriage is a significant social phenomenon. To capture another layer of the dynamics, it is important to examine how people relate to each other with respect to transnational marriages. To do this, I propose to consider women in this kind of relationship as a distinct social category.

An Emerging Social Category

The improved economic well-being and distinctive lifestyles of women living with Western husbands set them apart from other villagers, thereby putting them into a distinct social category. This section explores the criteria by which this emerging category can be considered a "class" of its own and the ways in which it affects the social order within the village hierarchical structure and social relations among villagers. To take a closer look at these dynamics, I employ social stratification analysis and draw particularly on Bourdieu's notion of class distinction (1984), which suggests that taste is a cultural and symbolic marker for class.

Social stratification is one of the mainstream theories in social analysis, among which Marxist and Weberian approaches to class analysis are most prominent (Wright 2005). In Marxist theory, class is a core concept and is defined in relation to production, more specifically to ownership of the means of production and to labour. This definition is less applicable to the emerging social category of *mia farang*, which is characterised by increased material wealth and enhanced consumption—oftentimes perceived as conspicuous consumption—rather than in relation to production in the Marxist sense. While Marxist analysis focuses basically on economic production, Weber distinguishes class as a function of economic order and the status groups associated with social honour and consumption; castes and ethnic groups are specific instances of endogamous status groups. Weber explicitly connects status or "honour" groups with a common style of life manifested in patterns of consumption and association. He points out that wealth is not necessarily the primary cause of status, although some forms of property ownership are linked to prestige (Cox 1950; Weber 1947).

In a sense, Bourdieu's notion of class distinction, like Weber's class stratification, focuses on consumption as the manifestation of taste. Bourdieu claims that taste—as manifested in consumer preferences and lifestyles—indicates an individual's status and reflects a symbolic hierarchy determined by the dominant class to reinforce their distinction from other classes in the society. Society incorporates "symbolic goods, especially those regarded as the attributes of excellence, [...as] one of the key makers of 'class' and also the ideal weapon in strategies of distinction" (Bourdieu

1984: 66). Bourdieu contends that class distinction "is most marked in the ordinary choices of every day existence, such as furniture, clothing or cooking, which are particularly revealing of deep-rooted and long-standing dispositions" (1984: 77). In this sense, taste becomes a class marker and is concerned with consumption. Taste/consumption is conditioned by a varying combination of economic capital (assets, cash), social capital (acquaintance, recognition, networks, relationships) and cultural capital (knowledge, skills, experiences, education, attitudes).[3] Bourdieu emphasises particularly the dominance of cultural capital as a class marker, to the effect that "differences in cultural capital mark the differences between the classes" (1984: 69). However, he does not ignore the importance of other forms of capital in the formation of cultural capital. For instance, he attributes the ability to create art and play music in relation not only to dispositions associated with long establishment in art and culture, but also to economic means and spare time (Bourdieu 1984: 75). This indicates that taste as cultural capital is linked to other forms of capital and that these various forms of capital are, to an extent, mutually convertible.

In Na Dokmai, as shown in the previous chapters, material improvement and consumption patterns symbolising middle-class ideals are amply manifested in the living standards and lifestyles of women married to Westerners and their natal families. Many of these women were able to augment their assets, such as a house, car and consumer goods as well as paddy land. Some also invested in local businesses such as bars, restaurants and internet cafés. Their daily behaviour and leisure activities constituted distinctive styles that set them apart from most other villagers, including those belonging to privileged groups in the village hierarchy. Similar observations regarding consumption and display of consumer goods in the natal homes of women married to Western men appear in Panitee's work (2009). Furthermore, this pattern of consumption was also common among labour migrants. Mills (1998: 304–7) observes that migrants and their families use their wages and remittances not only for food and other subsistence requirements but also for the acquisition of expensive commodity items—refrigerators, television sets, etc.—and the construction of new, urban-style houses. These material possessions not only underpin the "modern" sophistication and urban achievement of migrants and their families; they are also important symbols in migrant households' claims to

---

[3] See further discussion on three forms of capital and how the structure of their distribution represents the structure of the social world and determines practices in Bourdieu's work *The Forms of Capital* (1986).

status and prestige. Likewise, Panitee (2009) relates consumption patterns of Thai migrant wives to the Thai idea of life overseas, associating it with a modern Western and middle-class lifestyle, with visions of imagined places and the type of modernity local people fantasise about. According to Bourdieu, these kinds of consumption comprise a symbolic hierarchy and a marker for class.

The ethnographic descriptions of the village in Chapter Two show that many of the relatively new houses with gardens and lawns built in the style typical of urban-middle class owners belong to women married to *farang*. During my stay in the village, I visited a few of these women in their houses, which were furnished with expensive, factory-made furniture, a modern kitchen with a dining-room table set, a microwave oven and refrigerator, a living room with a sofa and matching chairs, large television and stereo equipment. These expensive factory-made commodities are different from the locally-made furniture found in most middle-class households in the village. From my observation, however, the women and their Thai family members living in the houses rarely used these spaces and this furniture. One woman explained that she preferred the Isan style of having meal sitting in a circle on a mat on the floor or with a low table. The dining table was used by her husband during his stay. He also used the modern kitchen in the house when he cooked, but she often cooked in an old kitchen outside the house. A similar story was told by the mother of another woman when she took me to see her daughter's house. She said that the living room, which was well furnished, was hardly used when her son-in-law was away in his home country. Usually, members of her family spent their daytime at an open-air place outside the house; they ate, chatted, socialised with the neighbours and sometimes took a nap there. The "modern" and luxurious furniture used minimally in these cases serves to indicate the status of the households and symbolises the distinction from other families. In this sense, these commodities constitute an index of class mobility.

In addition to consumption patterns typical of middle-class lifestyles, women with Western husbands and their natal families earned social recognition by contributing to the community and making merit, as shown in the previous chapter. During my time in Na Dokmai, it was often the case that these women were the top contributors in supporting communal, school and religious activities. The two influential women, Phin and Mon, are cases in point. Phin had been one of the main contributors to the village school's revolving fund since 2003 when she returned from the US and resettled in the village. Similarly, Mon had continuously contributed to community affairs. In 2009, she was one of the two sponsors who each gave a cow for the two top prizes in a village festival. The other sponsor was the district head (*kamnan*) who was running for another term. This situation is different from the past when contributing to the community and making merit by donating a considerable amount of money and other material resources were usually done by people at the top of the village hierarchy and the urban elite. As Bourdieu points out, financial contributions and merit-making are cultural markers for class distinctions, and at the same time, symbolise assets and recognition/merit. In other words, cultural markers for class become cultural capital that can be mutually converted into economic capital (assets) and social capital (recognition/merit). In the Weberian sense, such practices of community contribution and merit-making as well as (conspicuous) consumption are indications of social honour or status. Thus, in line with the theories of Bourdieu and Weber—but not Marx—the practices signify both economic mobility and enhanced social honour, and the social category of women married to *farang* could be construed as an emergent class.

While the conspicuous consumption practised by these women reflects their increased material wealth, local people, especially those in privileged positions (for example grocery shop owners, school teachers and local civil servants) and the urban-middle class regard the people associated with such highly visible forms of consumption as the "*nouveaux riches*". This idea is related to certain "folk" or "vernacular" perceptions of honourable/ meritorious behaviour (Sampson 1994). Local views, in this case, draw largely on such factors as social origin—rural, poor, marginally educated— and insinuations about working in the sex industry, etc. Put differently, the emergent class of women married to *farang* contains ambiguities derived from their enhanced material wealth and rising status on the one hand, and their generally low-class background and the stigma associating them with prostitution on the other.

This analysis is in line with Keyes's recent ideas about "cosmopolitan villagers", which underpin the articulations of Isan peasants with global dynamics. Keyes (2014) points out that the old elite remained rooted in the village whereas the peasants were on the move and became "cosmopolitan". By getting involved in extensive domestic and international mobility and absorbing a massive amount of information from the media, Isan peasants have come to see themselves as belonging to much larger worlds than their home villages. These dynamics mark the enormous degree of change in contemporary Isan society. Keyes elaborates on such transformations by relating cosmopolitan villagers' experience with the politics of populist democracy in Thailand. He argues that Isan villagers make a rational political choice, on the basis of their experiences, in supporting populist policies. The overwhelming support of the party promoting such policies in the 2011 election reflected a backlash against Thai politics which have long represented the middle-class and elite. In other words, Keyes's perspective speaks of the overturning of the old village and urban elites through electoral politics based on the new "cosmopolitan" peasant class.

Women married to Westerners are a perfect example of Keyes's "cosmopolitan villagers". The emergence of these women as a new social category—representing a new "class"—parallels the relative waning of the old "rooted" village elite, who increasingly experience a decline or a perceived decline in their prominence and impact. These dynamics impose tensions onto the existing class divisions in the village; specifically, they generate challenges to the old village social order. This situation has, in part, contributed to the multiplicity of local perceptions of and reactions to women married to Western men and current transnational marriages.

Conclusion

While the impacts of transnational marriages on material improvement, income growth and employment expansion in Isan are obvious, the social and cultural consequences are subtler and complex, especially with respect to gender and class. In term of gender dynamics, Bélanger et al. (2010) discuss the transformation of gender relations as an intrinsic part of cross-border marriages of Vietnamese women. The study centres on the changes in experience and perception regarding the gendered positioning of women married to foreign men in the eyes of their families and community members as well as women themselves. The present study focuses on another angle of gender dynamics and reveals that transnational marriage challenges traditional notions of gender in relation to marriage and sexuality. In particular, transnational marriage often places local men in vulnerable positions by highlighting the idea of desired partners as reliable and good family men, while categorising local men as unfit husbands. This idea is a powerful one; it motivates not only women whose previous relationships with local partners have failed, but also young, single women hoping for an ideal relationship, to seek transnational marriage. This idea also reinforces certain (Thai) constructions of femininity by allowing women to fulfil their filial obligations of bun khun, especially within the contexts of mixed-couple families.

The dynamics of class at the "local end" is one of the major contributions of this study as it adds original insight to the existing literature on transnational marriage. It addresses the emergence of a new "class" comprised of women with Western husbands as a key aspect of the dynamics in the sending community. This transformation is not confined to women's natal villages, but is part of the changes taking place in contemporary Isan society, and in Thailand generally. As transnational marriages have become popular among women of both rural and urban backgrounds, these changes will continue, intensify and expand.

The local dynamics reflected by the reactions of women's parents reveal a wide range of activities on their part in encouraging and assisting their daughters in marriage processes. Nonetheless, this does not mean that they have control over their children's choice of marriage partners or their sexuality. Rather, parents' authority in this regard is declining. Such involvement by parents highlights their roles as active players in supporting and making transnational connections become realisable, though their support varies. These people are not simply passive recipients benefiting from and affected by remittance and the social remittance that is generated through transnational processes. Rather, they are active agents with clear aims, purposes and intentions.

All in all, the current dynamics and subtle shifts going on in Na Dokmai generated by transnational marriage of village women are a part of the social transformations and (re)production of Isan communities taking place in the face of local and global encounters. The stories of these women, their husbands and the villagers of Na Dokmai presented in this book are remarkable examples of how people engage in and experience global opportunities, as well as of how such engagement influences their lives and the life of their community.

CHAPTER SEVEN

Conclusion and Contributions

The growing number of transnational marriages in Thailand—especially in Isan—is part of the phenomenon of global intimacies that have influenced dynamics at the "local end" in many ways, as this book has illustrated. The insights discussed throughout the book, which are shared with the existing literature[1] highlight the desires and experiences of individuals, mostly women, who engage in this global opportunity as well as their strategies and practices and the ways in which they negotiate and manipulate such intimate relationships. In addition, this book goes a step further by expanding the framework of analysis to include the "sending community". Thus, it focuses on the "local end" of transnational connections and those people who stay behind as much as those who engage in global intimacy.

Based on such analysis, this book offers four important contributions to the literature on transnational marriage. The first refutes the bimodal view of materiality and intimacy, by arguing that material benefits and romantic love are not the main factors upon which these transnational relationships are built. The current transnational marriage phenomenon is much more complex. The logics of desire compelling local women and Western men to opt for marriage as well as the relationships between mixed marriage couples and between these couples and the women's local kin are diverse, and are shaped by local and Western cultural norms regarding gender and marriage as well as gender fantasies about Western societies and lifestyles. The second contribution of this book involves the roles of people in women's natal villages who do not directly engage in these relationships but influence and facilitate them. In other words, it addresses the agency of the "left-behind" population of transnationalism. The third contribution addresses the consequences of transnational marriages on the "local end"

---

[1] Some of the recent works include Cheng (2010), Cheng, Yeoh and Zhang (2015), Faier (2009), Ishii (2016a), Malher and Lafferty (2014), Parreñas (2011), Rattana and Thompson (2013), Sirijit and Angeles (2013), Thai (2008), Thompson et al. (2016) and Yang and Lu (2010), which were discussed in the previous chapters.

of transnational connections, especially on the emergent social category constituted by women married to foreign men, which has imposed itself among the existing class divisions in the village and challenged the village elites. Alongside with class dynamics, women's choice of transnational marriage has often had the effect of relegating local men to a vulnerable position as they are perceived as unreliable and not good providers. The fourth outlines the historical perspective of transnational marriage. While the current marriage phenomenon is complex, its historical roots are also diverse and ingrained in historical and cultural specificities dating back several centuries. It is from the long familiarity with these marital relationships that the popularity of today's transnational marriages developed.

Historical Diversity and Current Complexity

In searching for insights into transnational marriages beyond financial motivations, this study began by exploring the historical roots of contemporary transnational marriages. Most, if not all, of the previous studies on marriages between Thai women and Western men are limited in their historical perspective in that they trace these relationships only as far back as the presence of American troops in Thailand during the Vietnam War in the 1960s and 1970s. The present work breaks new ground by showing that intermarriage in Thai society can be traced as far back as the thirteenth century, and that conjugal relations between Thai women and Western men were documented in the early sixteenth century with the arrival of Westerners in Ayutthaya.

From this historical perspective, it is clear that interracial marriages were shaped by the intersection of gender, class and ethnicity (Chapter One). Intermarriages often followed a gendered pattern and were linked closely with social class. Marriages between Thai women and Western men were observed among the general population, whereas marriages between Thai men and Western women occurred mainly among the elite and the royal family. Furthermore, while marriages between Thai women and Chinese men were promoted under assimilation policies, especially during the reign of King Rama V (1868–1910), those between Thais and Westerners were rather restricted due to the emphasis on nationalism by King Rama VI (1910–25), whose reign promulgated laws and regulations regarding Thai-Western marriages. The historical explorations also reveal an accepted utilitarian dimension to interracial marriages, which nevertheless did not exclude emotional factors. This utilitarian and social acceptance is the foundation upon which the popularity of current transnational marriage is built. The present phenomenon can be said to have its roots in interracial marriages dating back several centuries.

Today's transnational marriage phenomenon is context-specific, showing forms of conjugal unions that are different from those of the past. The increased popularity of this type of marriage and the regularity of contacts between women in these marriages (and their husbands) with their families in rural communities are the most prevalent characteristics of current transnational marriages. The family bonds and wider social relations within their home village are particularly crucial for the women. The continuous investment by women in their home communities is a determining factor in the success of the marriage. Inevitably, such transnational connections and practices shape perceptions and expectations of mixed couples and complicate social relationships between these women, their husbands and local people in the women's natal communities.

Another significant factor reflecting historical connections between today's transnational relations with those of the past is women's awareness of the possibility of escaping from situations resulting from marriage problems with local men, improving their living conditions and fulfilling their social obligations as dutiful daughters. To a great extent, such awareness was realised through the experiences of GIs' wives during the Vietnam War. Despite the ambivalent attitudes towards these women, who often experienced both admiration and jealousy for their material improvement and criticism for their connection to prostitution, their stories, especially of those who became influential local figures, have inspired women of later generations to seek Western husbands. Transnational marriages nowadays are perceived as the deliberate choices of individuals. This is quite different from interracial unions in the past, which were often viewed in association with the country's politics, modernisation and international relations. This dynamic is indicative of a change in perceptions and meanings of mixed marriages in Thai society; it emphasises individuals' (and their families') strategies in the face of local-global articulations rather than state concerns for international relations and development.

The highly-valued cultural idea of *bun khun*, according to which a dutiful daughter supports her parents and family, is another important factor in present-day transnational marriages. Gender roles determined by *bun khun* reciprocity underline a female's life-long obligations to her parents (and natal family). Fulfilling this norm by maintaining connections with and continuing support for her parents allows a woman to gain merit and social recognition. However, obligations shape the relationships and practices developed within women's natal families and their conjugal ones. It is precisely these dimensions—the women's strong sense of obligation to their families, the inability to let that go—and the relationships with their husbands that are most crucial in the success of these marriages.

In addition, tensions generated by the differences between this local norm and Western cultural ideas of the family, which emphasise the conjugal unit more than connections with the natal family, are often experienced by women married to Westerners, their husbands and relatives. This study reveals diverse reasons that motivate women to engage in a transnational marriage, including failure of an earlier marriage, local norms and practices regarding gender and marriage, and fantasies about Western society and "modernity". However, one motivation is always at the forefront: the obligations shaped by the dutiful-daughter notion. This is the case especially for women from limited-resource backgrounds. This is not to say that these women marry foreigners solely because of material incentives. Rather, I argue that there are diverse sets of motivations at play, associated with women's positions within power hierarchies, or what Mahler and Pessar (2001) call "social locations". In the case of women who marry Westerners, their "social locations" are defined by socio-economic status, educational background, age, marital status and marriage prospects. For some women their low education and low income status "locates" them in a position in which transnational marriage becomes a viable alternative to fulfil their roles as dutiful daughters. Other women situated in different positions engage in this type of conjugal relation for different reasons; nevertheless, they always uphold dutiful-daughter obligations.

Explanations of Thai women's contributions to their natal households drawing on the cultural norm of *bun khun* and the daughter's filial duty have long been the focus of scholarly works in the fields of labour migration, marriage migration and prostitution (Buapan et al. 2005; Mills 1999; Muecke 1992; Panitee 2009; Rattana and Thompson 2013; Sirijit and Angeles 2013; Sukanya 1988; Thisa 1980). While my study builds on these works, I also look at the way in which women associate their involvement in transnational marriage with *bun khun* reciprocity and a daughter's filial duty as a strategy in legitimising their decision. In this light, this local norm provides women with room to fulfil their obligation to be good daughters while also breaking free from the local limitations relating to gender relations and marriage possibilities.

Most women married to *farang*, in addition to nurturing close ties with their rural family, maintain good connections within the local community, especially through material contributions to religious and social causes. Such contributions allow them to maintain a village-based identity and reaffirm a commitment to their natal community. These contributions testify to their financial achievement as shown by their new roles as community benefactors. These benevolent acts are appreciated by fellow villagers and enhance women's sense of belonging and bring them social prestige. Together with the fulfilment of the *bun khun* obligation, such acts combine to mitigate the ambivalent attitudes toward these women.

Beyond Material Relations and Romantic Love

The stories of women and their Western husbands presented in this book involve a variety of factors shaping the marriage decisions and experiences of both women and men. They demonstrate that marrying a *farang* is not just a shortcut to wealth for women, nor do men become involved in this type of marriage solely because of romantic love. Rather, the "logics of desire" compelling women and men to opt for transnational marriage constitute a complex set of diverse motivations that cannot be attributed to either economic reasons or emotional ties alone. The experiences and sentiments of women and men involved in transnational marriages reveal that they are continuously weighing such factors as economic opportunities and constraints, filial obligations, "love", imaginings, individual experiences and desires that intermingle and shape their marriage decisions and conjugal relationships. This study shows that such factors extend far beyond material relations and romantic love. The experiences of women and men reflect the ideas of Zelizer, in "connected lives" (2005), which argue that people are actively engaged in negotiating such combinations in constructing their social lives.

The intermingling of sex, money and desire for a long-term relationship is also manifested in the associations and relationships between male tourists and local women in Pattaya, a "space of opportunity and hope" where the transnational ties of many women from Na Dokmai were initiated. Most of the bar girls and freelancers I spoke with perceived their work as a vehicle to meet and make connections with Western men, hoping that an association would result in a serious relationship. Women's strategies and tactics in managing, negotiating and maintaining associations with their customers clearly show that these women's investment in these relationships went beyond a mere exchange of money for sex. This is a path through which many women have been able to change their lives and attain a relatively secure future for themselves and their dependents, despite fact that others have not been successful in doing so.

The motivations propelling women and men to look for a serious relationship and the factors shaping their interactions and social relations within various contexts—for example a "space of opportunity and hope", a conjugal unit, and the women's natal family and community—reflect the importance given to economic resources with their meanings extending beyond monetary value. Such material support provided by a Western partner to his wife, her parents, children and relatives represents an expression of "love", care and commitment. Similarly, bar girls view the gifts and money that tourist men give them as a sign of serious interest and care. The allowance and other material resources that women provide to their parents symbolise their gratefulness as dutiful daughters. Likewise, community contributions made by women signify their belonging, commitment and social recognition. These transactions, apart from their economic significance, also have social and symbolic meanings as they are embedded in local norms and values, thereby influencing the social relations, expectations and practices of people involved in transnational marriages and their relatives.

Most studies on inter- and transnational marriages both in Thai and Asian contexts are conceptualised in relation to colonial culture, militarisation, gendered imaginations and the discourses of modernity and tradition, as I have discussed in the preceding chapters. Insights into how economic opportunities and intimate relationships not only play a part in the "logics of desire" but also complicate these relationships and practices, and bring a new dimension to the existing body of literature on the subject.

Transnational Marriage and Perspectives on Transnational Studies

Drawing on the "migration-left behind" perspective (Toyota et al. 2007) that includes the wider social environment of the women, this study calls attention to other important players in the field—parents, extended family members and other villagers living in the women's natal community. The motives and actions of women's parents in transnational marriage processes highlight the active roles of the "left behind". The parents are not passive recipients who merely benefit from and are affected by financial and social remittances. The encouragement and support they give to their daughters are a testimony to their desire for a secure future for their daughters and grandchildren, as well as for themselves. It is the intention, determination, involvement and the high degree of agency of those staying behind that make transnational connections and marriages possible.

The involvement of others not directly engaged in these marriages has been noted in various works (Abelmann and Kim 2005; Freeman 2005; Wang and Chang 2002), which reveal the roles of marriage brokers and government policies, as well as the groom's and the bride's parents in facilitating or limiting transnational marriages. Observations on the ways in which these kinds of transnational relations have been realised reveal diverse groups of people remaining in sending communities who have influenced, managed and controlled transnational activities. These insights suggest that the issue of agency in transnational studies should not be conceptualised in relation to geographical mobility alone—looking at who moves and who stays. Rather, one should take into account the various actors who support, initiate and control decisions and practices to engage in transnational activities in the framework of what Massey calls the "power geometry" (1993). Massey reminds us that the point of concern is not only those who move and those who do not, but that those who do the moving may not necessarily be "in charge" of the process. In fact, those who do not move may influence decisions and actions in transnational processes, as shown in the actions of the women's parents described in this book.

Insights on the complexity of "migration-left behind" perspective on transnational marriage (and international migration) would be more complete by taking into account both important players and the multiple roles and responsibilities of women under these transnational intimate relations. On the conceptual level, the diverse roles that women play, as wives, workers, mothers, daughters and citizens—either unintended or deployed as self-conscious strategies—are analytical categories (Piper and Roces 2003) that have to be explored in relation to women's decisions, experiences, practices and relationships with other players.

Another significant point related to transnationalism concerns the ways in which sex work has been conceptualised, especially within transnational tourist spaces. By focusing on interactions and associations between tourist men and local women working in Pattaya, I found that both of the main approaches applied to the analysis of sex work—one focusing on women's victimisation and oppression, the other arguing for women's agency and viewing sex work exclusively in relation to economic transaction—are limited in capturing the life realities of the women whom I met. These women were proud of their contributions to their natal families and communities as well as to their children's development. Some even spoke of their "good" marriage and their genuine love for their *farang* partners. Their experiences point to the fact that an approach which considers sex work solely in terms of either exploitation or economic exchange overlooks how it is used as a means to a specific end that is meaningful for women (and their dependents) and how the boundaries between money, sex and the imagining of possibilities for a better life overlap and dissolve. This perspective intersects with a number of scholarly works discussed in the previous chapters.

Thus, I propose a more nuanced approach in analysing sex work. By "more nuanced", I suggest looking at the place of sex work in a transnational marriage trajectory rather than considering this profession exclusively from a purely sexual slavery-oriented or economic perspective. This approach might serve as a useful tool to capture the realities of women's lives and to understand how women make sense of their own lives on their own terms. Sex work, in other words, is interwoven with a multitude of social relations. Therefore, a purely sex work or sexual slavery-oriented perspective looking at sexual commerce in isolation distorts the position of sex work in a transnational marriage trajectory.

Local Dynamics: Material Improvement and Gender and Class Challenges

In focusing on the women's natal village, this book demonstrates that transnational marriages represent more than women's strategies in coping with family crises and asymmetrical gender relations, or in fulfilling their personal desires. These marriages also serve as a conduit for women's natal families and rural residents to be involved in the interactions between local particulars and global processes. The material improvement in the village with the trappings of modernity such as urban-style houses, cars, large grocery stores, etc. together with improvements in public places such as schools, temples and communal places, are largely funded by mixed couples. Some families in Na Dokmai depend largely on financial support from their daughters or nieces to make ends meet. For others, remittances bring new wealth to be invested locally. Some people are able to travel to foreign countries for the first time to visit their daughters. Through regular contacts with their daughters, nieces, mothers and friends living in various parts of the world, as well as through modern telecommunications, many villagers, young and old, are instantly connected to the world beyond their home village and homeland. Along with economic changes are transformations in cultural norms and values that influence the social lives of local people.

While material improvements are easily observed, social and cultural transformations are often subtler, profound and complex. Transnational marriages could strengthen or challenge local norms and practices in various ways. The local norm of female obligations to parents is strengthened, as the marriage allows women to fulfil the Thai value of "dutiful daughters". Through these marriages women also extend their domestic roles to "global villages" in various parts of the world where they live with their husbands. Such practices reinforce the constructions of (Thai) femininity. Indeed, the idea of "desired partner" that developed upon the notion of "dutiful daughters" underpins the rejection of local men as unfit and thus legitimates women's engagement in transnational marriage. This emerging idea is a powerful one and it works for both women who have experienced failed marriages and for unmarried young women who prefer to have a Western husband. Local men's reactions to this situation reflect the pressure they feel. Thus, I posit that women's marriage alternatives outside of marrying locally challenge gendered power relations around the discourses of marriage and sexuality, thus placing local men in a vulnerable position.

Studies on cross-cultural and transnational marriages often discuss gendered power relations, women's negotiations and gender reconfigurations in the context of women's natal societies (Bélanger et al. 2010; Panitee 2009; Ratana 2010; Sirijit 2009). My research shares with the existing works on the issue of gender alteration in women's natal communities. In addition, it also reveals another dimension of local dynamics by focusing on the issue of class. The local transformations generated by transnational marriages of village women have taken place in the realm of social order and the village hierarchy. This dynamic is the emergence of a new "class" defined by improved economic well-being, distinctive lifestyles, and the social recognition and prestige that women with Western partners obtain by fulfilling social obligations as dutiful daughters and making contributions to their home villages. Drawing on Weberian-Bourdieuan social stratification analyses emphasising consumption in relation to status and "honour" groups (Weber 1947) as well as taste, manifested through consumption preferences and lifestyles, as a cultural and symbolic marker for class (Bourdieu 1984), I argue that women married to *farang* make up a new "class", though not a class in the Marxist sense. This emerging "class" accentuates class divisions in the village and challenges the well-to-do and well educated who feel or experience less importance in the changing hierarchical village structure. The overturning of the old village (and urban) elites runs parallel to Keyes's view on "cosmopolitan villagers" in which he points out the relative decline of the old "rooted" village elite as a part of ongoing social transformations in contemporary Isan society and in Thailand in general (Keyes 2014).

"*Mia farang*" as a class is inherently a complex social category. These women are challenging the existing village socio-economic hierarchy, making inroads into the ranks of villagers in privileged positions. This newly acquired status is something that these women and their relatives are proud of. Yet, local attitudes towards them are ambiguous. Despite their diverse backgrounds, women married to Western men are usually stereotyped. In contexts beyond the village, negative perceptions of them are even more obvious. Such perceptions have to do with the marginal status of Isan in the national context and the construction of "Thainess" as discussed in Chapter Two. Although a number of authors have observed a decrease in such social stigma and negative attitudes (Panitee 2009; Ratana 2010; Weisman 2000), I posit that the image of women married to Westerners is at best ambiguous and complex. Negative stereotypes associate these women with prostitution under the rubric of *mia chao* or tourist destinations catering to the sex industry. Moreover, official and academic discourses often treat transnational marriages as disguised trafficking operations and a threat to local traditions and the family institution. Paradoxically, the positive image of these women is built on fulfilling their filial obligations as dutiful daughters. For village leaders and local government staff, these women and their husbands are strategic resources for the development of their community. The ambiguities generated by such perceptions and attitudes create tensions and complicate the relationships and practices developed under this type of marital relationship, especially among these women, their spouses, local kin and the people within their village and beyond.

The ongoing transformations in Na Dokmai brought about by transnational marriages are realities with which the villagers have to come to terms. The current popularity of these marriages in Na Dokmai highlights the every day experiences of women married to *farang* men and village residents in negotiating local and global articulations. Such experiences may be shared by residents of other communities in Thailand and elsewhere as transnational marriage and migration have become more visible in many parts of the world in recent decades. This study reveals that any attempt to understand such marriages and their consequences would be incomplete if one failed to take into account the diversity of local and global processes that make these marriages imaginable and realisable, and the various ways in which people have engaged in and negotiated these relationships. These processes, though diverse and complex, are historically and culturally specific, thereby foregrounding the importance of their context.

The stories of these women, their parents, their husbands and people living in their natal villages highlighted in this book remind us that the phenomenon of transnational marriage is far more complex than a simple shortcut to wealth. Rather, these marriages are situated in the processes of social transition and reproduction in the face of local-global encounters, in which gender, class, lifestyles, norms and practices regarding marriage and family are put to severe test, along with imaginings about a better life for all concerned.

Interviewed Cases

Table 1: Interviewed Cases Divided by Sex

Category	Female	Male	Total	Remarks
1. The Village Setting				
Women married to *farang* husbands	26	–	26	1 woman is from other village. 18 women are currently in a relationship with a Western partner. 7 women have ended their relationships.
Women's parents	13	3	16	
Women's siblings	4	1	5	
Village residents	11	5	16	1 man and 2 women are from the village next to Na Dokmai.
Village leaders/ school teachers/ government officers	7	5	12	Some of the village school teachers and local government officers live in other villages, but have worked in Na Dokmai for some years.
Western husbands	–	11	11	2 men live with their wives in other villages.
Sub-total	**61**	**25**	**86**	
2. Pattaya				
Bar girls	7	–	7	3 women are from Na Dokmai.
Sub-total	**7**	**–**	**7**	
Total	**68**	**25**	**93**	

Background Information of Women Married to *Farang* Men and Their Husbands in Na Dokmai in 2008

Table 1: Ages of Women Married to *Farang* Men and Ages of Their Husbands

Age	Women		Men	
	Number	**Per cent**	**Number**	**Per cent**
18–20	2	1.2	0	0.0
21–30	29	18.2	6	3.8
31–40	85	53.6	25	15.7
41–50	28	17.7	46	29.0
51–60	12	7.5	31	19.5
61–70	2	1.2	24	15.1
More than 70	0	0.0	8	5.0
NA	1	0.6	19	11.9
Total	**159**	**100.0**	**159**	**100.0**

Table 2: Education of the Women

Level of Education	Number	Per cent
Po 4 (grade 4)	39	24.5
Po 6 (grade 6)	65	41.0
Mo 3 (grade 9)	31	19.5
Mo 6 (grade 12)	4	2.5
Po Wo Cho (Vocational education: 3 years after grade 9)	4	2.5
Po Wo So (Vocational education: 5 years after grade 9)	1	0.6
Bachelor's degree	3	1.9
Master's degree	1	0.6
NA	11	6.9
Total	**159**	**100.0**

Table 3: Settlement Locations (places where women have settled)

Location	Number	Per cent
Overseas: mainly partners' home countries	123	77.4
Na Dokmai	25	15.7
Thailand: outside Na Dokmai	11	6.9
Total	**159**	**100.0**

Table 4: Regions and Countries of Origin of the Foreign Husbands

Regions/Countries	Number (159)	Per cent
Europe	*130*	
Germany	30	
Sweden	21	
England	18	
Norway	12	
Italy	10	
France	7	
Denmark	6	*81.8*
Austria	6	
The Netherlands	5	
Switzerland	4	
Belgium	4	
Finland	3	
Iceland	2	
Luxemburg	1	
Greece	1	
US	*14*	8.8
Asia	*11*	
Japan	6	
Hong Kong	2	*6.9*
Singapore	1	
Korea	2	
Australia	*4*	2.5

Table 5: Occupations of *Farang* Husbands

Occupation	Number	Per cent
"Blue collar" work*	63	39.6
Professional work**	30	18.9
Business/self-employed***	9	5.7
Study	1	0.6
No job	1	0.6
Pensioner	20	12.6
NA	35	22.0
Total	**159**	**100.0**

Notes:
* "Blue collar" work includes professions such as car drivers, construction workers, mechanics, car mechanics, plumbers, chefs and salesmen.
** Professional work includes being an engineer, a policeman, an architect, a medical doctor, a language teacher, an accountant or a computer technician. These jobs require college education.
*** Business/self-employed includes working as a construction sub-contractor, running a restaurant or house-renting business and agriculture.

Glossary of Thai Terms

Note: Thai words do not indicate plurals in their spelling: so, for example, *mia* can mean both *wife* and *wives*.

bap	Buddhist demerit
bai-si su-khwan	soul-trying ceremony; traditional Isan rite of blessing
bun	Buddhist merit; moral merit
bun khun	debt of gratitude, especially between parents and children or patron and client
du thuk	to look down upon
faen	boy- or girlfriend(s)
farang	Westerner or white men/women
karma	the Buddhist concept explaining a result of actions in present and past lives; good actions earn moral merit (*bun*), bad/wrong actions gain demerit (*bap*)
kathin	a Buddhist ritual organised within 30 days of the end of the monks' three-month rainy season retreat (*phansa*)
khwam charoen	progress; often an emphasis on material progress
luk khrueng	children of mixed Thai-Western parents
mia/phanraya	a wife
mia chao	a "hired wife"
mia farang/ phanraya farang	a Thai wife of a Western man
mia noi	a minor wife
mo lam	an Isan folk performance including singing and dancing
mu baan	village(s)
pha pa	a Buddhist ritual to offer robes and objects for the monks' personal use such as soap, medicine, packaged drinks, toilet paper and cash gifts

rak tae	"real love"
rai	a measure of land area equal to approximately one-sixth of a hectare: 6 *rai* equals 1 hectare
sami/phua	husband(s)
saphai	daughter(s)-in-law
sinsot	bride payment which is given by the grooms to the bride's family
Songkran	a Thai festival held on 13–15 April, celebrating the traditional New Year; the most obvious activity is the throwing of water, and it is known as the water festival
taeng-ngan	marriage
thansamai	modern, up-to-date

Bibliography

Abdelhady, Dalia. 2006. "Beyond Home/Host Networks: Forms of Solidarity among Lebanese Immigrants in a Global Era". *Identities: Global Studies in Culture and Power* 13: 427–53.

Abelmann, Nancy and Hyunhee Kim. 2005. "A Failed Attempt at Transnational Marriage: Material Citizenship in a Globalizing South Korea". In *Cross-Border Marriages: Gender and Mobility in Transnational Asia*, ed. Nicole Constable. Philadelphia, PA: University of Pennsylvania Press, pp. 101–23.

Akin Rabibhadana. 1984. "Kinship, Marriage and the Thai Social System". In *Perspectives on the Thai Marriage*, ed. Apichat Chamratrithirong. Bangkok: Mahidol University, pp. 1–27.

_____. 1996. *The Organization of Thai Society in the Early Bangkok Period 1782–1873*. Bangkok: Bhumipanya Foundation and Thai Association of Qualitative Researchers.

Amara Phongsaphit. 1990. *Changing Family Pattern in Thailand*. Bangkok: Social Research Institute, Chulalongkorn University (monograph).

Anchalee Singhanetra-Renard and Nitaya Prabhudhanitisarn. 1992. "Changing Socio-economic Roles of Thai Women and Their Migration". In *Gender and Migration in Developing Countries*, ed. Sylvia Chant. London and New York: Belhaven Press, pp. 154–73.

Andaya, Barbara W. 1998. "From Temporary Wife to Prostitute: Sexuality and Economic Change in Early Modern Southeast Asia". *Journal of Women's History* 9(4): 11–34.

Appadurai, Arjun. 1996. *Modernity at Large: Cultural Dimensions of Globalization*. Minneapolis, MN: University of Minnesota Press.

Askew, Marc. 2009. "Sex and the Sacred: Sojourners and Visitors in the Making of the Southern Thai Borderland". In *Centering the Margin: Agency and Narrative in Southeast Asian Borderlands*, ed. Alexander Horstmann and Reed L. Wadley. New York: Berghahn Books, pp. 177–206.

Basch, Linda, Nina G. Schiller, and Cristina S. Blanc. 1994. *Nations Unbound: Transnational Projects, Postcolonial Predicaments, and Deterritorialized Nation-States*. Amsterdam: Gordon & Breach Science Publishers.

Bélanger, Danièle, Hye-Kyung Lee, and Hong-Zen Wang. 2011. "Ethnic Diversity and Statistics in East Asia: 'Foreign Bride' Survey in Taiwan and South Korea". *Ethnic and Racial Studies* 33(6): 1108–30.

Bélanger, Danièle, Tran G. Linh, Le B. Duong, and Khuat T. Hong. 2010. "From Farmer's Daughters to Foreign Wives: Marriage Migration and Gender in Sending Communities of Vietnam". In *Asian Gender under Construction: Global Reconfiguration of Human Reproduction*, ed. Emiko Ochiai. Kyoto: International Research Center for Japanese Studies, pp. 157–80.

Bencha Yoddumnern-Attig. 1992. "Conjugal and Parental Roles: A Behavioral Look into the Past and Present". In *Changing Roles and Statuses of Women in Thailand: A*

Documentary Assessment, ed. Bencha Yoddumnern-Attig, Kerry Richter, Amara Soonthorndhada, Chanya Sethaput, and Anthony Pramulratana. Nakhon Pathom, Thailand: Institute for Population and Social Research, Mahidol University, pp. 25–35.

Bishop, Ryan and Lillian S. Robinson. 1998. *Night Market: Sexual Cultures and the Thai Economic Miracle*. New York and London: Routledge.

Boonyong Chunsuvimol. 2004. "Multi-Racial Society: The Case of Chinese in Thailand". Presented at the Third International Symposium on Toward a Sustainable Society, 9 July, Tokyo University.

Bourdieu, Pierre. 1984. *Distinction: A Social Critique of the Judgment of Taste*, trans. by Richard Nice. London: Routledge.

_____. 1986. "The Forms of Capital". In *Handbook of Theory and Research for the Sociology of Education*, ed. J. Richardson. New York: Greenwood Press, pp. 241–58.

Bowie, Katherine. 2008. "Standing in the Shadows: Of Matrilocality and the Role of Women in a Village Election in Northern Thailand". *American Ethnologist* 40(1): 136–53.

Brennan, Denise. 2004. *What's Love Got to Do with It?: Transnational Desires and Sex Tourism in the Dominican Republic*. Durham and London: Duke University Press.

Buapan Promphakphing, Asok Phonbamrung, Nilwadee Promphakphing, Suphawadee Bunchua, Sumalai Phuangket, Kitiyawadee Sida, Phonphen Pankham, Phattharaphron Sriphrom, and Petsaraphorn Plangsaeng. 2005. *Kan taeng-ngan kham watthanatham khong phuying nai chonnabot Isan* [Cross-Cultural Marriage of Women in the Northeast of Thailand]. Khon Kaen, Thailand: Faculty of Humanities and Social Sciences, Khon Kaen University.

Cabezas, Amalia L. 2004. "Between Love and Money: Sex, Tourism, and Citizenship in Cuba and the Dominican Republic". *Journal of Women in Culture and Society* 29(4): 987–1015.

_____. 2009. *Economics of Desire: Sex and Tourism in Cuba and the Dominican Republic*. Philadelphia, PA: Temple University Press.

Cameron, Deborah. 1998. "Gender, Language, and Discourse: A Review Essay". *Signs* 23(4): 945–73.

Chanpen Saengtienchai, John Knodel, Mark VanLandingham, and Anthony Pramualratana. 1999. "'Prostitutes are Better than Lovers': Wives' Views on the Extramarital Sexual Behavior of Thai Men". In *Genders and Sexualities in Modern Thailand*, ed. Peter A. Jackson and Nerida M. Cook. Chiang Mai, Thailand: Silkworm Books, pp. 78–92.

Chapkis, Wendy. 1997. *Live Sex Acts: Women Performing Erotic Labor*. New York: Routledge.

Chatthip Natsupha. 1984. *Setthakit muban Thai nai adit* [Thai Villages' Economy in the Past]. Bangkok: Sangsan Press.

Chavivun Prachuabmoh. 1985. "The Role of Religious and Economic in Decision Making: The Case of Thai/Malay Women". In *Anuson Walter Vella*, ed. Ronald Renard. Honolulu, HI: Center for Asian and Pacific Studies, University of Hawaii at Manoa, pp. 295–315.

Cheng, Sealing. 2010. *On the Move for Love: Migrant Entertainers and the U.S. Military in South Korea*. Philadelphia, PA: University of Pennsylvania Press.

Cheng, Yi'En, Brenda S.A. Yeoh, and Juan Zhang. 2015. "Still 'Breadwinners' and 'Providers': Singaporean Husbands, Money and Masculinity in Transnational Marriage". *Gender, Place and Culture: A Journal of Feminist Geography* 22(6): 867–83. doi: 10.1080/0966369X.2014.917282.

Cohen, Erik. 1971. "Arab Boys and Tourist Girls in a Mixed Jewish-Arab Community". *International Journal of Comparative Sociology* 12: 217–33.

_____. 1996. *Thai Tourism: Hill Tribes, Islands and Open-Ended Prostitution*. Bangkok: White Lotus Press.

_____. 2003. "Transnational Marriage in Thailand: The Dynamics of Extreme Heterogamy". In *Sex and Tourism: Journeys of Romance, Love, and Lust*, ed. Thomas G. Bauer and Bob McKercher. New York: The Haworth Hospitality Press, pp. 57–82.

Constable, Nicole. 2003. *Romance on a Global Stage: Pen Pals, Virtual Ethnography, and "Mail-Order" Marriages*. Berkeley, CA: University of California Press.

_____, ed. 2005a. *Cross-Border Marriages: Gender and Mobility in Transnational Asia*. Philadelphia, PA: University of Pennsylvania Press.

_____. 2005b. "Introduction: Cross-Border Marriages, Gendered Mobility, and Global Hypergamy". In *Cross-Border Marriages: Gender and Mobility in Transnational Asia*, ed. Nicole Constable. Philadelphia, PA: University of Pennsylvania Press, pp. 1–16.

_____. 2009. "The Commodification of Intimacy: Marriage, Sex and Reproductive Labor". *Annual Review of Anthropology* 38: 46–64.

Cox, Oliver C. 1950. "Max Weber on Social Stratification: A Critique". *American Sociological Review* 15(2): 223–7.

Crawford, Mary. 2003. "Gender and Humor in Social Context". *Journal of Pragmatics* 35: 1413–30.

Dahles, Heidi. 2009. "Romance and Sex Tourism". In *Tourism in Southeast Asia: Challenges and New Directions*, ed. Michael Hitchcock, Victor T. King, and Michael Parnwell. Copenhagen: NIAS Press, pp. 222–35.

Dararat Mattariganond. 2007. "Kan taeng-ngan kham watthanatham: 'Thai' kap 'farang' nai prawatsat sangkhom sayam" [Cross-cultural Marriage: "Thai" and "*farang*" in Siamese Social History]. In *Kan taeng-ngan kham wathanatham: Kan sueksa sathanaphap ong khwam ru* [Cross-cultural Marriage: A Study of a Stage of Knowledge], ed. Patcharin Lapanun, Dararat Mattariganond, and Yaowalak Aphichatvullop. Khon Kaen, Thailand: Khon Kaen University, Center for Research on Plurality in the Mekong Region, pp. 12–56.

_____. 2009. "Nayobairat lae kan taeng-ngan kham watthanatham nai sangkhom sayam" [State Policy and Cross-cultural Marriage in Siamese Social History]. Presented at RDI Symposium, Research and Development Institute, Khon Kaen University, 24–26 August, Khon Kaen, Thailand.

Davidson, Julia O'Connell. 1995. "British Sex Tourist in Thailand". In *(Hetero) Sexual Politics*, ed. Mary Maynard and June Purvis. Bristol: Taylor & Francis, pp. 42–65.

De Albuquerque, Klaus. 1998. "Sex, Beach Boys and Female Tourists in the Caribbean". *Sexuality & Culture* 2: 87–111.

De Young, John E. 1958. *Village Life in Modern Thailand*. Berkeley, CA: University of California Press.

Doezema, Jo. 1998. "Forced to Choose Beyond the Voluntary vs. Forced Prostitution Dichotomy". In *Global Sex Workers: Rights, Resistance and Redefinition*, ed. Kamala Kempadoo and Jo Doezema. New York and London: Routledge, pp. 34–50.

Ehrenreich, Babrara and Arlie R. Hochschild, eds. 2002. *Global Woman, Nannies, Maids, and Sex Workers in the New Economy*. New York: Henry Holt and Company.

Enloe, Cynthia. 2000. *Bananas, Beaches and Bases*. Berkeley, CA: University of California Press.

Faier, Lieba. 2009. *Intimate Encounters: Filipina Women and the Remaking of Rural Japan*. Berkeley, CA: University of California Press.

Fouron, Georges and Nina G. Schiller. 2001. "All in the Family: Gender, Transnational Migration, and the Nation-State". *Identities* 7(4): 539–82.

Fox, Robin. 1967. *Kinship and Marriage*. Baltimore, MD: Penguin Books.

Freeman, Caren. 2005. "Marrying Up and Marrying Down: The Paradoxes of Marital Mobility for Chosonjok Brides in South Korea". In *Cross-Border Marriages: Gender and Mobility in Transnational Asia*, ed. Nicole Constable. Philadelphia, PA: University of Pennsylvania Press, pp. 80–100.

Garrick, Damien. 2005. "Excuses, Excuses: Rationalisations of Western Sex Tourists in Thailand". *Current Issues in Tourism* 8(6): 497–509.

Glazer, Nathan and Daniel P. Moynihan. 1963. *Beyond the Melting Pot: The Negroes, Puerto Ricans, Jews, Italians and Irish of New York City*. Cambridge, MA: MIT Press.

Glytsos, Nicholas P. 2002. "The Role of Migrant Remittances in Development: Evidence from Mediterranean Countries". *International Migration* 40(1): 5–26.

Gozdziak, Elzbieta M. and Elizabeth A. Collett. 2005. "Research on Human Trafficking in North America: A Review of Literature". In *Data and Research on Human Trafficking: A Global Survey*, ed. Frank Laczko and Elzbieta Gozdziak. Geneva: International Organization for Migration, pp. 99–128.

Guarnizo, Luis E. and Michael P. Smith. 1998. "The Location of Transnationalism". In *Transnationalism from Below*, ed. Michael P. Smith and Luis E. Guarnizo. New Brunswick: Transaction Publishers, pp. 3–34.

Hannerz, Ulf. 1998. "Transnational Research". In *Handbook of Methods in Cultural Anthropology*, ed. H. Russell Bernard. Walnut Creek, CA: Alta Mira Press, pp. 235–56.

Harrison, Rachel. 1999. "The Madonna and the Whore: Self/'Other' Tensions in the Characterization of the Prostitute by Thai Female Authors". In *Genders and Sexualities in Modern Thailand*, ed. Peter A. Jackson and Nerida M. Cook. Chiang Mai, Thailand: Silkworm Books, pp. 154–67.

Hendry, Joy. 2003. "An Ethnographer in the Global Arena: Globography Perhaps?" *Global Networks* 3(4): 497–513.

Hirsch, Philip. 1993. "Introduction: The Village Revisited". In *The Village in Perspective: Community and Locality in Rural Thailand*, ed. Philip Hirsh. Chiang Mai, Thailand: Social Research Institute, Chiang Mai University, pp. 1–8.

Hutchison, E.W. 1985. *Adventurers in Siam in the Seventeenth Century*. Bangkok: D.D. Books.

Ingram, James. 1971. *Economic Change in Thailand 1850–1970*. Palo Alto, CA: Stanford University Press.

Ishii, Sari K., ed. 2016a. *Marriage Migration in Asia, Emerging Minorities at the Frontiers of Nation-State*. Singapore: NUS Press.

_____. 2016b. "Marriage Migrants as Multi-marginalized Transnational Diaspora". In *Marriage Migration in Asia, Emerging Minorities at the Frontiers of Nation-State*, ed. Sari K. Ishii. Singapore: NUS Press, pp. 1–26.

Jiemin, Bao. 2003. "The Gendered Biopolitics of Marriage and Immigration: A Study of Pre-1949 Chinese Immigrants in Thailand". *Journal of Southeast Asian Studies* 34(1): 127–51.

Jones, Gavin W. 2012. "Marriage, Migration in Asia: An Introduction". *Asian and Pacific Migration Journal* 12(3): 287–316.

Jones, Gavin W. and Hsiu-hua Shen. 2008. "International Marriage in East and Southeast Asia: Trends and Research Emphases". *Citizenship Studies* 12(1): 9–25.

Kearney, Michael. 1995. "The Local and The Global: The Anthropology of Globalization and Transnationalism". *Annual Review of Anthropology* 24: 547–65.

Keely, Charles B. and Bao Nga Tran. 1989. "Remittances from Labor Migration: Evaluations, Performance and Implications". *International Migration Review* 23(3): 500–25.

Kempadoo, Kamala. 1998. "Introduction: Globalizing Sex Workers' Rights". In *Global Sex Workers: Rights, Resistance and Redefinition*, ed. Kamala Kempadoo and Jo Doezema. New York and London: Routledge, pp. 1–28.

Keyes, Charles F. 1967. "Isan: Regionalism in Northeastern Thailand". Cornell Thailand Interim Report Series No. 10, Data Paper No. 65, Southeast Asian Program, Department of Asian Studies, Cornell University, Ithaca, New York.

_____. 1976. "In Search of Land: Village Formation in the Central Chi River Valley, Northeast Thailand". *Contributions to Asian Studies* 9: 45–63.

_____. 1984. "Mother or Mistress but Never a Monk: Buddhist Notions of Female Gender in Rural Thailand". *American Anthropologist* 11(2): 223–41.

_____. 2014. *Finding Their Voice: Northeastern Villagers and the Thai State*. Chiang Mai, Thailand: Silkworm Books.

King, Russell, Mirela Dalipaj, and Nicola Mai. 2006. "Gendering Migration and Remittances: Evidence from London and Northern Albania". *Population, Space and Place* 12: 409–34.

Kirsch, Thomas. 1982. "Buddhism, Sex-Roles and the Thai Economy". In *Women of Southeast Asia*, ed. Penney Van Estrick. DeKalb, IL: Northern Illinois University, Center for Southeast Asian Studies, pp. 16–41.

_____. 1985. "Text and Context: Buddhist Sex Roles/Culture of Gender Revisited". *American Ethnologist* 12: 302–20.

Knodel, John, Chanpen Saengtienchai, Mark VanLandingham, and Rachel Lucus. 1999. "Sexuality, Sexual Experience and the Good Spouse: Views of Married Thai Men and Women". In *Genders and Sexualities in Modern Thailand*, ed. Peter A. Jackson and Nerida M. Cook. Chiang Mai, Thailand: Silkworm Books, pp. 93–113.

Kyle, David. 2000. *Transnational Peasants*. Baltimore, MD: The Johns Hopkins University Press.

Levitt, Peggy. 1996. "Social Remittances: A Conceptual Tool for Understanding Migration and Development". Cambridge, MA: Working Paper Series No. 96.04, Harvard Center for Population and Development Studies, Harvard University.

_____. 2001. *Transnational Villagers*. Berkeley, CA: University of California Press.

Levitt, Peggy, Josh DeWind, and Steven Vertovec. 2003. "International Perspectives on Transnational Migration: An Introduction". *International Migration Review* 37(3): 565–75.

Lightfoot, Paul and Theodore Fuller. 1984. "Circular Migration in Northeast Thailand". In *Strategies and Structures in Thai Society*, ed. Han ten Brummelhuis and Jeremy H. Kemp. Amsterdam: Anthropological-Sociological Centre, University of Amsterdam, pp. 85–93.

Lindholm, Charles. 2006. "Romantic Love and Anthropology". *Etnofoor* XIX(1): 5–22.

Long, Millard F. 1966. "Economic Development in Northeast Thailand: Problems and Prospects". *Asian Survey* 6(7) :355–61.

Lyttleton, Chris. 1994. "The Good People of Isan: Commercial Sex in Northeast Thailand". *The Australian Journal of Anthropology* 5(3): 257–79.

_____. 2000. *Endangered Relations: Negotiating Sex and AIDS in Thailand*. Bangkok: White Lotus Press.

Maher, Kristen H. and Megan Lafferty. 2014. "White Migrants Masculinities in Thailand and the Paradoxes of Western Privilege". *Social & Cultural Geography* 15(4): 427–48.

Mahler, Sarah J. 1998. "Theoretical and Empirical Contributions toward a Research Agenda for Transnationalism". In *Transnationalism from Below*, ed. Michael P. Smith and Luis E. Guarnizo. New Brunswick: Transaction Publishers, pp. 64–103.

Mahler, Sarah J. and Patricia R. Pessar. 2001. "Gendered Geographies of Power: Analyzing Gender across Transnational Spaces". *Identities* 7(4): 441–59.

Manderson, Lenore. 1992. "Public Sex Performances in Patpong and Explorations of the Edges of Imagination". *The Journal of Sex Research* 29(4): 451–75.

Manderson, Lenore and Margaret Jolly. 1997. "Sites of Desire/Economies of Pleasure in Asia and the Pacific". In *Sites of Desire, Economies of Pleasure: Sexuality in Asia and the Pacific*, ed. Lenore Manderson and Margaret Jolly. Chicago and London: University of Chicago Press, pp. 1–26.

Marcus, George E. 1995. "Ethnography in/of the World System: The Emergence of Multi-Sited Ethnography". *Annual Review of Anthropology* 24: 95–117.

Massey, Doreen. 1993. "Power-Geometry and Progressive Sense of Place". In *Mapping the Futures: Local Cultures, Global Change*, ed. John Bird, Barry Curtis, Tim Putnam, George Robertson, and Lisa Tickner. London and New York: Routledge, pp. 60–70.

McKay, Deirdre. 2003. "Filipinas in Canada—De-skilling as a Push toward Marriage". In *Wife or Worker? Asian Women and Migration*, ed. Nicola Piper and Mina Roces. Lanham: Rowman & Littlefield Publishers, pp. 23–51.

Mills, Mary B. 1998. "Gendered Encounters with Modernity: Labour Migrants and Marriage Choices in Contemporary Thailand". *Identities* 5(3): 301–34.

_____. 1999. *Thai Women in the Global Labor Force*. New Brunswick: Rutgers University Press.

Mizuno, Koichi. 1978 "The Social Organization of Rice-Growing Villages". In *Thailand: A Rice-Growing Society*, ed. Yoneo Ishii. Honolulu, HI: University Press of Hawaii, pp. 83–114.

Muecke, Marjorie A. 1992. "Mother Sold Food, Daughter Sells Her Body: The Cultural Continuity of Prostitution". *Social Science and Medicine* 35(7): 891–901.

Mulder, Niels. 1985. *Everyday Life in Thailand: An Interpretation*. Bangkok: Duang Kamol Publication.

Mulkay, Michael. 1988. *On Humour: Its Nature and its Place in Modern Society*. Cambridge and New York: Polity Press.

Murray, Alison. 1998. "Debt-Bondage and Trafficking: Don't Believe the Hype". In *Global Sex Workers: Rights, Resistance and Redefinition*, ed. Kamala Kempadoo and Jo Doezema. New York and London: Routledge, pp. 51–64.

Nakamatsu, Tomoko. 2005. "Complex Power and Diverse Responses: Transnational Marriage Migration and Women's Agency". In *The Agency of Women in Asia*, ed. Marshall Lyn Parker. Singapore: Marshall Cavendish Academic, pp. 158–81.

National Economic and Social Development Board (NESDB). 2004. "A Survey of Thai Women Marrying Foreigners in Northeast Thailand". National Economic and Social Development Board, Thailand. Unpublished paper (in Thai).

National Statistical Office (NSO). 2003. *Agricultural Census Survey, Northeastern Region*. Bangkok: National Statistical Office, Ministry of Information and Communication Technology. Monograph (in Thai).

Nencel, Lorraine. 2001. *Ethnography and Prostitution in Peru*. London: Pluto Press.

Odzer, Cleo. 1990. "Patpong Prostitution: Its Relationship to, and Effect on the Position of Women in Thai Society". PhD dissertation, Department of Political Science, University of Michigan, Ann Arbor.

Ong, Aihwa. 1985. "Industrialization and Prostitution in Southeast Asian". *Southeast Asia Chronicle* 96: 2–6.

Ooms, Arno. 2002. "Siamese Brides". Presented at the 8th International Conference on Thai Studies, 9–12 January, Nakhon Phanom, Thailand.

Ortner, Sherry. 2006. *Anthropology and Social Theory: Culture, Power and the Acting Subject*. Durham, NC: Duke University Press.

Oxfeld, Ellen. 2005. "Cross-Border Hypergamy? Marriage Exchanges in a Transnational Hakka Community". In *Cross-Border Marriages: Gender and Mobility in Transnational Asia*, ed. Nicole Constable. Philadelphia, PA: University of Pennsylvania Press, pp. 17–33.

Panitee Suksomboon. 2009. "Thai Migrant Women in the Netherlands: Cross-Cultural Marriages and Families". PhD dissertation, Faculty of Social and Behavioural Sciences, Leiden University.

Park, Robert E. 1928. "Human Migration and the Marginal Man". *The American Journal of Sociology* 33: 881–93.

Parreñas, Rhacle. 2011. *Illicit Flirtations: Labor, Migration and Sex Trafficking in Tokyo*. Palo Alto, CA: Stanford University Press.

Pasuk Phongpaichit. 1982. *From Peasant Girls to Bangkok Masseuses*. Geneva: International Labour Office.

Pasuk Phongpaichit and Chris Baker. 1995. *Thailand: Economy and Politics*. Kuala Lumpur, Oxford and New York: Oxford University Press.

Pataya Ruenkaew. 1999. "Marriage Migration of Thai Women to Germany". Presented at the 7th International Conference on Thai Studies, 4–8 July, Amsterdam.

_____. 2002. "The Transnational Prostitution of Thai Women to Germany: A Variety of Transnational Labour Migration?" In *Transnational Prostitution: Changing Patterns in Global Context*, ed. Susanne Thorbek and Bandana Pattanaik. London and New York: Zed Books, pp. 69–85.

Patcharin Lapanun. 2007. "Dynamics and Research Approaches: A Study of Cross-Cultural Marriage of Women in Esaan Society". *Journal of Mekong Societies* 2(3): 1–36.

_____. 2012. "It's Not Just About Money: Transnational Marriages of Isan Women". *Journal of Mekong Societies* 8(3): 1–28.

_____. 2018. "Masculinity, Marriage and Migration: *Farang* Migrant Men in Thailand". *Asian Journal of Social Science* 48(1): 111–31.

Piper, Nicola and Mina Roces, eds. 2003. *Wife or Worker? Asian Women and Migration*, Lanhan: Rowman & Littlefield Publishers.

Piper, Nicola. 2009. "The Complex Interconections of the Migration-Development Nexus: A Social Perspective". *Population, Place and Space* 19: 93–101.

Porpora, Douglas and Mah Hui Lim. 1987. "The Political Factors of Migration to Bangkok". *Journal of Contemporary Asia* 17(1): 76–89.

Portes, Alejandro. 1997. "Immigration Theory for a New Century: Some Problems and Opportunities". *International Migration Review* 31(4): 799–825.

Portes, Alejandro, Luis E. Guarnizo, and Patricia Landdolt. 1999. "The Study of Transnationalism: Pitfalls and Promises of the Emergent Research Field". *Ethnic and Racial Studies* 22(2): 217–37.

Potter, Sulamith H. 1977. *Family Life in a Northern Thai Village: A Study in the Structural Significance of Women*. Berkeley, CA: University of California Press.

Pramualratana, Anthony. 1992. "The Impact of Societal Change and Role of the Old in a Rural Community in Thailand". In *Changing Roles and Statuses of Women in Thailand: A Documentary Assessment*, ed. Bencha Yoddumnern-Attig, Kerry Richter, Amara Soonthorndhada, Chanya Sethaput, and Anthony Pramulratana. Nakhon Pathom: Institute for Population and Social Research, Mahidol University, pp. 44–54.

Ratana Tosakul. 2010. "Cross-Cultural Marriages: Experiences of Village Women from Northeastern Thailand with Western Men". In *Asian Cross-border Marriage Migration: Demographic Patterns and Social Issue*, ed. Wen-Shan Yang and Melody Chia-Wen Lu. Amsterdam: Amsterdam University Press, pp. 179–200.

Rattana Jongwiliawan and Eric C. Thompson. 2013. "Thai Wives in Singapore and Transnational Patriarchy". *Gender, Place & Culture* 20(3): 363–81.

Reynolds, Craig J. 1999. "On the Gendering of Nationalist and Postnationalist Selves in the Twentieth-Century Thailand". In *Genders and Sexualities in Modern Thailand*, ed. Peter A. Jackson and Nerida M. Cook. Chiang Mai, Thailand: Silkworm Books, pp. 261–74.

Rigg, Jonathan. 2007. "Moving Lives: Migration and Livelihoods in the Lao PDR". *Population, Space and Place* 13: 163–78.

Ryan, Chris and Michael C. Hall. 2001. *Sex Tourism: Marginal People and Liminalities*. London and New York: Routledge.

Said, Edward. 1978. *Orientalism*. New York: Vintage Books.

Salemink, Oscar. 2010. "Ritual Efficacy, Spiritual Security and Human Security: Spirit Mediumship in Contemporary Vietnam". In *A World of Insecurity: Anthropological Perspectives on Human Security*, ed. Ellen Bal, Thomas H. Erikson, and Oscar Salemink. London and Ann Arbor, MI: Pluto Press, pp. 262–90.

Sampson, Steven L. 1994. "Money Without Culture, Culture Without Money: Eastern Europe's Nouveaux Riches". *Anthropological Journal on European Cultures* 3(1) :7–30.

Saran Thongpan. 2003. "HRH Prince of Chumporn: The Man, The Myth and His Many Lives" (in Thai). *Sarakadee Magazine* 19(22): 77–97.

Sassen, Saskia. 2000. "Women's Burden: Counter-geographies of Globalization and the Feminization of Survival". *Journal of International Affairs* 53(2): 503–24.

Schein, Louisa. 2005. "Marrying out of Place: Hmong/Miao Women Across and Beyond China". In *Cross-Border Marriages: Gender and Mobility in Transnational Asia*, ed. Nicole Constable. Philadelphia, PA: University of Pennsylvania Press, pp. 53–79.

Schiller, Nina G., Linda Basch, and Cristina Blanc-Szanton. 1992 "Transnationalism: A New Analytic Framework for Understanding Migration". *Annals of the New York Academy of Sciences* 645(1): 1–24.

Schuerkens, Ulrik. 2005. "Transnational Migrations and Social Transformations: A Theoretical Perspective". *Current Sociology* 53(4): 535–53.

Seabrook, Jeremy. 1996. *Travel in the Skin Trade: Tourism and the Sex Industry*. London: Pluto Press.

Shorter, Edward. 1975. *The Making of the Modern Family*. New York: Basic Books.

Sinke, Suzanne M. 2006. "Gender and Migration: Historical Perspectives". *International Migration Review* 40(1): 82–103.

Sirijit Sununta. 2009. "Global Wife, Local Daughter: Gender, Family and Nation in Transnational Marriages in Northeast Thailand". PhD dissertation, University of British Columbia, Vancouver, BC.

_____. 2014. "Thailand and the Global Intimate: Transnational Marriage, Health Tourism and Retirement Migration". MMG Working Paper No. 14–20, Max Planck Institute for the Religious and Ethnic Diversity, Göttingen, Germany.

Sirijit Sunanta and Leonora C. Angeles. 2013. "From Rural Life to Transnational Wife: Agrarian Transition, Gender Mobility, and Intimate Globalization in Transnational Marriages in Northeast Thailand". *Gender, Place and Culture* 20(6): 699–717.

Skinner, William G. 1957. *Chinese Society in Thailand: An Analytical History*. Ithaca, NY: Cornell University Press.

Sobieszczyk, Teresa. 2002. "Local Meanings, Global Destinations: Constructing a Culture of International Labor Migration on Northern Thai Villages". Presented at the 8th International Conference on Thai Studies, 9–12 January, Nakhon Phanom, Thailand.

Stahl, Charles W. and Fred Arnold. 1986. "'Overseas Workers' Remittances in Asian Development". *International Migration Review* XX(4): 899–925.

Stengs, Irene. 2009. *Worshipping the Great Moderniser: King Chulalongkorn, Patron Saint of the Thai Middle Class*. Singapore: NUS Press.

Stoler, Ann. 1992. "Sexual Affronts and Racial Frontiers: European Identities and the Cultural Politics of Exclusion in Colonial Southeast Asia". *Comparative Study of Society and History* 34(3): 514–51.

Sukanya Hantrakul. 1988. "Prostitution in Thailand". In *Development and Displacement: Women in Southeast Asia*, ed. Glen Chandler, Norma Sullivan, and Jan Branson. Melbourne: Centre of Southeast Asian Studies, Monash University, pp. 115–36.

Sumalee Bumroongsook. 1995. *Love and Marriage: Mate Selection in Twentieth-Century Central Thailand*. Bangkok: Chulalongkorn University Press.

Supang Chantavanich, Suteera Nittayananta, Prapairat Rattana-olan Mix, Pataya Ruenkeaw, and Anchalee Khenkhruk. 1999. *Kan yai thin khong phuying thai pai Yoeraman: Sahet chiwit khwam penyu lae phonkrathop nai prathet Thai lae Yoeraman* [Migration of Thai Women to Germany: Courses, Living Conditions and Impacts for Thailand and Germany]. Bangkok: Faculty of Political Sciences, Chulalongkorn University.

Supawatanakorn Wongthanavasu, Wannapha Niwasarat, and Khanittha Nunthabuthara. 2005. *Phonkrathop khong kan taeng-ngan kham chat tho sathaban khropkhrua nai phak tawan-ok chiangnuea* [The Impact of Cross-cultural Marriages on Family Institutions in the Northeast of Thailand]. Khon Kaen: Faculty of Nursing, Khon Kaen University.

Suriya Smutkupt and Pattana Kitiarsa. 2007. "The Business of Marrying the Orient and Its Vicissitudes: Farang Husbands and Isan Wives on the Global Cultural Stage". Presented at the 20th Anniversary Celebration Conference on Religious, Ethnicity and Modernity: Identity and Social Practice in Asia, 5–6 October, Southeast Asia Center, University of Washington, Seattle.

Suzuki, Nobue. 2005. "Tripartite Desires: Filipina-Japanese Marriages and Fantasies of Transnational Traversal". In *Cross-Border Marriages: Gender and Mobility in Transnational Asia*, ed. Nicole Constable. Philadelphia: University of Pennsylvania Press, pp. 124–44.

Tambiah, Stanley J. 1970. *Buddhism and the Spirit Cults in North-east Thailand*. London: Cambridge University Press.

Taylor, Edward J. 1999. "The New Economics of Labour Migration and the Role of Remittances in the Migration Process". *Journal of Development Studies* 32: 899–912.

Ten Brummelhuis, Han. 1987. *Merchant, Courtier and Diplomat: A History of the Contacts between the Netherlands and Thailand.* Lochem: Uitgeversmaatschappij De Tijdstroom.

_____. 1994. "Mobility, Marriage and Sex Work: Thai in the Netherlands". Presented at the Seminar on Sexual Subcultures, Migrations and AIDS, 27 February–3 March, Bangkok, Thailand.

Terwiel, Barend J. 1994. *Monks and Magic: An Analysis of Religious Ceremonies in Central Thailand.* Bangkok: White Lotus.

Thai, Hung C. 2005. "Clashing Dreams in the Vietnamese Diaspora: Highly Educated Overseas Brides and Low-Wage U.S. Husbands". In *Cross-Border Marriages: Gender and Mobility in Transnational Asia*, ed. Nicole Constable. Philadelphia, PA: University of Pennsylvania Press, pp. 145–65.

_____. 2008. *For Better or For Worse: Vietnamese International Marriage in the New Global Economy.* New Brunswick, NJ and London: Rutgers University Press.

Thak Chaloemtiarana. 1979. *Thailand: The Politics of Despotic Paternalism.* Bangkok: Thai Khadi Institute, Thammasat University.

Thistlewaite, Aloysius B. 2006. *Money Number One.* 3rd ed. Kincumber, NSW: The Mitraphab Press.

Thitsa, Khin. 1980. *Providence and Prostitution: Image and Reality for Women in Buddhist Thailand.* London: Change International Reports.

Thompson, Eric C., Pattana Kitiarsa, and Suriya Smutkupt. 2016. "From Sex Tourist to Son-in-Law: Emergent Masculinities and Transient Subjectivities of Farang Men in Thailand". *Current Anthropology* 57(1): 53–71.

Thongchai Winichakul. 1994. *Siam Mapped.* Honolulu, HI: University of Hawaii Press.

Tolentino, Roland B. 1996. "Bodies, Letters, Catalogs: Filipinas in Transnational Space". *Social Text* 48: 469–76.

Toyota, Mika, Brenda S.A. Yeoh, and Liem Nguyen. 2007. "Editorial Introduction: Bringing the 'Left Behind' Back into View in Asia: A Framework for Understanding the 'Migration-Left Behind Nexus'". *Population, Space and Place* 13: 157–61.

Truong, Thanh-Dam. 1990. *Sex, Money, and Morality: The Political Economy of Prostitution and Tourism in South-East Asia.* London: Zed Books.

Van Esterik, Penny, ed. 1982. *Women of Southeast Asia.* DeKalb, IL: Northern Illinois University, Center for Southeast Asian Studies.

_____. 1996. "The Politics of Beauty in Thailand". In *Beauty Queens on the Global Stage: Gender, Contests, and Power*, ed. Colleen Ballerino Cohen, Richard Wilk, and Beverly Stoeltje. New York: Routledge, pp. 103–216.

_____. 2000. *Materializing Thailand.* Oxford, UK: Berg Publishers.

Vertovec, Steven. 1999. "Conceiving and Researching Transnationalism". *Ethnic and Racial Studies* 22(2): 447–62.

_____. 2001. "Transnational Challenges to the 'New' Multiculturalism". Presented at the ASA Conference, 30 March–2 April, University of Sussex, United Kingdom.

_____. 2004. "Migrant Transnationalism and Modes of Transformation". *International Migration Review* 38(3): 970–1001.

Walker, Dave and Richard Ehrlich. 1992. *"Hello My Big Big Honey!" Love Letters to Bangkok Bar Girls and Their Revealing Interviews.* Bangkok: Dragon Dance Publications.

Wang, Hong-zen and Shu-ming Chang. 2002. "The Commodification of International Marriages: Cross-border Marriage Business in Taiwan and Viet Nam". *International Migration* 40(6): 93–114.

Weber, Max. 1947. *The Theory of Social and Economic Organization*, trans. by A.M. Henderson and Talcott Parsons. New York: Free Press.

Weisman, Jan R. 2000. "Tropes and Traces: Hybridity, Race, Sex, and Responses to Modernity in Thailand". PhD dissertation, University of Washington, Seattle, USA.

Whittaker, Andrea. 1999. "Women and Capitalist Transformation on a Northeastern Thai Village". In *Genders and Sexualities in Modern Thailand*, ed. Peter A. Jackson and Nerida M. Cook. Chiang Mai, Thailand: Silkworm Books, pp. 43–62.

Wilson, David. 1966. "Introductory Comment on Politics and the Northeast". *Asian Survey* 6(7): 349–52.

Wright, Erik O. 2005. "Social Class". In *Encyclopedia of Social Theory*, ed. George Ritzer. Thousand Oaks, CA: Sage, pp. 717–24.

Wyatt, David K. 1975. "Education and the Modernization of Thai Society". In *Change and Persistence in Thai Society*, ed. G. William Skinner and A. Thomas Kirsch. Ithaca, NY: Cornell University Press, pp. 125–50.

_____. 1984. *Thailand: A Short History*. Bangkok: Thai Watana Panich.

_____. 1994. *Studies in Thai History: Collected Articles*. Chiang Mai, Thailand: Silkworm Books.

Yang, Wen-Shan and Melody Chia-Wen Lu, eds. 2010. *Asian Cross-border Marriage Migration: Demographic Patterns and Social Issues*. Amsterdam: Amsterdam University Press.

Yos Santasombat. 1992a. *Mae ying si khaitua: Chumchon lae kan kha praweni nai sangkhom thai* [Women Who Sell Themselves: Community and Commercial Sex in Thai Society]. Bangkok: Local Development Institute.

_____. 1992b. "Prologue". In *"Hello My Big Big Honey!" Love Letters to Bangkok Bar Girls and Their Revealing Interviews*, collected by Dave Walker and Richard Ehrlich. Bangkok: Dragon Dance Publications, pp. 14–27.

Zelizer, Viviana A. 1989. "The Social Meaning of Money: 'Special Moneys'". *The American Journal of Sociology* 95(2): 342–77.

_____. 2005. *The Purchase of Intimacy*. Princeton, NJ: Princeton University Press.

_____. 2006. "Money, Power and Sex". *The Yale Journal of Law and Feminism* 18: 303–15.

Newspapers

Kom Chad Luek, 4 March 2008.

Thai Rat, 7 February 2009.

Websites

https://en.wikipedia.org/wiki/United_States_Air_Force_in_Thailand, accessed 7 June 2008.

http://www.anglicanthai.org/alabaster.htm, accessed 27 June 2010 (site is no longer available).

http://www.udonmap.com/udonthaniforum/sin-sort-issue-t19318.html, accessed 23 March 2011.

http://www.talkstory.com, accessed 23 March 2011.

http://www.kanchanaburi-info.com/en/muang.html, accessed 2 March 2012.

http://www.awm.gov.au/encyclopedia/pow/general_info.asp, accessed 2 March 2012 (site is no longer available).

https://en.wikipedia.org/wiki/South-East_Asian_theatre_of_World_War_II, accessed 2 March 2012.

http://www.ieat.go.th/ieat/index.php, accessed 18 May 2012 (site is no longer available).

http://medical-dictionary.thefreedictionary.com/erotomaniac, accessed 25 May 2012.

https://www.youtube.com/watch?v=BtOH91HF1p4, accessed 10 March 2016.

http://service.nso.go.th/nso/web/statseries/statseries23.html, accessed 10 March 2016.

http://service.nso.go.th/nso/nso_center/project/search_center/23project-th.htm, accessed 15 July 2016 (site is no longer available).

Index